John McDowell

Philosophy Now

Series Editor: John Shand

This is a fresh and vital series of new introductions to today's most read, discussed and important philosophers. Combining rigorous analysis with authoritative exposition, each book gives a clear, comprehensive and enthralling access to the ideas of those philosophers who have made a truly fundamental and original contribution to the subject. Together the volumes comprise a remarkable gallery of the thinkers who have been at the forefront of philosophical ideas.

Published

Saul Kripke
Greg Fitch

John McDowell
Tim Thornton

Forthcoming

Nelson Goodman
Daniel Cohnitz & Marcus Rossberg

John Rawls
Catherine Audard

David Lewis
Daniel Nolan

Wilfrid Sellars
Willem de Vries

Thomas Nagel
Alan Thomas

Bernard Williams
Mark Jenkins

Hilary Putnam
Max de Gaynesford

John McDowell

Tim Thornton

McGill-Queen's University Press
Montreal & Kingston • Ithaca

*To Beth, for companionable pints in the Somerville Arms
throughout the many months of writing this book*

© Tim Thornton 2004

ISBN 0-7735-2882-2 (hardcover)
ISBN 0-7735-2883-0 (paperback)

Legal deposit third quarter 2004
Bibliothèque nationale du Québec

Published simultaneously outside North America
by Acumen Publishing Limited

McGill-Queen's University Press acknowledges the financial support of the
Government of Canada through the Book Publishing Development Program
(BPIDP) for its activities.

Library and Archives Canada Cataloguing in Publication

Thornton, Tim, 1966-
   John McDowell / Tim Thornton.

(Philosophy now)
Co-published by Acumen.
Includes bibliographical references and index.
ISBN 0-7735-2882-2 (bound).—ISBN 0-7735-2883-0 (pbk.)

   1. McDowell, John Henry. I. Title. II. Series: Philosophy now
(Montréal, Québec)

B945.M454T48 2004   192   C2004-903903-2

Designed and typeset by Kate Williams, Swansea.
Printed and bound by Biddles, King's Lynn.

Contents

Acknowledgements

I would like to thank members of the Department of Philosophy at the University of Warwick for the support they have given me, in particular Bill Fulford and Greg Hunt. I am grateful to a number of graduate students for helping maintain a vigorous intellectual life in the department. As well as for suggestions by a number of anonymous referees, I am grateful for detailed comments on the manuscript by Neil Gascoigne, Jakob Lindgaard, Alex Miller and Ben Smith. For unfailing support as well as sage editorial advice my thanks, as ever, to Lois. For delaying completion of the manuscript by generally getting in the way – and thus providing me with an excuse to linger in the area of McDowellian philosophy – thanks of a sort to Brix, the best cat in the world.

Throughout the book, quoted text is taken from the collected editions of McDowell's papers, *Meaning, Knowledge and Reality* (1998a) and *Mind, Value and Reality* (1998b) rather than from the original paper. For full listings, see the Bibliography.

Introduction

When John McDowell's *Mind and World* was published in 1994 it created great excitement in the world of philosophy. It was widely read and debated by professional philosophers and students alike. Many philosophy books are published each year but there was clear agreement that this one was exceptional. Of course, philosophy is a contested discipline. There was, and remains, widespread disagreement with many, perhaps all, of McDowell's key claims, but *Mind and World* has continued to exercise a powerful hold on the imagination of philosophers. Why did it generate such interest? I think there are three main reasons and these shed light on the significance of McDowell's philosophy more generally.

First, *Mind and World* addresses what is perhaps the central question of modern philosophy (since Descartes): what is the relation between mind and world? This large and rather abstract question is raised through a number of more specific, but still central, questions in philosophy. How is it possible for thoughts to be about the world, for *intentionality* to be possible? What must the world be like if it can be "taken in" by subjects in experiences? What is the connection between thought and experience: does thought presuppose experience? What role do the natural sciences play in describing the limits of the natural world, of what is really real? How does understanding through reasons relate to explanation by laws?

Secondly, the cast of characters is impressive. McDowell's account of the relation of mind and world draws on the work of, among others, Aristotle, Kant, Hegel, Frege, Russell, Wittgenstein, Sellars, Davidson and Evans. In *Mind and World*, an Aristotelian account of ethics is used to promote a broadly Kantian or post-Kantian picture of the

1

empirical world. Kant's slogan "Thoughts without content are empty, intuitions without concepts are blind" is combined with Sellar's attack on the myth of the given. Davidson's coherentist account of language and thought is contrasted with Evans's work on object-dependent thought and McDowell suggests a middle path. Wittgenstein's idea that thoughts need not stop short of the very facts they concern is reconciled with a neo-Fregean distinction between sense and reference. A number of minor characters make appearances, such as Strawson, Dummett and Kripke from the analytic tradition, but also Weber, Gadamer and even Marx. It is breathtaking that a work of contemporary philosophy should borrow so widely from the history of philosophy to attempt to present a coherent picture of our place in nature.

Thirdly, McDowell's philosophical approach in *Mind and World* is, at first, surprising and dramatic. Despite the number of influences from the philosophical canon, his aim is *not* a piece of substantial philosophical theory building. He aims not to bridge the gulf between mind and world, but to show that there is no gulf to be bridged. The dualisms that seem to generate such philosophical difficulty, and call for speculative philosophical theory to overcome them, are dismantled.

This approach shows McDowell's indebtedness to the later Wittgenstein's "therapeutic" or "diagnostic" model of philosophy. Wittgenstein famously rejected the view that there were any real philosophical problems to be solved. They were themselves the result of misunderstanding language and could be eased or explained away by proper attention to our use of words, rather than answered on their own terms. Wittgenstein's *Philosophical Investigations* (1953), however, contains hardly any explicit reference to the history of philosophy or any other philosopher. McDowell, by contrast, attempts to combine a therapeutic approach to philosophy with substantial reference to, and use of the terminology of, influential philosophers. This prompts the question: is that a coherent method for philosophy?

Although for many *Mind and World* was the first taste of McDowell's philosophy, he had already written on a number of different areas that culminate in and significantly inform that work. John McDowell was born in Boksburg, South Africa in 1942 and educated at University College of Rhodesia and Nyasaland and at New College, Oxford. He was a Fellow in Philosophy at Oxford from 1966 to 1986. Much of his work at Oxford drew on Greek philosophy, on broadly analytic philosophy of language and thought and on

Wittgenstein. He translated Plato's *Theatetus* and edited the late Gareth Evans's seminal work *Varieties of Reference* (1980), which defends a neo-Fregean approach to singular, or object-dependent, thoughts.

McDowell's work on Wittgenstein is his most significant for us in understanding his approach to philosophy. Although many commentators take Wittgenstein to offer a radical and revisionary view of meaning and mental content, McDowell argued that we should take seriously Wittgenstein's insistence that philosophy leave everything as it is. He rejected an interpretation that takes Wittgenstein's destructive arguments to be directed against meaning to leave scepticism about meaning. He argued instead that those arguments were directed against a misleading Cartesian assumption about the nature of mind that made meaning merely seem mysterious. With that assumption rejected, the place of meaning in our understanding of the natural world and thus the relation of mind and world become clearer.

A second aspect of McDowell's approach was apparent in another aspect of his discussion of meaning from this period. Although most Wittgensteinians shun the project of devising formal theories of meaning for languages, McDowell wrote several papers on Donald Davidson's highly systematic approach. These papers are effectively descriptions of the best way to interpret what Davidson was attempting and relate it to a neo-Fregean approach to thought. The aim is clear: philosophical problems about meaning can be shown to be merely apparent by paying attention to other philosophers, even if they themselves are systematic theory builders.

In 1986 McDowell moved to America, where he became, and remains, Professor of Philosophy at the University of Pittsburgh. Richard Rorty has described him as a member of the "Pittsburgh School of Neo-Hegelians" (alongside Robert Brandom and John Haugeland). While one misleading connotation of that label is an overemphasis on the similarity between McDowell's work and Brandom's, it does capture the increasing influence of Kant and Hegel on McDowell's work.

Another new influence is that of the American philosopher Wilfrid Sellars (1912–89) (already a strong influence on Brandom and Rorty) who himself used Kant to try to develop an account of intentionality. Sellars's views on the importance of experience in understanding how thought can connect with the world together with his rejection of epistemological foundationalism are central to McDowell's recent writing.

On his curriculum vitae, McDowell lists his major interests as "Greek philosophy (especially the ethics of Plato and Aristotle); philosophy of language, philosophy of mind, metaphysics; ethics (especially the borderlines with metaphysics and philosophy of mind)". This broad range of subjects, as well as the number of different philosophers whose work McDowell considers, raises practical problems for understanding McDowell. It is difficult to see the relation between the different debates: to see the continuity within the diversity. This problem is exacerbated by McDowell's writing style. First, with the exception of two longer lecture series (*Mind and World* and the Woodbridge Lectures (1998e)), his philosophy is spread through a number of discrete philosophical papers. Secondly, his prose is dense and difficult. Papers lack subheadings and the arguments are neither clearly indicated nor summarized. Repetition and redundancy are kept to a minimum. Although this produces a kind of austere elegance, it can also make things difficult for the reader.

A central aim of this book is thus to provide a careful account of the main claims that McDowell advances in a number of different areas of philosophy: the nature of meaning and mental content; ethics and values; formal theories of meaning; and singular thought and epistemology. I aim to set out the main features of these areas of his thought as clearly as possible and bring out the interconnections between the arguments advanced in different areas.

This list of subjects, however, disguises two major strands of continuity that run throughout McDowell's philosophy. One constant theme, which guides his philosophy of nature, is the question of how the world can be brought within the "space of reasons" in Sellars's influential phrase. McDowell's aim is to reconcile reason and nature (McDowell 1994: 86) to dismantle a dualism that he thinks has a damaging effect on much contemporary philosophy. This dualism places, on one side, the normative conceptual structure of having reasons and responding to them and, on the other, brute meaningless nature as successfully described by modern science. It is a dualism of the "space of reasons" and the "realm of law" (*ibid.*: 70–71). McDowell aims to show how both aspects can form part of a broader conception of a "partly re-enchanted" (*ibid.*: 85) nature.

The second theme is metaphilosophical and concerns the nature of philosophy. McDowell holds that philosophy should be practised in a broadly therapeutic, non-theoretical manner. Philosophical problems should be diagnosed as resting on mistaken assumptions rather than answered through the construction of philosophical theories.

Dualisms should be dismantled rather than bridged. This raises the question of whether McDowell is actually successful in this aim and whether a therapeutic approach to philosophy, owing much to the later Wittgenstein, is consistent with the substance of McDowell's discussion of nature, which is set out using the vocabulary of other philosophers from the canon, including, centrally, Kant.

In this introduction I aim to provide a brief overview of these two important themes before, in the main chapters of the book, examining in detail McDowell's contributions to contemporary philosophical debates.

I The philosophy of nature

One broad aim of McDowell's philosophy is the reconciliation of reason and nature. In this section I shall outline two aspects of this reconciliation. The first is McDowell's opposition to a Cartesian dualism of mind and world; the second is McDowell's advocacy of a broadly post-Kantian account of the world, which contrasts with a Humean view of it as a structureless lump.

The Cartesian conception of mind

McDowell criticizes the Cartesian view of the mind as a kind of inner space. On the Cartesian view, mental states are thought of as freestanding occupants of a separate inner realm and ontologically independent of the world outside. It is the view of "an inner realm as self-standing, with everything within it arranged as it is independently of external circumstances" (McDowell 1998a: 243). It contrasts with a view in which mental states are essentially relational and thus not independent of the outer world.

Because, on the Cartesian account, mental states are independent of the outer world, the outer world could be different from the way we take it to be without affecting those states. McDowell suggests that this motivates Descartes's sceptical thought experiment based on the evil genie. Even if there were no outer world of material objects, our thoughts could be just the same, although now systematically false.

McDowell suggests that Descartes's motivation for this view of the mind is the:

plausible aspiration to accommodate psychology within a pattern of explanation characteristic of the natural sciences ... It seems scarcely more than common sense that a science of the way organisms relate to their environment should look for states of the organisms whose intrinsic nature can be described independently of the environment; this would allow explanations of the presence of such states in terms of the environment's impact, and explanations of interventions in the environment in terms of the causal influence of such states, to fit into a kind of explanation whose enormous power to make the world intelligible was becoming clear with the rise of modern science ...   (*Ibid*.: 243)

The motivation to equate psychological explanation with the kind of causal explanation central to the natural sciences naturally leads to a view of mental states as inner causes of actions. The same motivation is at play in many contemporary materialist approaches to the philosophy of mind. These also construe mental states as literally inner neurological states. Descartes's immaterialist theory of mind is replaced by a materialist account. But, McDowell suggests, the shared assumption that mental states are entities that can exist independently of the outer world shows a profound similarity between materialism and immaterialism.

McDowell, however, raises the following objection to any account that shares this view of mental states (see Ch. 4). Once mental states are thought of as freestanding inner states, how can they be about anything? How can they possess intentionality or have a bearing on the world? By starting with items (mental states) that have no essential connection to the outer world, such an account has to provide a substantial philosophical explanation of how they come to have some such connection. Why do they not remain, for example, merely internal causal states with no "aboutness" at all? McDowell suggests that they would be "blank" or "blind" (McDowell 1998a: 243) or "dark" (*ibid*.: 249). No "light" (*ibid*.: 250), by which he means intentionality or meaning, can enter the picture.

McDowell's fundamental objection to this broadly Cartesian account is thus *not* that it cannot explain how *knowledge* is justified in the face of the sceptical possibilities raised by the evil genie or by more recent worries that we might be brains in a vat. The deeper problem is rather that intentionality does not seem to be possible at all.

McDowell suggests that there is a connection between this Cartesian assumption about the nature of mind and the target of Wittgenstein's discussion of understanding meaning, mental content and rules (see Ch. 1). The target is the assumption that understanding is *encoded* in an internal representation that comes before the mind's eye. Understanding the meaning of a word might, for example, be encoded in a picture of what the word stands for. But as Wittgenstein argues, any such internal representation – such as an inner picture – would itself only connect to something in the world under a specific *interpretation*. Understanding that interpretation would also, on the same assumption, have to be explained as being encoded by a further inner representation. This generates a vicious regress of interpretations, which has been taken by some commentators to amount to a sceptical attack on the very idea of meaning (e.g. Kripke 1982). With the assumption in play, the only alternative to scepticism would be what McDowell calls "rampant Platonism", which postulates an interpretation that somehow, magically, needs no further interpretation: it can be understood in only one way.

McDowell suggests, by contrast, that Wittgenstein's target coincides with the Cartesian picture of mind set out above. On the Cartesian picture, mental states are freestanding states that merely *can be interpreted* to be world-involving but are not essentially world-involving. McDowell calls this the "master thesis" (1998b: 270). Wittgenstein's arguments provide a further reason for rejecting that thesis. Once it is rejected there is no need for either a general scepticism about meaning or (rampant) Platonism.

In the place of a dualist separation of mind and world, McDowell aims to show how they "interpenetrate" (1998a: 241). For him, the mind is not an enclosed inner space; it is instead constitutively or essentially open to the world. I shall now outline three elements of this claim based on:

- singular or object-dependent thoughts;
- a "disjunctive" model of experience;
- an identity theory of true thoughts and facts.

One indication of the interpenetration of mind and world is the phenomenon of singular, or object-dependent, thoughts, when correctly understood (see Ch. 4). These are thoughts – expressed for example by *"This* cat is the best in the world!"* – that, according to McDowell, are *constituted* by perceptual relations to worldly objects. They contrast with descriptive thoughts which I shall outline first.

Descriptive thoughts aim to single out an object via a description. The most famous example is "The present king of France is bald". But whether or not there is an entity that, uniquely, satisfies the description "the present king of France", then, according to the most influential analysis, something is still successfully thought. Russell argues that the thought expressed by "The present king of France is bald" is currently false rather than meaningless. This is because the thought itself does not depend for its constitution on a relation to such a person. It is, instead, analysed as a conjunction of general quantified claims (there is at least one present king of France; there is at most one present king of France; and every present king of France is bald). Descriptive thoughts are thus independent of the world and consistent with the Cartesian picture of mind described above.

By contrast, according to McDowell, singular thoughts depend for their very identity on contextual relations to the world. In the case of singular thought, "which configurations a mind can get itself into is partly determined by which objects exist in the world". Thus the "topology of psychological space, so to speak", is not "independent of the contingencies of worldly existence" (McDowell 1998a: 230). Singular thoughts are thus counter-instances to a Cartesian picture of the mind.

A second aspect of the interpenetration of mind and world is McDowell's advocacy of a "disjunctive" account of experience (*ibid*.: 240) rather than a "highest common factor" account (*ibid*.: 386) (see Chs 4 and 5). The latter, according to McDowell, is motivated by a common response to the argument from illusion that runs as follows. The argument from illusion stresses the fact that true (veridical) experiences and illusions can be indistinguishable to a subject. Because they seem qualitatively identical, it is tempting to assume that there must be an element common to both that explains this similarity. But if so, there is no more to true experience than to illusory experience, as far as a subject is concerned. The only difference is that in the former case a further fact happens also to hold (the fact that the experience is supposed to be about). But this further fact lies outside the experience itself. It is "blankly external" to it (*ibid*.: 391). Thus it does not seem possible for experience, construed on the highest common factor model, to underwrite perceptual *knowledge* of the world. Knowledge is non-accidentally true belief but whether the external fact holds or not is merely an accident as far as a subject's experience is concerned. In the case of veridical experience, causal theories add a causal connection to a fact to the elements common to veridical and illusory experiences. But this is not a part of the experience itself and thus cannot contribute to the subject's justification.

McDowell suggests instead that we should think of experience disjunctively: as either veridical or illusory, rather than sharing elements common to both. While illusory experience is merely experience of an *appearance*, veridical experience "does not stop short" (McDowell 1994: 27) of the *fact* it concerns. In other words, veridical experience is *constituted* by a relation to a worldly fact; it makes that fact available to the subject. Rather than being an internal mental state, experience is a form of openness to the world.

This idea also plays an important role in *Mind and World*. McDowell argues that meaning or representational content is only possible in general because facts are made available to subjects through experience. He calls this view "transcendental empiricism" (McDowell 2000b: 6). This is not to say that McDowell aims to show how representational content is constructed from something else. The emphasis is rather that without a connection to perceptual experience – thought of as direct access to the world – such content would be mysterious. I shall shortly outline McDowell's development of this idea in *Mind and World*.

A third aspect of the interpenetration of mind and world concerns the connection of true thoughts (rather than just experiences) and facts (see Ch. 6). According to McDowell, facts, the very elements that make up the world, can be embraced in thought. In *Mind and World* he summarizes this by saying: "[T]here is no ontological gap between the sort of thing one can mean, or generally the sort of thing one can think, and the sort of thing that can be the case. When one thinks truly, what one thinks *is* what is the case" (McDowell 1994: 27). This brief statement summarizes a view that has been called an *identity* theory of thoughts and facts. It contrasts with, for example, the idea of *correspondence* between these two sides: between thoughts or sentences, on the one hand, and "sentence-shaped piece[s] of non-linguistic reality" on the other (Rorty 1991: 4). Anticipating the charge of idealism, McDowell is careful to distinguish between "thinkables" and acts of thinking. Facts are equated not with acts of thinking but with thinkable contents. Correct judgements have to be accountable to something independent of (acts of) human thinking but not independent of what is thinkable. In Chapter 6, I shall return to whether this is enough to turn aside a charge of idealism.

Having outlined three aspects of McDowell's criticism of the Cartesian dualism of mind and world, I shall now turn to the second aspect of McDowell's philosophy of nature, which dovetails with the identity of thoughts and facts: the post-Kantian conception of the world.

John McDowell

The post-Kantian conception of the world

McDowell's most direct articulation and defence of a broadly post-Kantian conception of the world stems from his rejection of another dualism: the dualism of a conceptual scheme and its content, described and criticized by Davidson (1984: 183–98). McDowell's *Mind and World* starts with an argument against that dualism based on its application to experience, which further develops his account of the disjunctive conception of experience described above. I shall outline that argument and then turn more broadly to the post-Kantian conception of the world it helps support.

Scheme–content dualism is a model of the relation of, on the one hand, language or thought and, on the other, the world. It assumes that the totality of empirical beliefs that constitute a worldview results from the interplay of two elements, each of which can be understood in isolation from the other. On the one hand there is the structure of the scheme of concepts. On the other, there is the world, construed as a structureless lump. Empirical beliefs result from organizing the world, using the concepts that make up the scheme.

One feature of this dualism is that the world is construed as utterly *independent* of human subjectivity. All the structure evident in talk of facts, or, for example, of objects and properties, is the result of subsequent organization by something that does depend on subjectivity: our conceptual scheme. A consequence of this dualism is that it implies the coherence of a form of relativism. There may be different conceptual schemes that organize the same structureless world in different ways.

As I shall describe in more detail in Chapter 6, McDowell objects to this dualism for the following reason. Empirical beliefs are rationally accountable to the world. But the dualism of scheme and content makes this rational accountability impossible. Consider the resources that are available on the scheme side. One can imagine that there might be relations between elements of the scheme that underpin rational inferences. Judgements using particular concepts might imply or justify or make probable other judgements using related concepts. But without also invoking elements from the content side – whether thought of as parts of the world or of experiences – the transitions on the scheme side cannot be thought of as responses to the world. They remain merely conditionals: if a judgement that p is justified then so is the judgement that q.

The only way to construe transitions on the scheme side of the dualism as answering to how the world actually is involves adding in elements from the content side. But McDowell points out that because the content side is thought of as lacking structure it cannot provide a *rational* constraint on empirical beliefs. The reason for this is that the materials that make up rational connections have been placed wholly on the other side of the dualism. Our only model of such rational connection is that which holds between items that are conceptualized or lie within the space of reasons. Thus the dualism of conceptual scheme and extra-conceptual content cannot account for the rational responsiveness of a worldview to the world.

In *Mind and World*, McDowell attempts to describe the position left once the dualism of scheme and content is rejected. He suggests that it is "encapsulated in the familiar Kantian tag: 'Thoughts without content are empty, intuitions without concepts are blind'" (McDowell 1999: 87). It appears at first sight that this slogan merely recapitulates the dualism of scheme and content. But McDowell suggests that it is nevertheless helpful to follow Kant in claiming that empirical knowledge is the result of cooperation between the faculties of receptivity and spontaneity (responsible for intuitions and concepts respectively). But this is helpful only "if we can achieve a firm grip on this thought: receptivity does not make an even notionally separable contribution to the co-operation" (McDowell 1994: 9).

Holding on to the thought that receptivity and spontaneity do not play separable roles requires construing experience as always already having a conceptual content. The capacity for conceptual thought – the faculty of spontaneity – is drawn on automatically or passively in experience. Thus the most world-involving elements of human thought – perceptual experiences – are already conceptualized; no elements of thought or experience are less connected with human subjectivity. In other words there is nothing corresponding to an unstructured Humean impression or a pure Kantian intuition that has subsequently to be clothed with conceptual form. Experiences as well as judgements have conceptual structure. That is a consequence of dismantling scheme–content dualism as it applies to experiences. I shall now turn to its broader consequences for a conception of the world.

As an example of the conceptual nature of experience, McDowell considers the act of perceiving "*that things are thus and so*" (*ibid.*). This, he points out, is the sort of thing that one might also endorse in an active judgement. But the example suggests that what can be taken in is how things are. Since, however, the experience is conceptualized and also takes in how the world is, then the world itself must be constitutively apt for conceptualization. It is this idea that is connected to a broadly Kantian or post-Kantian philosophy of nature. (I call the position that results *post-Kantian* because McDowell expresses some concern that Kant's noumenal realm – the realm of things in themselves – is an example of the content side of scheme–content dualism. McDowell sometimes credits post-Kantian German Idealists with greater insight than Kant himself.)

McDowell suggests that Kant, unlike Hume, realized that the world cannot be a structureless lump for the following reason. An acceptable world picture is structured by concepts into facts. But, if true, a world picture also answers to how the world is. McDowell then argues that "we cannot suppose [with Hume] that intelligible structure has completely emigrated from the world ... we have to suppose that the world has an intelligible structure, matching the structure in the space of *logos* [the space of reasons or concepts]" (McDowell 1998b: 178). The argument for this is that if empirical beliefs are conceptually structured but also mirror the world then the world must itself fit the structure of those beliefs: "But mirroring cannot be *both* faithful, so that it adds nothing in the way of intelligible order, *and* such that in moving from what is mirrored to what does the mirroring, one moves from what is brutely alien to the space of *logos* to what is internal to it" (*ibid.*: 179). In other words, the world itself cannot be thought of as lying outside the space of reasons. To be a world at all it has to possess the kind of structure that we, as rational subjects, can find intelligible. There is no prospect of adopting a "sideways-on" perspective (McDowell 1994: 34) that charts the relation of language and thought, on the one hand, and an extra-conceptual world, on the other, from outside both language/thought and the world.

McDowell makes a broadly similar point in the context of the philosophy of language. An influential approach in the philosophy of language has been, following Davidson, the project of articulating the general shape – if not the details – of a formal axiomatized theory of a natural language. In Chapter 3, I discuss the debate between McDowell and Michael Dummett on the nature of this project. The focus of their disagreement is whether a formal theory should "full-bloodedly" (Dummett 1993: 5) attempt to explain the meaning of the basic words or concepts of a language in, for example, practical, non-linguistic terms. McDowell argues, in support of modesty, that full-bloodedness presupposes the possibility of a perspective on the connection between language and the world from outside: a perspective of "cosmic exile" (McDowell 1998a: 329). But from that perspective, the rational structure of language cannot be recovered.

If a sideways-on perspective, from which the interconnections between language and world can be charted, is a philosophical myth, what understanding can we have of language and world? McDowell suggests that learning a first language is interdependent on acquiring a worldview. Interpreting a second language is then not a matter of viewing the connections between it and the world from an external perspective but, rather, charting those connections from within. It involves a fusing of horizons (see McDowell 1994: 146–53).

In fact, McDowell makes similar comments about the perspectives required to understand normatively structured or rule-governed behaviour (Ch. 1), moral judgements (Ch. 2) and linguistic behaviour (Ch. 3). In each case an understanding of the phenomena requires the adoption of a perspective *within* the relevant practice, the relevant tract of the space of reasons. The judgements and concepts involved cannot be grasped from outside that perspective. This marks McDowell's rejection of reductionist forms of naturalism, as I shall describe in Section II.

Given these objections to the idea of trying to step outside our practices to chart their interconnection with the world, we can make nothing of the idea that the world does not have the intelligible structure it is represented as having. Equally, we can make nothing of a vindication of those practices in independent, non-question-begging terms. But this suggests the following general worry about McDowell's philosophy of nature. Can it succeed in representing the world as objective and independent of our judgements about it? If aspects of the world are somehow connected to human subjectivity, are they really objective features of the world? As I shall describe, McDowell's response to this threat is nuanced.

The worry can be given a more specific focus. In discussing theories of meaning (Ch. 3) and singular thought (Ch. 4), McDowell stresses the importance of a neo-Fregean notion of sense. Only a theory of meaning that captures the characteristic ways in which speakers think of objects will be able to make sense of their speech and action. This means that the theory will need to take account of more than just the reference of words. Equally, McDowell's account of singular thought rejects the tradition based on Russell's idea of acquaintance with objects, which interprets the relation between a subject and the objects they are acquainted with to be purely referential. McDowell's focus stresses a subjective aspect to the relation of mind and world.

The mind does not stand in a merely referential relation to the world. But this raises the worry that the counterpart to the mind is not an objective world but a world somehow dependent on minds.

This threat of idealism, to which I shall return, is raised rather than lowered in passages such as: "On a proper understanding of the Fregean apparatus, my exploitation of Wittgenstein's 'truism' . . . can indeed be reformulated by saying thought and language meet in the realm of sense" (McDowell 1994: 180). I shall attempt to show, however, that although there is some tension in combining Wittgensteinian and neo-Fregean ideas, this is not a fatal objection to McDowell's philosophy of nature.

II The nature of philosophy

McDowell's view of the nature of philosophy contains three important interlocking elements:

- a rejection of scientistic and reductionist views of naturalism and hence the philosophical method it promotes;
- a therapeutic rather than a substantial, constructive or reductionist conception of philosophy;
- an emphasis on the importance of certain key thinkers in the philosophical canon for removing philosophical confusion.

In this section, I shall outline each of these in turn.

The rejection of reductionist naturalism

One aspect of McDowell's metaphilosophical views is the rejection of the prevalent metaphysical view "philosophical naturalism", which promotes a view of philosophical method, as I shall explain. (In general, there is no sharp division between McDowell's metaphilosophy and his ground-level philosophical views, because one informs the other.)

In a recent work called *Philosophical Naturalism* (1993), David Papineau considers what the term means. He suggests that it is typically taken to involve a number of different elements:

- continuity between philosophy and empirical science;
- rejection of dualism;
- externalism in epistemology.

Papineau suggests, however, that there is a further and more fundamental strand to naturalism: "the thesis that all natural phenomena
are, in a sense to be made precise, physical" (Papineau 1993: 1). It is
this thesis that plays such an important role in much contemporary
philosophy, and is rejected by McDowell.

In a book on meaning and intentionality, the assumption that all
natural phenomena are physical is shaped by Jerry Fodor into an
explicit argument that is worth quoting at length.

> I suppose that sooner or later the physicists will complete the
> catalogue they've been compiling of the ultimate and irreducible
> properties of things. When they do, the likes of *spin, charm* and
> *charge* will perhaps appear upon their list. But *aboutness* surely
> won't; intentionality simply doesn't go that deep. It's hard to see,
> in face of this consideration, how one can be a Realist about
> intentionality without also being, to some extent or other, a
> Reductionist. If the semantic and intentional are real properties
> of things, it must be in virtue of their identity with (or maybe of
> their supervenience on?) properties that are *neither* intentional
> *nor* semantic. If aboutness is real, it must be really something
> else. (Fodor 1987: 97)

Fodor's argument takes it for granted that a complete catalogue of
physical properties is a complete catalogue of nature. With this
assumption in place, a necessary condition for a property to be a genuine or real feature of the world is either that it is found in that catalogue of physical properties or that it can, at least, be related to properties found there. If, by contrast, there is no such relation then the
problematic concepts cannot describe genuine features of the world.

This *metaphysical* view gives rise to a characteristic *metaphilosophical* view. Philosophy should aim to *naturalize* problematic
concepts, ideas or phenomena by relating them back to the more
basic vocabulary of natural science or physics that serves as a standard or benchmark. Showing how a philosophically puzzling phenomenon can be reduced to (or constructed from) something more basic
and not puzzling should ease philosophical confusion. Naturalism so
understood is a form of reductionism.

The idea that a physical description of the world can serve as a
benchmark for what is real is applied in a number of different areas; I
have already mentioned the philosophy of mind. But it also underpins
neo-Humean approaches to ethics. These assume that ethical judgements have to be understood as projections of sentiments onto a value-

free physical world rather than as responses to genuine moral facts (see Ch. 2). Something akin to this idea underpins some views of human behaviour and language use (Chs 1 and 3). The philosophers of language Michael Dummett and Crispin Wright aim to account for normative language through norm-free descriptions of behaviour. The aim is to account for something apparently supernatural (meaning and intentionality) in less supernatural terms (norm-free descriptions of behaviour).

McDowell, however, suggests a different response to the prospect of the failure of a reduction of philosophically puzzling concepts to more basic physical concepts. Rather than regarding such failure as impugning the reality, or worldliness, of the properties or concepts concerned, it may merely show that reductionists have started with an impoverished conception of what is real or part of nature. He suggests that although the assumption that what is real is exhausted by the natural sciences is itself a natural one, it is by no means compulsory.

> What is at work here is a conception of nature that can seem sheer common sense, though it was not always so; the conception I mean was made available only by a hard-won achievement of human thought at a specific time, the time of the rise of modern science. Modern science understands its subject matter in a way that threatens, at least, to leave it disenchanted ...
>
> (McDowell 1994: 70)

One reason for saying that science leaves its subject matter "disenchanted" is that the medieval idea that nature comprised a book of moral lessons has been rightly rejected. But in addition, McDowell suggests that the modern conception of nature threatens to limit what is real to what he calls the "realm of law". This contrasts with those phenomena that have to be fitted within a different pattern of intelligibility: the space of reasons (in Sellars's phrase), which describes the rational pattern of intentional states. He suggests that nature should not be equated just with the realm of law but should also be taken to include the space of reasons.

By suggesting that nature includes more than just what lies within the realm of law, McDowell does not aim to slight the success of science. Nor does he suggest that there should be no place for a disenchanted view of nature within scientific method.

But it is one thing to recognise that the impersonal stance of scientific investigation is a methodological necessity for the achievement of a valuable mode of understanding reality; it is quite another thing to take the dawning grasp of this, in the modern era, for a metaphysical insight into the notion of objectivity as such, so that objective correctness in any mode of thought must be anchored in this kind of access to the real ... [It] is not the educated common sense it represents itself as being; it is shallow metaphysics. (McDowell 1998b: 182)

Thus one important element of McDowell's metaphilosophy turns on the rejection of a metaphysical assumption shared by most contemporary forms of naturalism. What, then, is put in place of philosophical reductionism as a philosophical method?

A therapeutic conception of philosophical method

A second strand in McDowell's metaphilosophy is a Wittgensteinian emphasis on philosophy as therapy rather than philosophy as a constructive theory-building enterprise. The aim is to diagnose apparently compelling philosophical problems as actually resting on mistaken assumptions. Once those assumptions are brought to light through careful examination, the apparent need to answer the problems directly subsides. Philosophy can find a kind of peace.

Wittgenstein puts the claims that philosophy should be non-revisionary and descriptive in a typically bald manner.

Philosophy simply puts everything before us, and neither explains nor deduces anything.

Since everything lies open to view there is nothing to explain. For what is hidden, for example, is of no interest to us.

(Wittgenstein 1953: §126)

Philosophy may in no way interfere with the actual use of language; it can in the end only describe it.

For it cannot give it any foundation either.

It leaves everything as it is. (*Ibid.*: §124)

McDowell shares this approach. In a section of *Mind and World* summarizing his view of Wittgenstein's discussion of rules, he sets out a model for his own philosophical project. He suggests that Wittgenstein is concerned with a fundamental dualism of norm, or reason, and nature. Conventional modern philosophy is concerned with dualisms that are derivative of this one, such as between subject

17

and object, or thought and world. But conventional philosophy approaches these in a characterisatically constructive way.

> Ordinary modern philosophy addresses its derivative dualisms in a characteristic way. It takes its stand on one side of a gulf it aims to bridge, accepting without question the way its target dualism conceives the chosen side. Then it constructs something as close as possible to the conception of the other side that figured in the problems, out of materials that are unproblematically available where it has taken its stand. Of course there no longer seems to be a gulf, but the result is bound to look more or less revisionist.
>
> (McDowell 1994: 94)

This passage, reminiscent of P. F. Strawson's account of conventional philosophical method (Strawson 1992), highlights the kind of objection McDowell has to the idea that philosophy should aim to bridge the dualism of mind and world. The objection turns on the idea of accepting the terms of the dualism and then trying to bridge the gulf between them. This same approach is taken by those philosophers who interpret Wittgenstein as defending a radical and revisionary view of meaning. Such commentators take for granted a distinction between norms and nature. Norms are construed as requiring a form of *rampant Platonism*, such that "the rational structure within which meaning comes into view is independent of anything merely human, so that the capacity of our minds to resonate to it looks occult or magical" (McDowell 1994: 92). Nature is construed as "disenchanted": completely describable by resources from the realm of law. Given the terms of this dualism, the normativity of meaning appears to be *supernatural*. Constructive philosophy is then needed to show how, using only resources from the realm of law, something that approximates to our pre-philosophical view of meaning can be rebuilt and thus accommodated within what is taken to be natural.

McDowell, by contrast, argues that Wittgenstein's rejection of substantial philosophy should be respected (see Ch. 1). What is needed is the rejection of the presuppositions of the dualism. If nature can be expanded beyond the area described by natural science then there will be no need to see the normativity of meaning as supernatural. This expansion requires abandoning the ungrounded metaphysical assumption that nature is limited to the disenchanted realm of law.

In *Mind and World*, McDowell introduces the idea of *second nature* using the term *"Bildung"*. It is part of our nature as human

beings that we can be initiated into conceptual capacities. This initiation requires education, training and the moulding of our characters.
But given that initiation, then we can be enabled to respond to the
demands of reason, including both the norms associated with meaning and those of ethics. Our eyes are "opened to reasons at large by
acquiring a second nature" (*ibid.*: 84).

This discussion, which I examine in Chapter 1, is important in two
respects. First, it highlights McDowell's (ground-level philosophical)
view that the fundamental dualism to be dismantled is that between
reason and nature. Secondly, it reveals a characteristic approach to
the onus of proof. The dualism that produces philosophical unrest is
diagnosed as depending on an assumption. In this case it is the
assumption that nature is disenchanted. Because that assumption is
ungrounded, it is rejected, and the everyday phenomenology of norms
is reinstated without the need for further justificatory philosophy.

A similar strategy is followed in the case of moral philosophy (see
Ch. 2). McDowell diagnoses the assumptions that lie behind both
neo-Humean projectivist accounts of moral philosophy and Kantian
principles-based approaches. The former depend on a disenchanted
view of nature that, as I have just described, McDowell rejects. The
latter depend on a mistaken assumption that cognition must be
grounded in principles, a grasp of which compels judgement in
particular cases.

Once both of these assumptions are rejected, McDowell suggests
that the phenomenology of value judgement can reassert itself. Moral
judgement is made in response to features in the moral environment
and cannot be codified into a set of principles. But no further positive
justification is offered for this position. (Unlike Jonathan Dancy, Mc-
Dowell offers no explicit argument for *particularism* in moral
philosophy. His "argument", such as it is, is that, once misguided
philosophical resistance is diagnosed, a rejection of a thoroughgoing
principles approach is the obvious interpretation of the moral
phenomenology. McDowell does not, however, reject the use of principles completely.) Thus while he can be seen as defending a form of
moral realism, McDowell sees himself as attacking anti-realism (Mc-
Dowell 1998b: x).

McDowell thus suggests that the major theme of his philosophy is
the dismantling of the dualism of reason and nature. He summarizes
this in the following passage.

My proposal is that we should try to reconcile reason and nature,
and the point of doing that is to attain ... a frame of mind in

which we no longer seem to be faced with problems which call on philosophy to bring subject and object back together. If we could achieve a firm hold on a naturalism of second nature, a hold that could not be shaken by any temptation to lapse back into ordinary philosophical worries about how to place minds in the world, that would not be to have produced a bit of constructive philosophy ... In Wittgenstein's poignant phrase, it would be to have achieved "the discovery that gives philosophy peace".

(McDowell 1994: 86)

The role of the philosophical canon

McDowell's Wittgenstein-inspired therapeutic style of philosophy is, however, unusually combined with the third metaphilosophical characteristic outlined earlier: the assumption that the history of philosophy can be of positive help in forming a correct understanding of our place in nature. By contrast with the tenor of much broadly Wittgensteinian philosophy – which follows Wittgenstein's own written example of not explicitly addressing itself to, or locating itself within, the history of philosophy – McDowell draws widely from the philosophical canon. Among the philosophers whose work he uses – not uncritically – are Davidson, Evans, Sellars, Wittgenstein, Kant and Aristotle.

Perhaps the most pervasive on this list is Kant, who provides the central framework for McDowell's work on the relation of mind and world. McDowell recruits Kant to shed light on how access to the world should not be seen as problematic.

It is a fundamentally Kantian thought that the truth about the world is within the reach of those who live in the realm of appearance ...   (McDowell 2000c: 112)

One of my main aims is to suggest that Kant should still have a central place in our discussion of the way thought bears on reality.   (McDowell 1994: 3)

The role that Kant plays in McDowell's own philosophy is made most explicit at the beginning of the 1997 Woodbridge Lectures on intentionality (1998e), where he says, "there is no better way for us to approach an understanding of intentionality than by working toward understanding Kant" (McDowell 1998e: 432). In fact, in these lectures McDowell pursues the project of understanding intentionality by exploring Sellars's understanding of Kant, including both his positive insights and the ways in which his interpretation is unfortunately warped by his own mistaken assumptions. (This book adds a third layer.)

> I believe we can bring into clearer focus the way Kant actually thought about intentionality, and thereby – given that first belief – how we ourselves ought to think about intentionality, by reflecting on the difference between what Sellars knows Kant wrote and what Sellars thinks Kant should have written.
>
> (*Ibid.*: 432)

McDowell's reading of Sellars is both sympathetic and critical. The same goes for his account of Kant. Although McDowell approves Kant's claim that the world is constitutively apt for conceptualization, he rejects Kant's transcendental account of how this comes about through interaction with something that lies outside the space of reasons: the "in-itself".

This approach does, however, present a tension that will be a continuing, if implicit, theme throughout this book. To what extent can the therapeutic approach to philosophy be combined with the philosophical machinery that seems implicit in the philosophical works McDowell appropriates? Michael Friedman raises a lingering worry in a paper, most of the other points of which are convincingly rebutted by McDowell:

> In light of the historical–philosophical tangles produced by Mc-Dowell's attempt to bring Wittgensteinian "quietism" into some kind of explicit relation with the philosophical tradition nonetheless, one can only conclude, in the end, that Wittgensteinian quietism may itself make sense only in the context of Wittgensteinian philosophical method.   (Friedman 2002: 48)

III The structure of the book

In order to emphasize McDowell's central ideas about the philosophy of nature and the nature of philosophy, I have not followed the chronology of his written work. That would have required starting with McDowell's work in the philosophy of language on Davidsonian theories of meaning. Instead I begin with McDowell's interpretation of Wittgenstein set out in his "Wittgenstein on Following a Rule" (1984b). This is a difficult place to start. McDowell's paper is both complex in itself and also a critique of two commentaries on some difficult passages from Wittgenstein's *Philosophical Investigations* (1953). But the paper also exemplifies many of the ideas and virtues of McDowell's philosophy.

Chapter 1 thus sets out McDowell's interpretation of Wittgenstein's discussion of understanding a rule or a meaning. Rules are important to McDowell's project because they are *normative*. They prescribe correct and incorrect moves. Thus they exemplify the normativity of thought – of mental states like intentions – and of the space of reasons more generally. McDowell's interpretation of Wittgenstein contrasts with the interpretations of Kripke and Wright in defending Wittgenstein's claims about the non-revisionary nature of philosophy. Rather than construing grasp of rules as a mysterious phenomenon that has to be explained or reconstructed using non-normative terms, McDowell aims to show how it only appears mysterious because of mistaken assumptions about the nature of mind. One consequence of this approach, however, is that there is no hope for a philosophical account of meaning that attempts to describe it from an external perspective. A prior grasp of meaning has to be presupposed.

One central aspect of this diagnosis involves the rejection of the master thesis: that the mind is populated with items that merely *can be interpreted* as world involving. Rejection of this thesis forms part of McDowell's attack on Cartesian accounts of the mind. Another important aspect of the diagnosis turns on the rejection of one conception of objectivity, in which a genuine fact must be a matter of the way things are in themselves, utterly independently of us. McDowell argues that a consequence of Wittgenstein's account of meaning is that human subjectivity is "necessarily implicated" both in judgements about the facts and thus also in the facts themselves. McDowell describes his interpretation of Wittgenstein as support for a form of German Idealism, by which he means the broadly post-Kantian philosophy of nature described earlier in this introduction.

Chapter 2 sets out McDowell's defence of moral realism (more precisely, his anti-anti-realism). This builds on the idea of nature just described because moral realism requires a moral realm that is, on the one hand, sufficiently independent of judgements to count as a moral standard and underpin moral truth, but, on the other hand, is not "wholly independent of our subjectivity and set over against it" (McDowell 1998b: 159). In order to make this broad conception of nature more intuitive he suggests comparison with an Aristotelian view of moral judgement together with the notion that proper education and training moulds our "second natures" in such a way that we learn to respond to this new tract of the space of reasons. Second nature also underpins our ability to respond to the normative demands that make up the broader space of reasons.

While McDowell distinguishes primary from secondary qualities, and suggests that moral properties are more like the latter than the former, nevertheless the idea that the moral world is not "utterly independent" of human minds or subjectivity serves as a model for the kind of realism that McDowell advocates generally. He invokes a Kantian picture of the philosophy of nature to make space for this moral realm. One consequence is that the moral realm can only be charted from *within* a moral perspective.

Chapter 3 examines the debate, touched on above, about the elucidation of the nature of meaning offered by a systematic theory that articulates how words in a grammar determine the meaning of whole sentences. McDowell argues that Davidson provides the minimal resources required for developing a neo-Fregean theory of sense for a language. A Davidsonian theory makes rational sense of the speech and action of subjects. It can do this without having to postulate senses as entities or construe them as epistemic routes to the world. But, *contra* Dummett, it should only be interpreted as a *modest* theory. It is one that charts the structure of language and world from within a perspective that takes meaning for granted. It cannot explain grasp of meaning as an achievement described in independent terms. It cannot explain meaning from a position of cosmic exile.

Chapter 4 considers a further aspect of the connection between the structure of the space of reasons and the world by examining object-dependent thoughts. McDowell argues that charting the rational structure of an encounter with the world should not be reduced to charting the structure of internal mental representations. Instead, a neo-Fregean theory should include singular or *de re* senses. Furthermore, the very existence of object-dependent thoughts suggests that the Cartesian separation of mind and world and the idea that the mind can only make contact with the world via a "blueprint" or description are both false. Instead, mind and world interpenetrate and the world can be taken in directly in experience (the disjunctive account of experience described above). This dovetails with rejection of the master thesis.

Chapter 5 examines the consequences for knowledge of the disjunctive account of experience described in Chapter 4. In "Knowledge and the Internal" (1995a), McDowell contrasts two views of justification. In one, a successful justificatory move within the space of reasons is an internal matter in the following way: to be justified does not require any luck or favours from the world. On such an account, however, the separation of truth and justification makes knowledge a mere matter of chance. Instead, McDowell argues that epistemic good standing (justification) is a primitive notion that cannot be understood in world-independent terms.

Chapter 6 outlines the way a number of strands of McDowell's philosophy are brought together in *Mind and World*. McDowell's key idea is that a proper understanding of the nature of experience relieves a transcendental anxiety. The anxiety concerns how representational content or objective purport is possible. The resolution involves insisting that experience is always already conceptualized and thus plays a role in the space of reasons while also insisting that nature is not exhausted by the realm of law. McDowell's position is, however, open to the objection that it is idealist. I argue that the combination of Wittgenstein and Frege in the resources McDowell deploys presents a tension, but one that can be resolved.

A number of characteristic semi-technical terms or phrases that McDowell uses are defined in the Glossary.

Chapter 1

Wittgenstein on philosophy, normativity and understanding

In this chapter, I shall examine McDowell's interpretation of Wittgenstein's discussion of normative rules that govern, among other things, the meaning of words. Given that McDowell's central project is shedding light on the relation of mind and world, concentrating on rules in this chapter may seem to be heading in a different direction. But McDowell thinks that what makes the relation of mind and world seem problematic is a deeper dualism between norms and nature. By norms he means normative rules. The deeper dualism is between the kind of intelligibility exemplified in what Sellars calls the "space of reasons", which is structured by normative rules, and what McDowell calls the "realm of law". So a proper understanding of rules and their place in nature promises to ease the dualism of mind and world.

There are two other reasons for starting this book with McDowell's interpretation of Wittgenstein's philosophy. It informs the central focus of his own work in two key respects:

- Metaphilosophically, McDowell's account of Wittgenstein serves as a model of his own therapeutic conception of philosophy in general. By contrast with commentators who advance philosophical theses in Wittgenstein's name, McDowell respects Wittgenstein's injunction that philosophy should leave everything as it is. Having diagnosed the misleading assumption that makes normative rules problematic, McDowell is able to remove the apparent need for a philosophical theory.
- Substantially, McDowell's interpretation of Wittgenstein involves key philosophical ideas, which recur throughout his positive account of mind and world.

As I shall describe below, the central difficulty in giving an account of rules is in escaping a dilemma that seems inevitable. It seems that rules either exert a genuine constraint on human practice that is underpinned supernaturally through a form of Platonism, or do not exert a genuine constraint after all. Thus the choice is between Platonism and scepticism. McDowell argues, however, that this choice is underpinned by a master thesis that the mind is populated with freestanding states. Such states are states of "inner space", independent of the outer world.

On this model, understanding a rule is a mental phenomenon that stands there "like a signpost" (Wittgenstein 1953: §85). The idea is that a signpost is just a board with some writing or a diagram on it. In itself it seems incapable of sorting human behaviour into that which is in accord – perhaps going in a particular direction – and that which is not. It seems that something else needs to be added to a description of the sign to achieve this: an interpretation of the writing or diagram that says what it means. If mental states were like that then they too would need further interpretation to come to be about anything. That would lead either to the notorious regress of interpretations, which in turn leads to scepticism, or to a form of rampant Platonism if one postulated an end to that regress through an interpretation that somehow interpreted itself. So one part of McDowell's diagnosis is to reject that master thesis.

Unlike sceptical commentators such as Saul Kripke (discussed below), McDowell does not think that Wittgenstein expresses any hostility to our pre-philosophical understanding that norms – such as those implicit in meaning, or the continuation of a mathematical series – have a degree of autonomy. They are ratification-independent. That is, norms do not depend on the ongoing judgements of rule-followers to create, for example, what should count as the correct continuation of a mathematical series. Rather, the series itself determines what rule-followers ought to judge is the correct next number in a particular case.

Articulating this view of rules introduces a number of McDowell's central concerns in the rest of his philosophy. He suggests that one lesson from this area of philosophy is that norms can be part of nature, when both are properly understood, without having to be explained in non-normative terms. For this reason he advocates a form of "naturalized" (by contrast with "rampant") Platonism to characterize the partial autonomy of rules and hence of the space of reasons. But he suggests that the right way to understand nature so as to accommodate that understanding of concepts is a form of German Idealism: a view that the world is constitutively apt for conceptualization. This helps undermine a stark contrast between reason on the one hand and non-normative nature on the other. And the right way to understand our ability to "resonate" to the partially autonomous normative demands of the space of reasons and our ability to hear them expressed in the utterances of others is to think of it as part of what he calls our "second nature". I shall introduce these ideas towards the end of this chapter.

I The background: Wittgenstein on normativity

McDowell begins "Wittgenstein on Following a Rule" with the comment that "We find it natural to think of meaning and understanding in, as it were, contractual terms" (McDowell 1998b: 221). The idea of a contract evokes a commitment or obligation. When one understands the meaning of a word, one is obliged to use it in a particular way, a way that accords with the meaning.

By stressing the natural contractual view, McDowell places normativity at the heart of the discussion to come. His aim is not to offer a substantial philosophical theory about meaning but to remove obstacles to a clear view of the matter. One key obstacle is misconstruing the nature of the contractual obligation involved in, for example, understanding the meaning of a word. In this short section I shall outline some of the connections between Wittgenstein's discussion of rules, meaning and intentional mental states by focusing on normativity. These will be developed further in Section II as I set out McDowell's complex discussion.

McDowell's discussion of meaning and understanding follows Wittgenstein's central emphasis on the importance of rules. Baldly, this emphasis on rules helps us to focus on the normativity of meaning and content. Thus Wittgenstein discusses rules as a way of more generally discussing meaning, thought and intentionality, or "aboutness". Elucidating the nature of the standard that a rule imposes on moves made in accord with it – and how we can understand that constraint both in a flash and as manifest over time – sheds light on the connection between thought and world.

Michael Luntley sets out a very similar general starting-point thus:

Meaning is normative. That is the starting point to our investigations. The normativity of meaning comes from the fact that the content of our utterance or thought is something assessed as true or false ... Without adding anything further about the nature of the concept of truth, this basic fact about meaning forces the following constraint. For any utterance or thought to possess meaning its meaning must be such that it demarcates between those conditions that would render the utterance true and those that would render it a failure in aiming for truth.

(Luntley 1991: 171–2)

A *rule* is explicitly normative: it *prescribes* the moves that accord with it and those that do not. Understanding the rule for the correct use of a word prescribes its correct use. But other intentional mental states are similar in that they too prescribe those acts, or events, that are in accord with or satisfy them. So having a mental state, like an expectation, imposes a standard by which the world can be judged. In the case of an expectation, subsequent events will either satisfy or frustrate it, and what that depends on is determined by the expectation itself.

These everyday observations on understanding rules and forming mental states suggest a philosophical question: how is it possible to grasp or to take on such an orientation or obligation? Wittgenstein's discussion, in a hundred or so paragraphs in the *Philosophical Investigations*, starts with the following observations and questions:

But we *understand* the meaning of a word when we hear or say it; we grasp it in a flash, and what we grasp in this way is surely something different from the "use" which is extended in time!

(Wittgenstein 1953: §138)

[I]sn't the meaning of the word also determined by this use? And can these ways of determining meaning conflict? Can what we grasp *in a flash* accord with a use, fit or fail to fit it? And how can what is present to us in an instant, what comes before our mind in an instant, fit a *use*? (*Ibid.*: §139)

Later, Wittgenstein describes the normative constraint more generally:

A wish seems already to know what will or would satisfy it; a proposition, a thought, what makes it true – even when that thing is not there at all! Whence this *determining* of what is not yet there? This despotic demand? (*Ibid.*: §437)

Wittgenstein considers a range of substantial explanations of this kind of connection. These explanations are, in general, attempts to connect the understanding that can happen in a flash with subsequent events or actions at a distance. But each substantial explanation fails. Typically they fail either because they do not sustain the normativity of the connection, or because they smuggle that normativity into the explanation in a question-begging manner. Explanations that postulate an inner mental mechanism fail to distinguish the normative notion of a *correct* response from a merely causal disposition to act in some way. Explanations that postulate inner signs or symbols that encode the understanding or mental content generate an infinite regress of interpretations.

Thus, in outline, Wittgenstein emphasizes the close connections between meaning, intentional states and normativity. He raises the question of how one can adopt such normative obligations (in understanding a rule or forming a mental state). And he rejects explanations based on causal mechanisms or interpreting inner signs.

The challenge this leaves to interpreters is this. If Wittgenstein rejects explanations of the connection between understanding a word and applying it over time, what is the purpose of that criticism and what account of meaning and normativity can survive that criticism? As I shall set out in Section II, Kripke and Wright both interpret Wittgenstein as offering a radical and revisionary account of meaning. They both undermine the natural contractual view of meaning: the view that understanding imposes a specific obligation on word use, for example. Against them, McDowell argues that it is only a misunderstanding of the nature of that contract that should be rejected.

II Opposing interpretations of Wittgenstein

Here and in Sections III and IV, I shall summarize, in some detail, the key features of the interpretation of Wittgenstein that McDowell puts forward in his paper "Wittgenstein on Following a Rule". Overall, McDowell presents Wittgenstein as a *therapeutic* philosopher who does not advance claims that aim to transform our everyday understanding of the relation of mind and world. He argues that Wittgenstein's discussion of rules is revelatory not of a successful philosophical *theory* of the relation of mind and world, but of why there need be no such theory.

John McDowell

McDowell sets out his own interpretation of Wittgenstein's work by contrasting his account of Wittgenstein with Kripke's and Wright's accounts. In this section I shall outline Kripke's and Wright's views as they feature in McDowell's paper, his criticisms of them and his diagnosis of where they diverge from a proper interpretation of Wittgenstein.

Kripke's Wittgenstein

Kripke's influential account takes Wittgenstein to advance a new form of scepticism about meaning. It is directed against the idea that rules can exert a constraint on, for example, the correct use of words. Because McDowell's account is very brief, I shall summarize Kripke's argument as presented in his *Wittgenstein on Rules and Private Language* (1982).

Kripke casts doubt on what appears, pre-philosophically, to be an everyday metalinguistic fact: the fact that one can mean something by a word. He considers the case of meaning *addition* by the word "addition" and asks the question: what justifies the claim that answering "125" is the correct response to the question "What does 68 + 57 equal?" Two simplifying assumptions are made:

- that "correct" means "in accordance with the standards of one's previous usage of the signs involved";
- that one has never calculated that particular result before. In fact Kripke assumes that one has "added" no number larger than 57.

If called upon to justify the answer "125", one might usually give two sorts of response. Arithmetically, one might ensure that one has carried out the computation correctly. Metalinguistically, one might assert: "that 'plus', as I intended to use that word in the past, denoted a function which, when applied to the numbers I call '68' and '57', yields the value 125" (*ibid.*: 8). Kripke now introduces the sceptical hypothesis that in the past one might have followed a different mathematical function, the *quus* function. This is defined to give the same number as the plus function for all pairs of numbers smaller than 57. For numbers greater or equal to 57, the application of quus gives the answer 5. Kripke now presses the question: what facts about one's past performance show that one was calculating in accordance with the plus function rather than the quus function?

There is a further condition on any satisfactory answer to the question. It must show why it is *correct* to respond 125 rather than 5. It must have the right normative properties. This precludes citing facts about one's education or training that now dispose one to answer 125. It may be true that one has such a disposition, but that will not show that one is correct to answer 125. (One may equally be disposed to make mistakes when adding large columns of figures.)

Kripke then deploys broadly Wittgensteinian arguments to show, apparently, that no facts about one's past actions, utterances or dispositions can justify an answer (*ibid*.: 7–54). Anything one did or said in the past could be interpreted as following the quus rule. It appears that nothing that one does or says or thinks to oneself can justify the claim that answering "125" is going on in the same way.

Consider two initially attractive lines of thought. Although it seems that the problem is set up so that one's past *actions* might equally be interpreted as according with the plus or quus function, one might still settle the issue if one previously said or thought to oneself "Now I'll *add* these numbers". But this would only answer the sceptic if there were an independent way to settle the correct *interpretation* of these words. Perhaps they meant *quad*. Suppose, now, that one had explicitly added, *sotto voce*, "And by add I mean a function based on *counting* in the following normal way ...". Whatever follows would also depend on the interpretation given to the word "count". Perhaps it meant *quount*, defined as the same as counting except in the case of the combination of numbers 57 and 68.

By such means, Kripke argues that there are no facts about one's past behaviour nor one's past mental history that allow one to infer the further fact that one has, in the past, followed the addition rule and meant addition by the word "addition". Thus nothing makes it correct to answer "125" today. Generalizing from this, he argues that there are no facts about meaning anything by any word.

> There can be no such thing as meaning anything by any word. Each new application we make is a leap in the dark; any present intention could be interpreted so as to accord with anything we may choose to do. So there can be neither accord, nor conflict.
>
> (*Ibid*.: 55)

This sceptical interpretation of Wittgenstein is reinforced by Kripke's reading of *Philosophical Investigations*, where Wittgenstein writes:

> This was our paradox: no course of action could be determined by a rule, because every course of action can be made out to accord

with the rule. The answer was: if everything can be made out to accord with the rule, then it can also be made out to conflict with it. And so there would be neither accord nor conflict here.

(1953: §201)

Kripke goes on to suggest what he calls a "sceptical solution" to the sceptical problem that he thinks is implicit in Wittgenstein's discussion. A sceptical solution "begins . . . by conceding that the sceptic's negative assertions are unanswerable" (Kripke 1982: 66). Unlike a "straight solution", it does not disprove scepticism but it suggests a way that the negative conclusions can be tolerated. The key idea in this case is that facts about meaning are not genuinely ushered back on to the stage. Rather, individuals can be dignified as rule-followers by the wider community providing they do not conflict with the community.

> It is essential to our concept of a rule that we maintain some such conditional as "If Jones means addition by '+', then if he is asked for '68 + 57', he will reply '125'" . . . the conditional as stated makes it appear that some mental state obtains in Jones that guarantees his performance of particular additions such as "68 + 57" – just what the sceptical argument denies. Wittgenstein's picture of the true situation concentrates on the contrapositive, and on justification conditions. If Jones does *not* come out with "125" when asked about "68 + 57", we cannot assert that he means addition by "+". (*Ibid.*: 94–5)

> What follows from these assertability conditions is *not* that the answer everyone gives to an addition problem is, by definition, the correct one, but rather the platitude that, if everyone agrees upon a certain answer, then no one will feel justified in calling the answer wrong. (*Ibid.*: 112)

It is not that agreement with the community constitutes someone's meaning something by their use of a word. There are still no facts about meaning. The role of the community is purely negative. Some uses of a word are ruled out as divergent without implying that there is a substantial standard for what using a word correctly consists in. This provides a method of construing normal talk about what words mean without contradicting the sceptical conclusion that there are no facts about meaning. That revisionary conclusion is supposed to follow from a self-contained argument implicit in Wittgenstein's discussion of rules.

McDowell summarizes Kripke's main sceptical argument thus:

[W]hatever piece of mental furniture I cite, acquired by me as a result of my training in arithmetic, it is open to the sceptic to point out that my present performance keeps faith with it only on one interpretation of it, and other interpretations are possible. So it cannot constitute my understanding "plus" in such a way as to dictate the answer I give. Such a state of understanding would require not just the original item but also my having put the right interpretation on it. But what could constitute my having put the right interpretation on some mental item? And now the argument can evidently be repeated. (McDowell 1998b: 226–7)

Wright's Wittgenstein

Wright also ascribes a radical view to Wittgenstein: "there is in our understanding of a concept no rigid, advance determination of what is to count as its correct application" (Wright 1980: 21, quoted in McDowell 1998b: 222). This is a radical view because it revises our pre-philosophical understanding of the normative connection between (understanding) the meaning of a word and its correct use. It is supposed to follow from a conflict between, on the one hand, what McDowell terms the natural contractual view of meaning, in which understanding the meaning of a word commits one to a pattern of linguistic usage, and, on the other, an attack on the very idea that such a pattern could have any sort of independent existence. McDowell goes on to argue, by contrast, that Wittgenstein's target is *not* "the very idea that a present state of understanding embodies commitments with respect to the future, but rather a certain seductive misconception of that idea" (1998b: 223).

Wright argues that Wittgenstein's view of meaning is revisionary because it involves an attack on the idea that grasping a meaning involves fidelity to a particular pattern of use, at least as this is ordinarily understood. On his view, the kinds of arguments that Wittgenstein uses to show that any stretch of behaviour, or speech, could be interpreted in different and conflicting ways, show that a pattern of use cannot be definitively explained to other people.[1] Thus a defender of the idea of meaning as a pattern of use is forced instead

---

1. Explanations by paraphrase or synonyms beg the question of their correct interpretation. Explanation by example can always be variously interpreted, as Kripke emphasizes.

to think of that pattern as being communicated only through the inspired *guesses* of individuals (cf. Wittgenstein 1953: §210). A speaker has to guess what the real point of an explanation of the use of a word is because no explanation can determine a specific pattern. Genuine understanding, on this picture, would have to be an individual matter: a form of individual idiolect.

According to Wright, however, this individualistic idea cannot work. The problem is that it cannot sustain a distinction between merely thinking that one's use of a word correctly follows the grasped pattern and it actually adhering to that pattern. For an individual speaker, that distinction – between being right and merely seeming right – will collapse (cf. *ibid.*). Thus there will not be a genuine notion of correctness. Something like the notion of correctness is only available by considering the speaker as a member of a community and thus liable to communal agreement and disagreement. But this does not, on Wright's account, save the idea of a ratification-independent pattern that the community is following. It merely gives an idea of being in step with one's fellows, not an idea of the community answering to an independent constraint imposed by a rule. (Elsewhere, Wright talks of meaning as being "plastic in response to speakers' ongoing performance" (1986: 289).)

Wright's positive suggestion is to revise the idea of fidelity to a pattern by construing the pattern as itself constituted by ongoing communal practice. Such patterns are not ratification-independent. Neither are they idiolectic. Rather, what truth there is in the idea of pattern is given by the ongoing actual use of words made by a linguistic community. But an important restriction is placed on the description of this unfolding practice that prevents one reading into it standards for future (or counterfactual) use. (I shall return to McDowell's account of the source of this restriction later.)

More recently, Wright has developed a different, although related, account of meaning based on the idea of the "judgement dependence" of intentions. Wright starts with the question: how does an intention that can be arrived at in a flash normatively constrain those actions that would accord with it in the future? As I have suggested above, the normative connection between an intention and what accords with it seems as mysterious as that between understanding a rule and its correct applications. Wright, in other words, re-emphasizes the fundamental connection between the problem of linguistic meaning and that of mental content that Wittgenstein sets out. Wright deploys a form of constructivism to explicate both problems.

According to Wright:

> One of the most basic philosophical puzzles about intentional
> states is that they seem to straddle two conflicting paradigms: on
> the one hand they are avowable, so to that extent conform to the
> paradigm of sensation and other "observable" phenomena of
> consciousness; on the other they answer constitutively to the ways
> in which the subject manifests them, and to that extent conform to
> the paradigm of psychological characteristics which, like irritabil-
> ity or modesty, are properly conceived as dispositional . . . It seems
> that neither an epistemology of observation – of pure introspection
> – nor one of inference can be harmonised with all aspects of the
> intentional. (1991: 142)

Intention is only one example of a general phenomenon that also
includes understanding, remembering and deciding. In each case,
the subject has a special non-inferential authority in ascribing these
to herself that is, nevertheless, defeasible in the light of subsequent
performance. Wittgenstein's attack on reductionist explanations of
such states shows that they cannot be modelled on a Cartesian
picture of observation of private experiences. But if understanding,
intending and the like are to be modelled on abilities instead, as Wittgenstein seems to suggest, how can the subject have special authority
in ascribing these to herself in the light of his attack on reductionist
explanation?

Constructivism appears to provide a solution to this problem. The
basic idea is to deny that there is any inner *epistemology* and to
devise a constructivist account of intention instead:

> The authority which our self-ascriptions of meaning, intention,
> and decision assume is not based on any kind of cognitive advan-
> tage, expertise or achievement. Rather it is, as it were, a *conces-
> sion*, unofficially granted to anyone whom one takes seriously as
> a rational subject. It is, so to speak, such a subject's right to
> declare what he intends, what he intended, and what satisfies
> his intentions; and his possession of this right consists in the
> conferral upon such declarations, other things being equal, of a
> *constitutive* rather than descriptive role. (Wright 1987a: 400)

All other things being equal, a speaker's sincere judgements constitute the content of the intention, understanding or decision. They
determine, rather than *reflect*, the content of the state concerned. In
the next chapter I shall set out the conditions that a form of judge-

ment has to satisfy to play this determining role. For now what matters is just the general shape of the idea. The meaning of a word or the content of an intention is constituted by the ongoing judgements a speaker makes.

Two points stand out. One is that the account does not support the natural contractual view of meaning that McDowell emphasizes. It is instead a revisionary view that attempts to build something akin to norms out of something supposedly more basic: ongoing judgement. In other words, it remains the case that meaning is moulded by ongoing use. But at the same time, however, it presupposes facts about the *content* of judgements that share the very normative properties of meaning that it was supposed to explain. Nothing further has been added to make the normativity of mental content less mysterious. Thus I do not think that Wright's more recent accounts of meaning undermine McDowell's criticisms which I will describe below. (For more substantial criticism of Wright see Thornton (1998: 80–88).)

Objections to Kripke and Wright

McDowell raises a number of objections to the interpretations of Wittgenstein set out by Kripke and Wright. First, Kripke's and Wright's radical pictures of meaning conflict with Wittgenstein's explicit hostility to philosophical theorizing. They conflict with passages where Wittgenstein seems to be arguing not so much against the view that meaning determines correct use as against particular explanations.

Secondly, their accounts of meaning undermine the very idea of the objectivity of our judgements in general. This follows from the idea that without something like the advance determination of what *would* be the *correct* thing to say in some circumstance (whatever is actually said), then the idea that there can be determinate states of affairs independent of actual judgements also fails. In other words, what might look at first sight to be merely an attack on the nature of meaning and language is in fact a form of idealism.

In a paper summarizing interpretations of Wittgenstein's discussion of rules, Paul Boghossian codifies this objection in the following brief argument (1989: 524). Non-factualism amounts to the claim that for any sentence *S* and propositional content, or meaning, *p*, "*S* means that *p*" is not truth-conditional: it is neither true nor false. This claim about the meaning of *S* has implications for what makes it true or false because the truth-condition of a sentence is in part a function of its meaning. This implies that for any S and p, "S has truth-condition p" is itself not truth-conditional: it is neither true nor false. From this it follows that "S has truth-condition p" is never true. And from that, "S" is neither true nor false. Thus, assuming that possession of factuality implies the possession of truth-conditions, the denial of factuality concerning rules or meaning implies a universal lack of factuality. If there are no facts about meaning, there are no facts at all.

This argument has been criticized by Wright on the grounds that it presupposes that even a substantial concept of truth has disquotational properties. These license the transition from the fact that a mentioned sentence lacks a truth-condition to its lack of truth, and from that to a denial of the content of the sentence (Wright 1992: 214–20). Wright suggests that in the context of a debate about realism this cannot be assumed. If one distinguishes a substantial notion of truth (amounting to normativity and something more such as a correspondence theory) from a more minimal notion of correctness (normativity alone), it is far from clear that these transitions hold good. The fact that a sentence lacks substantial truth need not justify the denial of the mere correctness of its content. But in this case, because Kripke's and Wright's accounts do not preserve even a minimal notion of truth – normativity is replaced by something much weaker – the objection is not relevant.

Thirdly, McDowell argues that while Kripke and Wright both aim to respect the normativity of the connection between meaning and application, having started from a position that eschews linguistic norms, they cannot achieve an account that involves more than an *illusion* of being subject to norms. McDowell illustrates this objection by considering the explicitly normative connection between an order and what accords with it. Wittgenstein rejects (1953: §460) the view that the connection between, for example, the order to bring a yellow flower and bringing a yellow flower might be explained by an intervening feeling of satisfaction. He points out that there is a difference between the order to bring a yellow flower and the order to bring a flower that evokes a particular feeling. The same sort of argument would apply to the best account that Wright (and equally Kripke) might provide. Rejecting any idiolectic account of the constraint that an order might place on its fulfilment, Wright's account of the connection is instead based on what action, by an individual, would secure communal approval. But the order to bring a flower of which everyone approves is not the same as the order to bring a yellow flower. In fact,

Wittgenstein explicitly stresses the difference between "This is yellow" and "This would be called 'yellow' by (most) speakers of English".

For this reason it is not clear that Kripke or Wright can preserve the basic idea of an action of calling something "yellow", of aiming to respect the rules governing the use of "yellow" in accordance with what it *means*. Instead, their accounts merely involve making a particular noise, feeling constrained and sharing propensities to vocalize with a community. The thought here is that the kind of constraint described by Kripke and Wright has nothing to do with the *content* or meaning of an utterance. This is why McDowell argues that, at best, Kripke and Wright have given an account of being under an *illusion* that one is subject to rules or norms.

McDowell argues, however, that both Kripke and Wright have misunderstood Wittgenstein's aim. Section 201 of Wittgenstein's *Philosophical Investigations* (quoted above) only appears to present a dilemma for understanding meaning if one has already made a mistaken assumption about the nature of meaning. In fact, Wittgenstein continues that passage as follows:

> It can be seen that there is a misunderstanding here from the mere fact that in the course of our argument we give one interpretation after another; as if each one contented us at least for a moment, until we thought of yet another standing behind it. What this shews is that there is a way of grasping a rule which is *not* an *interpretation*, but which is exhibited in what we call "obeying the rule" and "going against it" in actual cases.
>
> (Wittgenstein 1953: §201)

If, with Kripke, one assumes that facts about meaning have to underwrite an *interpretation* of linguistic expressions, then one faces a choice between equally unpalatable options. One is faced either with the scepticism of the regress of interpretations, which Kripke successfully describes, or one has to embrace what Wittgenstein argues is merely a mythology: the idea of a final interpretation, an interpretation that cannot or need not be further interpreted. But, McDowell argues, this dilemma can be avoided by *rejecting the underlying assumption that understanding is a species of interpretation.*

Before turning to what an account that rejects this assumption might look like and why one might adopt it in the first place, McDowell points out that this alternative view of the significance of the dilemma allows two features which Wright finds in Wittgenstein to be recontextualized:

- If the assumption of the foundational role of interpretation were correct, then Wright's suggestion that an interpretation would be a piece of *individual* understanding or idiolect would seem plausible. It seems that one would have to "hit on" an interpretation of any explanation of the use of a word for oneself. One would have to hit on it for oneself and get others merely to *guess* one's drift. But, because he denies the key assumption, McDowell disagrees with Wright about why this matters. The point is not so much to show that a community is a precondition of rule-following – as a kind of social pragmatic philosophy – but to show that understanding does not turn on mediating interpretation. I shall turn shortly to whether McDowell satisfactorily shows that meaning requires a community.

- Wright's description of Wittgenstein's supposed attack on the very idea of a pattern of use is instead an attack on the mythology of a last interpretation. It is an attack on the idea that the pattern extends *itself*. In *Mind and World*, McDowell uses the phrase "rampant Platonism" (which is contrasted with a preferred naturalized Platonism) to describe the radical independence of this discarded view. On his own reading, one is only driven to adopt rampant Platonism having already adopted an interpretation-based account of understanding and in an attempt then to escape the sceptical regress of interpretations. I shall return to the nature of rampant Platonism below.

III McDowell's interpretation

So far I have set out Wright's and Kripke's views of meaning derived from their interpretations of Wittgenstein. I have briefly sketched McDowell's objections to the plausibility of their accounts and his initial hints about how they have misunderstood Wittgenstein's real target: the assumption that understanding is a species of interpretation. In this section I shall describe both McDowell's diagnosis of the motivations of Wright's and Kripke's misreading of Wittgenstein and the development of his alternative view.

There are two main elements to McDowell's strategy for undermining an attachment to the assumption that understanding is a species of interpretation: a diagnosis of its attractions and a sketch of an alternative view of Wittgenstein's purpose.

- By comparing understanding meaning with understanding an order and with the possession of intentional mental states (wishes, expectations, intentions), McDowell undermines the intrinsic or independent plausibility of the assumption that understanding is a species of interpretation. Furthermore, he diagnoses that the thesis depends for its plausibility on a questionable Cartesian view of the mind as a world-independent realm: the master thesis.
- By invoking practical abilities, he suggests a different way of responding to Wittgenstein's dilemma.

Diagnosis

McDowell's rejection of Kripke's and Wright's master thesis turns in part on considering other cases of normative relatedness. It is implausible that, for example, the connection between an order and what fulfils it has to be mediated by an interpretation. This is suggested in the discussion of orders described in Section II. It is also evident in a passage, cited by McDowell (1998b: 239 n.26), in which Wittgenstein aims to undermine any of this idea's temptation: "The absent-minded man who at the order 'Right turn!' turns left, and then, clutching his forehead, says 'Oh! Right turn' and does a right turn. What has struck him? An interpretation?" (Wittgenstein 1953: §506).

The motivation for the thesis, and thus a clearer way of seeing what is at stake in rejecting it, is given elsewhere by McDowell. The thesis turns on a Cartesian assumption about what populates the mind. In a later paper, "Meaning and Intentionality in Wittgenstein's Later Philosophy" (1992b), McDowell puts it this way. In order to feel a philosophical difficulty with the very idea of understanding meanings and thus feel the need of substantial (and possibly revisionary) philosophical theorizing, one has to start with the assumption that "the contents of minds are items that, considered in themselves, just 'stand there like a sign-post', as Wittgenstein puts it (§85)" (McDowell 1998b: 264). If the mind contains objects of that sort, then they would indeed need to be interpreted to be about anything in the world.

But the assumption that the mind is populated with items whose identity does not turn on essential normative relations to the objective world is itself optional and counterintuitive.

We get a more radical divergence from Kripke, however, if we suppose that the thrust of Wittgenstein's reflections is to cast doubt on the master thesis: the thesis that whatever a person has in her mind, it is only by virtue of being interpreted in one of various possible ways that it can impose a sorting of extra-mental items into those that accord with it and those that do not.

It is really an extraordinary idea that the contents of minds are things that, considered in themselves, just "stand there". We can bring out how extraordinary it is by noting that we need an application for the concept of accord, and so run the risk of trouble from the regress of interpretations if we accept the master thesis, not just in connection with grasp of meaning but in connection with intentionality in general. An intention, just as such, is something with which only acting in a specific way would accord. An expectation, just as such, is something with which only certain future states of affairs would accord. Quite generally, a thought, just as such, is something with which only certain states of affairs would accord.   (*Ibid.*: 270)

Thus the assumption that understanding is a form of interpretation is an instance of the master thesis that the mind is populated with items that merely *can be interpreted* as relating to the world. But if this idea is extraordinary, why is it attractive? The origins of the idea are treated at length in "Singular Thought and the Extent of Inner Space" (McDowell 1986), and will be discussed in Chapter 4. Briefly, McDowell suggests there that it is a form of Cartesianism in which the mind is characterized as containing self-standing entities whose existence is independent of external circumstances. (This is what is meant by standing there like a signpost.)

Why might Descartes have found this idea tempting? And why should the temptation have first become pressing around Descartes's time? Both these questions can be answered in terms of a plausible aspiration to accommodate psychology within a pattern of explanation characteristic of the natural sciences ... It seems scarcely more than common sense that a science of the way organisms relate to their environment should look for states of the organisms whose intrinsic nature can be described independently of the environment; this would allow explanations of the presence of such states in terms of the environment's impact, and explanations of interventions in the environment in terms of the causal influence of such states, to fit into a kind of explanation whose enormous power to make the world intelligible was becoming clear with the rise of modern science ...   (McDowell 1998a: 243)

Thus the aim of a scientific account of the mind, fitting with the pattern of explanation present in developing modern natural science, drew Descartes to a conception of mental states that fits the master thesis. A scientific account required mental states to be freestanding internal states. But if mental states are intrinsically independent of the world, they can only be normatively related to that world through an interpretation. This motivates the key assumption that McDowell takes to be central to Wittgenstein's discussion. Furthermore, once that assumption – that understanding requires a mediating interpretation – is dropped, then the need for substantial philosophy will also subside.

I shall return to McDowell's argument against this Cartesian picture of inner space in Chapter 4. For now it is worth noting both that it leads to scepticism or rampant Platonism in the philosophy of content and that it is not compulsory. McDowell suggests that since this picture of mind is counterintuitive and, indeed, extraordinary, and since it is only this that motivates the otherwise implausible master thesis, it can be given up. In so doing the need for philosophical theorizing about meaning also lapses.

I began this chapter with McDowell's comment that we find natural a *contractual* picture of meaning: a picture in which grasp of a meaning imposes an obligation to use it a specific way. What is left of that idea if the master thesis is rejected? Luntley suggests that one of Wittgenstein's targets is the contractual view of meaning itself (Luntley 1991). A proper understanding of Wittgenstein's views involves, therefore, an appreciation of how he attempts to undermine contractualism. Luntley's reconstruction of Wittgenstein's argument is, however, very similar to McDowell's. He uses "contractualism" to name an *explanation* of mental content that ties inner states to the world through a kind of contract. Platonism is then a subsidiary target for criticism once a contractualist model is in play as a supposed contract that needs no interpretation. Thus the real difference between Luntley and McDowell is one of labelling. McDowell is happy to use the notion of a contract not as an *explanation* of the normativity of mental content but simply to label the *normativity* in question. Meaning can innocently be thought of as contractual in the sense that grasp of a meaning contracts one to use a word in a specific, albeit open-ended, way over time. The key and common target of criticism is a conception of the mind in which freestanding mental items are connected to the world via interpretations: the master thesis.

Sketch of an alternative view: practice

So far I have dealt with McDowell's diagnosis of the attraction of the master thesis. By the start of Section 7 of "Wittgenstein on Following a Rule", McDowell has argued that Kripke and Wright have mistaken the strategic purpose of the dilemma Wittgenstein sets out in *Philosophical Investigations* (§201) and that their own accounts of the normative connection between mind and world are satisfactory neither in their own right nor as an interpretation of Wittgenstein. McDowell begins to outline a different response to the dilemma. This is what I called the *second* element of his strategy. It begins with Wittgenstein's suggestion that obeying a rule is not an interpretation but a practice.

Wittgenstein's problem is to find a way to reject the "insidious assumption" (McDowell 1998b: 239) that there must be an interpretation between an order (or the explanation of a word) and an action (or the use of the word). Thus he talks of obeying rules *blindly* and of being *trained to react* to, for example, signposts. This might prompt an objection that such talk describes merely a matter of cause and effect rather than rule-governed behaviour. In reply Wittgenstein stresses that training is *initiation into a custom*. McDowell takes this to be an important indication of the kind of account of rule-following that Wittgenstein thinks possible.

The point here is that Wittgenstein does *not* aim to give an account of norms using concepts that are not themselves norm-presupposing. He does *not* attempt to dig beneath a bedrock of already normative behaviour. This is why he describes following a rule as *fundamental* to our language. It is also why he adds, to the well-known comment that reasons or justifications come to an end, the further claim that using an expression without a justification does not mean using it without a right. The ground-level moves made are always within the sphere of norms.

Thus, according to McDowell, Wittgenstein presents three nested pairs of choices. Either understanding has to be mediated by an interpretation or it does not. The motivation for thinking that it does is a conception of the mental as a domain of world-independent items. But if it does, then one has the unsatisfactory choice between scepticism or the mythology of rampant Platonism. On the other hand, rejection of the assumption that understanding is mediated by an interpretation appears to lead to another unpalatable option. It may seem that the only alternative to mediating by interpretations is rule-free and norm-free descriptions of behaviour, perhaps in purely causal terms. But there is another option. Blind but still rule-governed behaviour is behaviour that forms part of a *custom, practice* or *institution*.

This set of choices can be summarized thus:

* Must understanding be a species of interpretation or not?
  – If yes, then there is a further choice between scepticism and rampant Platonism.
  – If no, then the choice is between norm-free descriptions of behaviour and rule-governed customs.

So on the assumption, for the moment, that a custom requires a community of agents, McDowell's invocation of the community differs strategically from that of Kripke. Kripke deploys it to make the pair of choices "interpretation" and "scepticism" less unattractive. McDowell deploys it as a method of avoiding an interpretation-based account in the first place.

With the alternatives set out like this, what is striking about McDowell's paper is how much less attention he directs against rampant Platonism than he does against scepticism (or constructivism). I think that this is the result of two factors:

* McDowell has already argued that Platonism is the result of adopting the master thesis which is only plausible in the light of an extraordinary view of the mind.
* Platonism is an explicit target of Wittgenstein's *Philosophical Investigations*. He considers at length natural expressions of it. One example is the idea that continuing a mathematical series involves fidelity to "rails invisibly laid to infinity" (Wittgenstein 1953: §218). Another is that diagrams of simple machines somehow contain within them the possible movements of the parts (*ibid.*: §193). Wittgenstein rejects all such ideas as explanations of rule-following. Scepticism, by contrast, has been proposed as an interpretation of his philosophical conclusions. Thus it is scepticism that needs more comment.

Nevertheless, given that McDowell does not deny that there can be ratification-independent patterns of use, it is worth asking: what is wrong with Platonism?

In *Mind and World*, McDowell distinguishes between what he calls rampant Platonism and naturalized Platonism. Working with Sellars's idea that our conceptualized thought forms a rational structure called the space of reasons, McDowell introduces rampant

Platonism as "picturing the space of reasons as an autonomous structure – autonomous in that it is constituted independently of anything specifically human" (1994: 77). He goes on to contrast this idea with naturalized Platonism, which he advocates:

> In rampant platonism, the rational structure within which meaning comes into view is independent of anything merely human, so that the capacity of our minds to resonate to it looks occult or magical. Naturalized platonism is platonistic in that the structure of the space of reasons has a sort of autonomy; it is not derivative from, or reflective of, truths about human beings that are capturable independently of having that structure in view. But this platonism is not rampant: the structure of the space of reasons is not constituted in splendid isolation from anything merely human. The demands of reason are essentially such that a human upbringing can open a human being's eyes to them.
>
> Now rampant platonism figures as a pitfall to avoid in Wittgenstein's later writings about meaning and understanding. And I think naturalized platonism is a good way to understand what Wittgenstein is driving at there.   (*Ibid.*: 92)

Thus, on McDowell's reading, part of the point of Wittgenstein's analysis is to bring out the importance of the human subject in underpinning the conceptual order. I will return to the role of contingent human abilities at the end of Section IV and the implications of this for realism in Section V. But one aspect of McDowell's metaphilosophy is already clear in this interpretation. While Wright accepts a dualism of the supernatural ratification-independent rules and natural norm-free actions and thus attempts to reconstruct norms as far as possible using the latter, McDowell attempts, through the idea of naturalized Platonism, to dissolve that distinction. This is a key theme of *Mind and World* already present in "Wittgenstein on Following a Rule".

IV Hearing meaning directly in speech

So far I have set out McDowell's suggestions for the general lessons to be learnt from Wittgenstein's discussion of meaning and normativity. A natural contractual understanding of what it is to grasp a rule or form an intentional mental state can appear to be threatened by Wittgenstein's discussion of the regress of interpretations. The regress of interpretations, in turn, can seem to call for a substantial philosophical account of meaning, reconstructing it from less problematic notions and, perhaps, connecting it to communal judgements. But, in fact, the regress of interpretations is directed, in the first place, against a master thesis that understanding meaning, like any mental state, depends on interpretation. That, in turn, is part of a particular, broadly Cartesian, view of the mind. If the mind were populated by items whose existence were independent of the outer world then those items would indeed need to be reconnected to the world by interpretations. But that picture of the mind can be rejected. If so, Wittgenstein's account of meaning and normativity need not be revisionary.

In this section I shall examine McDowell's disagreement with Wright over the description of speech behaviour. This provides a further diagnosis of the reasons for their disagreement over Wittgenstein. But it also provides an important clue for understanding McDowell's view of experience (see Chs 4 and 5) and the place of meaning in nature, which will be further developed in Section V. Wright assumes that the only way to avoid a form of *psychologism* is to describe speech behaviour in thin, norm-free terms and then attempt to reconstruct a notion of normativity from this description. By contrast, McDowell argues that norm-rich meaning can be *expressed* in speech. Once one is initiated into this area of the space of reasons, one hears more in utterances than someone who does not understand language. This provides a model for initiation into the space of moral reasons and the perceptual model of moral judgements described in Chapter 2.

In the last four sections of "Wittgenstein on Following a Rule", McDowell attempts to diagnose why Wright is drawn to the interpretation he offers of Wittgenstein by examining the central "semantic anti-realist" argument on which it depends. McDowell argues that this itself turns on an assumption about the ground rules for philosophy of language, which themselves run counter to Wittgenstein's views.

McDowell ascribes to Wright an argument of the *modus tollens* form: if *p* then *q*, and not *q*; therefore not *p*. He says:

> Wright's reading of Wittgenstein hinges on this conditional: if possession of a concept were correctly conceived as grasp of a (ratification-independent) pattern, then there would be no knowing for sure how someone else understands an expression.
> (McDowell 1998b: 246)

The major conditional premise of the *modus tollens* argument thus appears to be:

1* If possession of a concept were correctly conceived as the grasp of a ratification-independent pattern, then there would be no knowing for sure how someone else understands an expression.

and the minor premise would thus have to be:

2* It is not the case that there is no knowing for sure how someone else understands an expression.

In fact the major premise McDowell ascribes to Wright is:

1   If possession of a concept were correctly conceived as the grasp of a ratification-independent pattern, then that understanding would have to be idiolectic (i.e. a matter of individual understanding).

And the minor premise is:

2   Idiolectic meaning is an illusion.

Premise 2 is justified by the claim that in a merely idiolectic context there would be no difference between merely thinking that one was in accord with a pattern and actually being so. This in turn depends – in a manner of dependence characteristic of semantic anti-realism – on the thought that one cannot distinctively *manifest*, again even to oneself, such a distinction.

Premise 1 is also underpinned by emphasis on what can be manifested: "What underlies the major premise – the conditional – is the anti-realist conception of what it is to manifest understanding to others" (McDowell 1998b: 247). This follows from the fact that one is apparently forced to an idiolectic conception of what it is to grasp a pattern as a result of Wittgenstein-inspired arguments as interpreted by Kripke. It seems that anything that can be manifested as understanding a pattern could be reinterpreted in a different way. One is thus left with the idea of "cottoning on" to a pattern for oneself and getting others to guess its essential shape. As will become clearer, this move depends on an anti-realist restriction on what can be manifested. And this in turn underpins the conditional on which McDowell said Wright's reading depended (1* above).

What makes the manifestation challenge substantial is an anti-realist restriction on how it can be met. This will also be discussed in Chapters 3 and 5, where it plays a role in the debate about theories of meaning for language and in accounts of knowledge of other minds. But in this case the restriction limits the possibilities for manifesting, to others, one's understanding of an idiolectic pattern.

> According to that conception, the behaviour that counts as manifesting understanding to others must be characterisable, in such a way as to display its status as such a manifestation, without benefit of a command of the language in question.
>
> (McDowell 1998b: 247)

This means that in ascribing a pattern of word-use to a speaker, a listener cannot deploy phrases such as "He is using the word to express the concept red". The pattern or regularity has to be picked out in some other way:

> Now what – besides itself – could be fully manifested by a piece of behaviour, or a series of pieces of behaviour, described in accordance with the anti-realist requirement? Perhaps the behaviour would license us to attribute a disposition; but how can we extrapolate to a determinate conception of what the disposition is a disposition to do? Our characterisation of the manifesting behaviour is not allowed to exploit understanding of the language in question; so even if, in our innocence, we start out by conceiving that as grasp of "a network of determinate patterns", we are debarred from extrapolating along the pathways of the network. It seems clear that within the rules of this game any extrapolation could only be inductive, which means that if we accept the requirement that understanding be fully manifested in behaviour, no extrapolation is licensed at all. The upshot is this: the anti-realist requirement of manifestation precludes any conception of understanding as grasp of a network of patterns. And this is precisely the conclusion Wright draws. (*Ibid.*: 247–8)

Wright's conclusion is not mandatory, however. The alternative (discussed in McDowell's "Wittgenstein on Following a Rule" (§11)) turns on finding a way to escape the assumptions that make the manifestation challenge substantial and compelling.

The anti-realist restriction on what can be taken to be manifested is a response to what is generally described as a form of psychologism. Anti-realism rejects the view that assigning meaning to others is a matter of *hypothesis* about something concealed behind surface linguistic behaviour. It restricts its attention to that surface behaviour. But McDowell suggests that it is merely optional to restrict description of that surface behaviour to the thin and norm-free language favoured by Wright. On McDowell's suggested alternative, the outer surface of linguistic behaviour has to be characterized as itself *expressing* thoughts and thus requiring description in terms of the *contents* of utterances made.[2]

McDowell's preferred view – in which meaning is part of the outer surface of speech behaviour, at least to those with eyes to see and ears to hear it – stands in a different relation to the contingencies on which communication depends than the view that is often associated with Wittgenstein. This latter view starts with the thought that beneath the bedrock of linguistic behaviour lies a set of contingencies concerning behaviour and the mind that can be described in norm-free language. These include shared human responses to explanations, for example, of direction by a pointing finger. Jonathan Lear expresses this view by saying that

> one becomes aware that there is nothing to guarantee one's continued correct language use beyond the fact that one happens to share with one's fellow man routes of interest, perceptions of salience, feelings of naturalness etc. From this perspective, one's continued hold on the world appears the merest contingency.
>
> (Lear 1982: 386)

With this awareness of the underlying contingencies in place, the following tempting dilemma can be put forward, either horn of which makes meaning precarious or fragile:

- On the assumption that grasp of meaning is a grasp of a pattern of use, it seems that a claim to know what another speaker means by a word is at best an *induction* that their use will continue to coincide with one's own. This inductive judgement will depend on merely contingent similarities in behavioural dispositions.
- On the other hand, one can give up an idiolectic conception and argue that agreement consists simply in marching in step right

---

2. This thought will return in McDowell's preferred view of systematic theories of meaning and in his account of how it is possible to know the content of other people's minds. In the former context, McDowell discusses and rejects a further, third, option favoured by Dummett: construing other people's speech as *guided* by *implicit* knowledge. In the latter context, the idea that behaviour expresses mental states is deployed by McDowell to bring such states within another person's epistemic grasp. Thus, while one person's inner states do not themselves fall within the experience of an observer, the fact that the subject of the mental states is *expressing* them in his or her behaviour, does. This idea of expression is *not* one that is consistent with the *absence* of inner states.

now, with no implications from past use and for future use. This is Wright's view.

Both of these options confuse levels of description that should be kept distinct. It is only by blurring these levels that the potentially revisionary view of the fragility of our conceptual order comes about. The problem is this. If the description of the underlying contingencies – concerning human responses, behaviour and abilities – is framed in norm-free terms, the kind of regularities that are present in, say, the pattern of the use of the word "red" will not be apparent. It would not be possible to chart the pattern of the use of the word "red" by saying that it was being used to pick out *red* things because that assumes a description in normative terms. Thus it seems that the conceptual order is more fragile than it really is.

The correct reading of the underlying contingencies is to concede that were certain facts not the case there would be no conceptual order. Future changes in the underlying facts that underpin our abilities to be language users would not make our *present* understanding precarious. If such changes were to come about they would prevent us *in the future* from understanding one another, but that would not retrospectively undermine present understanding.

So much, then, for the restriction that precludes the idea that a suitably educated subject can hear the meaning in another's utterances. But what positive account can be given? In a suggestive early passage McDowell puts the positive idea like this:

> How are we to make room for the phenomenological insight that one hears more, in speech in a language, when one has learned the language? How can drilling in a behavioural repertoire stretch one's perceptual capacities – cause one to be directly aware of facts of which one would otherwise not have been aware?
> ... The natural metaphor for the learning of a first language is "Light dawns". For light to dawn is for one's dealings with language to cease to be blind responses to stimuli: one comes to hear utterances as expressive of thoughts, and to make one's own utterances as expressive of thoughts ... And light does not dawn piecemeal over particular sentences: "Light dawns gradually over the whole" – a more or less coherent totality, that is, of sentences that one has been drilled into simply accepting. A difficulty in saying anything satisfying about the phenomenology of understanding is thus that working one's way into language – or

better, being cajoled into it – is, simultaneously, working one's
way into a conception of the world ...   (McDowell 1998a: 333)

This is an early suggestion of a view that McDowell develops in
later papers and in *Mind and World*. Subjects are initiated into the
space of reasons by being initiated into a worldview. They learn to
hear meanings in words and to respond to the rational connections
between meaningful words. What they acquire, however, cannot be
systematically related back to a stance that lacks the acquired
conceptual resources. And thus, as I shall describe in Chapter 5,
there is no hope of describing a route from mere patterns of noise (the
detection of which might be thought of as more epistemically secure)
to grasp of their meanings (the detection of which – via an inference –
might be thought of as less epistemically secure).

This epistemological account of the direct perception of meaning
presupposes the naturalized Platonism described at the end of Section
III. It is only by denying a contrast between a supernatural conception
of the space of reasons – rampant Platonism – and a realm of nature,
described in norm-free terms, that the capacity for perceiving rational
connections can seem unproblematically natural. Naturalized Platonism allows such rational connections, exemplified in rules governing
meanings, to have partial autonomy. They do not need to be reconstructed from human responses described in norm-free terms. But nor
are they completely independent of human abilities and behaviour.

One further aspect of McDowell's discussion deserves comment.
McDowell assumes that the practice-based alternative to the master
thesis requires *communal* practice. Why? First, recall that on McDowell's account the community is not invoked to reconstruct an ersatz
version of norms from thinner terms. The norms are implicit in communal practice. But could they have been implicit in individual practice,
as Simon Blackburn (1984a) suggests? McDowell argues that it is "precisely the notion of *communal* practice that is needed, and not some
notion that could equally be applied outside the context of a community"
(1998b: 254). The argument for this seems to be summarized in his preceding passage:

> Wittgenstein's problem was to explain how understanding can be
> other than interpretation ... This [i.e. McDowell's] non-anti-realist
> conception of a linguistic community gives us a genuine right to the
> following answer: shared command of a language equips us to
> know one another's meaning without needing to arrive at that
> knowledge by interpretation, because it equips us to hear someone

else's meaning in his words. Anti-realists would claim this right too, but the claim is rendered void by the merely additive upshot of their picture of what it is to share a language. In the different picture I have described, the response to Wittgenstein's problem works because a linguistic community is conceived as bound together, not by a match in mere externals (facts accessible to just anyone), but by a capacity for a meeting of minds.   (*Ibid.*: 253)

But this is far from clear. While McDowell undermines an anti-realist argument against being able to have genuine non-interpretative shared meaning, this does not establish that practice must be communal. In other words, he does not offer a decisive argument against escaping the master thesis by invoking *individual* practice, even if, as a matter of fact, linguistic practice is communal.

I have now sketched out the main themes in McDowell's interpretation of Wittgenstein's discussion of rules. McDowell rejects philosophical accounts that ascribe revisionary views of meaning to Wittgenstein. He argues that Wittgenstein's target is not the normativity of meaning or mental content but a conception of that normativity that requires the interpretation of freestanding inner states to connect them with the external world: the master thesis. Instead, by invoking the idea of practice, McDowell suggests how norms can be part of the foundation of human life. Further, once one is initiated into linguistic practices, one's experience can contain the meanings expressed by others in their utterances. Meaning can be part of a developed human nature.

In Section V, I shall examine two aspects of the form of naturalism that McDowell espouses as a result of his interpretation of Wittgenstein, and sketch the connection he draws between Wittgenstein and a post-Kantian understanding of nature. This will begin to show how ideas described in this chapter connect to McDowell's more recent work, especially *Mind and World*.

V German Idealism, scheme–content dualism, realism and nature

In Sections II–IV, I summarized the main arguments contained in McDowell's "Wittgenstein on Following a Rule". By contrast with Kripke's and Wright's interpretations, McDowell argues that Wittgenstein neither advances nor needs to advance a substantial account of meaning or intentionality in general. Instead, once the master thesis – that the mind is populated with freestanding items that need interpreting to be about anything – is rejected, then the philosophical problems in this area vanish. (I shall return to contrast McDowell with other philosophers who reject his claim that there need be no substantial philosophy shortly. In part the disagreement turns on disagreement about the nature of *nature*.)

In this section, I shall draw on two other papers to shed light on some comments at the end of "Wittgenstein on Following a Rule" that suggest some more general conclusions about the relation of thought and world. This will further help locate McDowell's version of Wittgensteinian philosophy within a broadly post-Kantian tradition. Post-Kantian philosophy shapes McDowell's thinking in *Mind and World* and the implicit picture of nature developed in much of McDowell's later philosophy. This section will thus help link this chapter with the rest of this book, in which the nature of nature is a repeated theme.

McDowell argues that Wittgenstein's account of rules has consequences for a proper conception of realism (1984b: §12) and thus, as I shall begin to describe, of nature. He says:

> Wittgenstein's reflections on rule-following attack a certain familiar picture of facts and truth, which I shall formulate like this. A genuine fact must be a matter of the way things are in themselves, utterly independently of us. So a genuinely true judgement must be, at least potentially, an exercise of pure thought; if human nature is necessarily implicated in the very formation of the judgement, that precludes our thinking of the corresponding fact as properly independent of us, and hence as a proper fact at all.
>
> We can find this picture of genuine truth compelling only if we either forget that truth-bearers are such only because they are meaningful, or suppose that meanings take care of themselves, needing, as it were, no help from us. This latter supposition is the one that is relevant to our concerns. If we make it, we can let the judging subject, in our picture of true judgement, shrink to a locus of pure thought, while the fact that judging is a human activity fades into insignificance ...
>
> When we say "'Diamonds are hard' is true if and only if diamonds are hard", we are just as much involved on the right-hand side as the reflections on rule-following tell us we are. There is a standing temptation to miss this obvious truth, and to suppose that the right-hand side somehow presents us with a possible fact, pictured as an unconceptualised configuration of things in themselves. (McDowell 1998b: 254–5)

In this context, the idea of meanings that "take care of themselves" with no help from us is rampant Platonism. What stands opposed to it, and to the shrinking of the judging subject to a locus of pure thought, are both the contingencies that underpin our abilities as rule-followers and language users, and the normative practices and customs that underpin those abilities and fit naturalized Platonism. But these navigational pointers still leave the question: what is meant by the claim that we are *involved on the right-hand side* of "'Diamonds are hard' is true if and only if diamonds are hard"? The right-hand side, after all, seems to invoke a worldly fact: something in which we are not involved except at the cost of idealism.[3] The answer lies in a connection to two other philosophical ideas, which McDowell invokes: the rejection of scheme–content dualism and the adoption of what he briskly labels "German Idealism". I shall describe the connection McDowell makes between post-Kantian philosophy and the private language argument, and the rule-following considerations.

The private language argument and post-Kantian philosophy

Surprisingly for a paper apparently describing Wittgenstein's argument about labelling sensations, and thus apparently a contribution to the philosophy of mind, "One Strand in the Private Language Argument" begins with the comment:

> This paper belongs in a general investigation of dualism of conceptual scheme and pre-conceptual given: that is, of the philosophical temptation to suppose that the conceptual structures that figure in experience (to put it neutrally) are the result of our imposing conceptual form on something received in pre-conceptual shape – intuitions, in a roughly Kantian shape. It is becoming a familiar suggestion in modern philosophy that this dualism is a mistake.
> (McDowell 1998b: 279)

The general idea expressed in McDowell's paper is that the passages in *Philosophical Investigations* that are generally called the "Private Language Argument" (for simplicity, the private language

---

3. The quoted sentence is an instance of a Tarskian *T* schema, used in formal theories of meaning. I shall describe the role of such instances in theories of meaning in Chapter 3.

argument in what follows) are directed against a view that grudgingly accepts a broadly Wittgensteinian and Kantian account of experience of the outer world but denies it in the case of inner experience. So by looking at McDowell's account of the apparent need for this rearguard action, and the correct response to it, I can make clearer the general picture he presents of Wittgenstein's relation to post-Kantian philosophy and German Idealism.

McDowell suggests that the best way to understand the private language argument is by placing Wittgenstein in the context of German Idealism. The key to this suggestion starts with a claim about Kant who "established that the world ... cannot be constitutively independent of the space of concepts, the space where subjectivity has its being" (McDowell 1998b: 306). This picks up the same point as the rejection, in the above quotation from "Wittgenstein on Following a Rule", of the idea that a fact is "an unconceptualized configuration of things in themselves" (*ibid.*: 255).

According to McDowell in "One Strand in the Private Language Argument", however, Kant undermines this claim about the world by suggesting that the world, which is not independent of subjectivity, results from an interplay of a noumenal realm and a transcendental subject. This spoils the insight by suggesting that genuine objectivity applies more properly to the noumenal realm. But the subsequent – and in McDowell's view laudable – tradition of German Idealism preserved the idea that the world is not independent of the space of reasons while doing away with the realm of the thing-in-itself. This is the broadly post-Kantian tradition to which McDowell wishes to enlist Wittgenstein.

McDowell now suggests that the private language argument is directed against an anti-Kantian philosophical position with the following form. The position accepts that our experience of the *outer* world is always already conceptualized – it has "a conceptual shape, an articulable experiential content" (McDowell 1998b: 279) – but it disagrees that this also applies to *inner* experience. In the case of inner experience, this anti-Kantian backlash takes one's stream of consciousness to consist of non-conceptual items about which judgements have subsequently to be made. In having a pain, for example, one encounters an item that is independent of any subsequent conceptualized judgements. Thus the anti-Kantian reaction claims that the "inner world is a lived refutation of idealism" (McDowell 1998b: 307).

On McDowell's interpretation, the private language argument is directed against this position. It argues that, for language users, even non-intentional inner states such as pains or tickles stand in relations (internal, normative) to the outer world (of behaviour, expression, action). It can thus be seen as adding to the discussion of rules and understanding. Whereas the discussion of rules is directed against construing understanding as based on the idea of mental items that are themselves unconnected with the world and have to be interpreted – the master thesis – the private language argument argues against a world-independent conception of non-intentional inner states.

Charting the philosophical territory in this way allows a further understanding of Wittgenstein's criticism of rampant Platonism. Seeing the inner realm as providing a direct refutation of idealism puts in place a particular view of what can come to mind. But "if this picture captures what it is for anything to come to mind, how could a meaning come to mind?" (McDowell 1998b: 308). Unlike sensations, meanings have explicit connections to the world. "But it is clear that a brute chunk of the 'in itself' could not have the internal links to performance that a grasped meaning would need to have" (*ibid.*). Thus it would stand in need of further interpretation and this leads to the dilemma of either sceptical regress or rampant Platonism described in the previous sections.

With the suggestion that Wittgenstein should be seen as a kind of German Idealist, McDowell is able to provide a unified account of the discussion of intentionality and of non-intentional mental items. In effect, he argues that all mental items have necessary connections to the world. Mental states – whether intentions, expectations or tickles – are all "constitutively apt for conceptual representation, not something set over against a conceptual scheme" (*ibid.*: 310–11). In the case of intentional states, this means that they do not simply stand there like signposts. In the case of sensations, they have connections to characteristic behaviour and expression.

But so far I have said nothing about outer sense except to say that the notional supporter of the rearguard action against German Idealism has already conceded to it that the outer world is constitutively dependent on the space of concepts. What is the connection between Wittgenstein's discussion of understanding rules and post-Kantian philosophy? I shall answer this question by briefly sketching an argument from McDowell's *Mind and World*, to which I shall return at greater length in Chapter 6.

Rule-following considerations and post-Kantian philosophy

In *Mind and World*, McDowell suggests that his "proposal is that we should try to reconcile reason and nature" (1994: 86). It is because of this apparent dualism that other dualisms between subject and object, mind and world seem compelling. By finding space for reason *in* nature, these other dualisms can be dismantled. So one important thread in McDowell's broader project is to show how, once the normatively structured space of reasons is construed in line with naturalized rather than rampant Platonism, the opposition between nature and reason can be shown to be false.[4]

This broader claim, which is discussed throughout this book, can be further clarified by connecting it both to Davidson's attack on scheme–content dualism and to McDowell's invocation of the Kantian slogan: "Thoughts without content are empty, intuitions without concepts are blind". As I described in the Introduction, McDowell takes this slogan to express an important insight into the possibility of having thoughts about the world or empirical content in general. But, he suggests, the slogan can be misinterpreted as lending support to the myth of the given by construing it as breaking empirical content down into two separable elements: a conceptual structure and a non-conceptual experience. The latter is the *given* and McDowell devotes several pages of *Mind and World* to arguing that it makes the rational connection of thought and the world impossible (see Ch. 6). McDowell's suggested cure is to realize that there is no notionally separable contribution to a full experience of a pre-conceptual response to the world. Using Kantian vocabulary, he puts this point by saying that "receptivity does not make an even notionally separable contribution to the co-operation" (McDowell 1994: 9). McDowell takes it that recognizing the always-already conceptualized nature of experience is a fundamentally Kantian idea.

The separation of experience into a conceptual and a non-conceptual element is one aspect of another broader philosophical myth: scheme–content dualism. In "On the Very Idea of a Conceptual Scheme" (Davidson 1984: 183–98), Davidson argues against a picture of the relation of language and the world that takes language to comprise a scheme of concepts that organizes an otherwise unstructured world.

---

4. This is *not* to say that the space of reasons can be reduced to the structure of the realm of law, the structure deployed in the natural sciences. There is no reason to restrict reason to that structure.

According to the picture the scheme of concepts can be understood independently of the world to which it can give a structure. This picture – to use a metaphor that will recur throughout this book – presupposes a sideways-on perspective to chart the connection or relation between language and the world. Its rejection is a central claim of McDowell's *Mind and World*. Whereas Davidson's specific argument against the idea of conceptual schemes takes the form of an attack on the metaphors that sustain the picture of an independent scheme and worldly content, the same conclusion can be mapped onto an interpretation of Wittgenstein on rules. This will further show the connection between McDowell's Wittgensteinian and Kantian influences.

Using the distinction between conceptual scheme and worldly content, one can see Wright and other semantic anti-realists as describing rules and language while focusing only on the scheme side. This is implicit in their attempt to give an account of linguistic practices without making use of the world-involving meaning of what is being said. Wright, in fact, also places restrictions on the nature of the scheme itself. It cannot take the form of a ratification-independent pattern. With this in mind one might construe rampant Platonism as a contrasting philosophical theory also about the conceptual scheme, but one that allows the conceptual scheme to be ratification-independent: to extend by itself. But in the case of rules governing empirical classificatory terms, rampant Platonism could also be used to label a position that takes the world as it is in-itself to guide classification.

McDowell argues, by contrast, that it is hopeless to ascribe priority either to the scheme side or the content side of a dualism of scheme and content. Instead, for the Wittgensteinian reasons described in this chapter, a description of the patterns of linguistic use has to employ a description of the world-involving content of the pattern. In the context of a denial of a distinction between conceptual scheme and empirical content, McDowell's interpretation of Wittgenstein turns on a denial that one can make sense of meaningful sentences and of worldly facts independently. Instead, in learning a language, one is initiated into a worldview at the same time. This is the claim that unites McDowell's Wittgensteinian and broadly Kantian influences.

This also explains McDowell's comments about our involvement on both sides of the sentence "'Diamonds are hard' is true if and only if diamonds are hard" and other instances of the Tarskian T schema. No priority can properly be granted to our understanding of either side. The articulation of the world into facts and the articulation of language into meaningful elements are interdependent. This is not an assertion of a form of idealism but merely a denial that any position that is outside language and the world, and that seeks to chart their interconnection, is possible.

In *Mind and World*, McDowell invokes a term from Max Weber in this context. A methodological assumption behind the rise of natural science was that the world should be thought of as *disenchanted*. McDowell goes on to suggest that an insight of broadly Kantian and post-Kantian philosophy is that the world has an intelligible structure and that the only way to capture this thought is partially to *re-enchant* the world. As I shall discuss in Chapter 6, Wittgenstein's discussion of rules and Davidson's critique of scheme–content dualism provide a clue as to what such re-enchantment involves. One cannot think of the world as containing no structure, as lying outside the space of concepts, and only subsequently clothed in conceptual form. Instead the world itself shares a conceptual structure. "Partial re-enchantment" is a label for this Wittgensteinian and Kantian insight.

I shall end this chapter with a brief comment on the way McDowell's post-Kantian view of nature contrasts with much contemporary naturalism. Consider again the following characteristic observation from Fodor (quoted in the Introduction):

> I suppose that sooner or later the physicists will complete the catalogue they've been compiling of the ultimate and irreducible properties of things. When they do, the likes of *spin, charm* and *charge* will perhaps appear upon their list. But *aboutness* surely won't; intentionality simply doesn't go that deep. It's hard to see . . . how one can be a Realist about intentionality without also being, to some extent or other, a Reductionist. If the semantic and intentional are real properties of things, it must be in virtue of their identity with . . . properties that are *neither* intentional *nor* semantic. If aboutness is real, it must be really something else.
>
> (1987: 97)

Fodor's argument turns on the assumption that nature is exhausted by the physical sciences. Thus if a property is a genuine feature of nature it must be possible either to find it in, or relate it to, a description provided by a future physics.

Fodor's explanation of the intentionality, meaning or content of mental states is based instead on a *causal* theory of meaning or reference. The underlying motivation for a causal theory is the fact that effects can sometimes carry information about their causes. One can say "those spots mean measles" or "smoke means fire". Paul Grice called examples like these cases of natural meaning (Grice 1957). Fodor deploys the same idea to argue that states of mind, or, rather, the brain, mean or refer to what they do because they are caused by their subject matter. Thus a particular type of neurological state might encode the meaning or content "Cow!" because it is caused (or "caused to be tokened") by the presence of cows.

However, this kind of *simple* causal theory cannot account for a key feature of mental content: its normativity. It cannot account for those occasions where having a mental representation corresponds to a *false* belief. In such cases, representations are caused by states of affairs that they do not depict or to which they do not refer. A simple causal theory will, however, include *all* these causes as parts of the content that a mental representation encodes. The mental representation will stand for a *disjunction* of all its possible causes and misrepresentation will be impossible. Hence the label "disjunction problem". Thus one condition of adequacy of causal theories is that they are able to discriminate between two kinds of circumstance in which a mental representation is produced in the mind. There must be occasions where the cause and the content coincide and occasions of "deviant" causation where the mental representation is caused by something from outside its extension.

Fodor's preferred solution to the disjunction problem is elegant and minimal. It is to distinguish between causal connections that are constitutive of content and those that are not, in terms of asymmetric dependence (Fodor 1987). A type of mental representation has the content "horse" if horses cause it to be tokened in the "belief box" of a thinker and if those occasions on which it is caused by non-horses depend asymmetrically on the connection to horses in this way. If the causal connection between horses and the mental representation had not existed then the connection between non-horses and the mental representation would not have existed either, but not vice versa. Occasions when non-horses cause the "horse" mental representation to be tokened can now be counted as errors.

Fodor's proposal has received much critical attention. There are published articles that attempt to show that Fodor's theory gives the wrong result in particular circumstances (e.g. Loewer & Rey 1991). But there is another more general problem highlighted by Peter Godfrey-Smith (1989). He asks what resources a *purely causal* theory has for distinguishing between the independent causal relation that determines the content of a mental representation and those dependent causal relations that correspond to error.

Consider a mental representation that is caused by normal-looking horses, athletic cows, muddy zebras and so forth. One obvious interpretation of this is that the representation encodes horse-thoughts and that the connections between it and some cows and zebras asymmetrically depend on the connection between the representation and horses. But there is another interpretation that is equally plausible given only the facts about causal connections. That is that the mental representation encodes a disjunctive content including normal-looking horses, and some cows and zebras. There is, after all, a *reliable* causal connection between those animals and the representation. It is only *given* the content of the mental representation that one can determine which connections are fundamental and which are dependent, which would hold in similar possible worlds and which would not. What this suggests is not just that there is a problem with Fodor's particular solution but that there is something generally wrong with attempts to reduce intentional notions to purely causal ones. Something is omitted by the causal account: it cannot determine which is the *correct* application.

A Wittgensteinian view of mind and meaning, by contrast, makes no effort to reduce normative to non-normative concepts. On the contrary, Wittgenstein provides arguments against the very possibility of reproducing normative relations in non-normative terms. (He, for example, rejects the view of understanding as a causal mechanism.) For this reason, McDowell describes his view of norms as naturalized Platonism. But in order to overcome Fodor's argument, more needs to be said about why the conflation of what is natural to what is describable in the concepts of physical science is mistaken. McDowell has two main suggestions, which I shall describe in Chapter 2:

- The assimilation stems from a misunderstanding of the significance of the fact that adopting a disenchanted view has been very successful in describing the world using the resources of the realm of law. A methodological strategy is misconstrued as a metaphysical insight. But a proper understanding of the Kantian insight that the world has an intelligible structure helps undermine this assumption.
- An Aristotelian model of ethics suggests a model of second nature. Human beings, and presumably any other rational subjects, have a natural ability, given a suitable education, to have their eyes opened to normative connections or requirements. With this in

place, we can begin to see how naturalized Platonism can form a part of an expanded conception of nature not limited to the concepts that belong in the realm of law.

In Chapter 2, I shall examine McDowell's account of moral judgement and shed light on these broader metaphysical themes.

Chapter 2

Value judgements

In this chapter, I shall describe McDowell's account of the moral world. Roughly, McDowell supports a form of moral realism. He argues that the world includes moral features as well as the features described by the physical sciences. More precisely, he characterizes his aim rather as defending "anti-anti-realism" (McDowell 1998b: viii). The distinction between realism and anti-anti-realism will become clear in this chapter.

The moral world is not, however, pictured as completely independent of us, or of subjectivity. Moral features do not "belong, mysteriously, in a reality that is wholly independent of our subjectivity and set over against it" (*ibid*.: 159). But this interrelation between us and the moral world – a relation McDowell likens to that between siblings rather than parent and offspring – is not a form of projectivism, where the appearance of a moral world is really the result of projecting human reactions, as though spreading the mind on to the external world. Thus his account attempts to tread a middle ground between the radical independence and the complete dependence of the moral world on moral subjects. As I shall describe in Section I, this middle ground is made a little clearer by an analogy with secondary qualities. Moral judgements are likened to judgements about secondary qualities, which, according to McDowell, have to be characterized via subjective responses to them but nevertheless can form part of the fabric of the world. But this distinction between primary and secondary qualities interpreted as sensory qualities is not without criticism.

In Section II, I sketch the broader post-Kantian account of nature and its connection to the space of reasons, of which moral judgement forms a part. This post-Kantian picture is introduced in *Mind and World* through a digression on moral judgement. The central claim that the world is constitutively apt for conceptualization – rather than comprising extra-conceptual things-in-themselves – dovetails with McDowell's defence of moral realism. I suggest that this context makes criticisms of McDowell's account of secondary qualities interpreted as sensory qualities less important to the overall account of moral judgements than they might otherwise have been.

As well as outlining the role of a post-Kantian picture of nature in general in McDowell's thinking (by contrast with a Kantian view of specifically moral judgement), Section II will introduce the idea of *second nature*. This is in the context of understanding Aristotle's relaxed naturalism about the moral realm. Both a post-Kantian picture of nature and the idea of second nature come together in the project of describing how the world makes itself known to human subjects. Thus McDowell subscribes to a form of moral *cognitivism*.

Invoking a world of moral properties is one way to give an account of how moral judgements can be correct or incorrect. Correct judgements track features of the world. This view contrasts with another position: correct moral judgements are those that accord with a system of general moral principles. McDowell's defence of moral realism accords with his criticism of a generalist or principles-based account of morals, which I discuss in Section III. Drawing on a reading of Aristotle, McDowell argues that this tract of the space of reasons – the reasons that can be given for moral judgements or actions – resists codification in any system of principles.

The resulting anti-principles position within moral philosophy is often called "particularism". It is taken by many, including Dancy, to be a radical and revisionary view. I will not, however, present McDowell's views as a part of a revisionary philosophical theory. His is instead merely a denial of the superstition that genuine cognition always requires that judgements answer to a codifiable set of principles. Once the assumptions that hold that superstition in place are exposed, then Aristotle's claim that moral judgements are not in fact codifiable becomes more mundane. Furthermore, the idea of "moral vision", using the title of David McNaughton's book (1998), can play a role in moral judgement. Judgement is underpinned by perception of real moral features in the world. But that is not to say that moral principles play no role.

Aside from articulating McDowell's views of the moral realm, my main aim in this chapter is to describe and then assess the broader metaphysical picture of the relation of mind and world that is first presented in McDowell's papers on moral philosophy and Aristotle and of which particularism plays only a supporting role. The overall question I shall highlight is: what account is given of the world or of nature and its measured independence from subjectivity?

McDowell has devoted a number of papers to discussion of the moral world, of which, perhaps, four are most central: "Aesthetic Value, Objectivity, and the Fabric of the World" (1983), "Values and Secondary Qualities" (1985b), "Projection and Truth in Ethics" (1987b) and "Two Sorts of Naturalism" (1995b). The key elements I shall explore in Section I are drawn from the first and last on that list. I shall describe McDowell's examination of the motivation for denying that the world might contain anything other than the kind of facts discovered by science. In Section II, I shall examine the broader and complementary, although less straightforward, arguments against an entirely "disenchanted", or meaning-free, nature. In Section III, I shall illustrate the relation between McDowell's particularism and his account of rule-following, discussed in Chapter 1.

I A world of moral and aesthetic features

Neo-Humeanism

In order to defend a broad view of nature that can include moral and aesthetic properties, McDowell has to undermine a narrower "neo-Humean" view in which values, like secondary properties (colours, tastes, smells and so forth), are only mistakenly thought to be "out there". The onus of proof here is taken to lie with such revisionary philosophical views. If they can be shown to be question-begging then the everyday phenomenology of responding to a world containing values can be taken at face value. The argument against those views will also outline a correct understanding of the relation between moral properties and our sensibilities.[1]

The arguments I shall set out in this section depend on the deployment of an analogy between moral judgements and judgements

---

1. McDowell himself denies that he attempts to provide a suitable basis for moral realism (2000c: 112). Instead, he says, he attempts to remove (at least) one obstacle to the thesis that moral judgements can be true and thus in that sense objective. I hope that this nuanced emphasis is clear in what follows but I shall talk, for convenience, of a defence of moral realism.

of secondary qualities thought of as sensory qualities. Having drawn the distinction between primary and secondary qualities in this way, McDowell uses it to reject John Mackie's error theory of moral judgements. He then goes on to reject a broader claim that sensory qualities cannot be genuine features of the real world. Describing this will involve describing Bernard Williams's absolute conception of reality. In Section II, I shall describe how the resultant view of moral properties fits into McDowell's broader post-Kantian view of nature in general.

One motivation for a neo-Humean view is the scientistic version of naturalism mentioned at the end of Chapter 1. I quoted Jerry Fodor's argument that, on the assumption that physical science will eventually arrive at a complete account of "the ultimate and irreducible properties of things", if another set of properties is real it must be reducible to the properties in that account. Fodor assumes, in other words, that physics has a privileged access to reality. Clearly, physics is unlikely to deploy moral properties. Thus, if Fodor's assumption is correct, moral properties have to be either related to physical properties or convicted of unreality. A neo-Humean view of ethics reflects something like Fodor's view of the importance of physics in charting the limits of nature.

A broadly neo-Humean moral philosophy can, however, take a number of forms. Perhaps the most famous example is emotivism. In *Language, Truth and Logic*, A. J. Ayer gives the following statement of an emotivist position:

> The presence of an ethical symbol in a proposition adds nothing to its factual content. Thus if I say to someone, "You acted wrongly in stealing that money", I am not stating anything more than if I had simply said, "You stole that money". In adding that this action is wrong I am not making any further statement about it. I am simply evincing my moral disapproval of it. It is as if I had said, "You stole that money" in a peculiar tone of horror, or written it with the addition of some special exclamation marks. The tone, or the exclamation marks, adds nothing to the literal meaning of the sentence. It merely serves to show that the expression of it is attended by certain feelings in the speaker.
>
> (Ayer 1946: 107)

On Ayer's account, such statements *evince* rather than *state* moral disapproval. Accounts like this are sometimes called "boo–hooray" theories because they construe moral judgements as neither true nor false, like a cry of "Boo!" or "Hooray!" Blackburn's quasi-realism, by contrast, aims to rehabilitate the truth of moral judgements (Blackburn 1984b). But he agrees with the basic neo-Humean assumption about the limits of nature in that quasi-realism builds "the features of moral language (or of the other commitments to which a projective theory might apply) which tempt people to realism" on the "slender basis" of projecting "internal sentiments" onto the world (*ibid*.: 171). A third example, Mackie's error theory, shares the same assumption about nature. He agrees with Blackburn that moral judgements make claims that could be true or false but he argues that they are all in fact systematically false because they take the world to contain features it does not (Mackie 1977).

Although there are significant differences between these positions, they share an underlying view of the place of moral features in the world. Moral properties do not form part of the "fabric of the world". Whether or not some notion of truth can be reconstructed for moral judgements, or whether or not talk of moral features is a systematic error, moral judgements are not accountable to moral features found in the world. The world contains less than might at first appear to be the case. This general view can usefully be called neo-Humean. In combating a neo-Humean view in general, and therefore defending a cognitivist account of moral judgement, McDowell takes the specific example of Mackie's *Ethics: Inventing Right and Wrong* (1977) as his main target.

Mackie concedes that the characteristic phenomenology of value judgements is one of responding to the value found in objects. Nevertheless, he argues that phenomenology embodies a systematic error. Really, value is not to be found in the world. It is not, in that sense, objective (although, as I shall describe shortly, this is not how McDowell uses "objective"). This claim applies both to ethical and aesthetic value. McDowell's aim is to dislodge this conception of the limits of what is natural by undermining Mackie's error theory. (In fact, one of McDowell's criticisms is that his opponents make no attempt to say what in principle might properly be taken to fix those limits.)

The first element of McDowell's diagnosis is to suggest that the assimilation of what is part of the fabric of the world with what is *objective* is not itself innocent. While value is subjective, and thus, in one sense, not objective, this does not imply that it cannot form part of the world. So what does McDowell mean by subjective and objective? I shall now describe McDowell's account of secondary properties and how it fits into his defence of moral realism.

Secondary qualities

McDowell defines a subjective property thus:

> A subjective property, in the relevant sense, is one such that no adequate conception of what it is for a thing to possess it is available except in terms of how the thing would, in suitable circumstances, affect a subject – a sentient being.
>
> (McDowell 1998b: 113)

He defines a secondary quality:

> A secondary quality is a property the ascription of which to an object is not adequately understood except as true, if it is true, in virtue of the object's disposition to present a certain sort of perceptual appearance: specifically, an appearance characterisable by using a word for the property itself to say how the object perceptually appears. (*Ibid.*: 133)

Thus, subjective, secondary and sensory are assimilated. As I shall explain in the rest of this section, McDowell's basic argumentative strategy is to claim that secondary or sensory qualities differ from primary qualities in a way that makes an analogy with value judgements appropriate because both depend on subjective responses. At the same time, however, secondary qualities are genuine features of the world and thus value judgements can also answer to parts of the real world.

This way of drawing a distinction between primary and secondary qualities has some difficulties, however. McDowell says that he is "heavily indebted to" Gareth Evans's account (*ibid.*: 134 n.11; Evans 1982), so further light can be shed by briefly examining Evans's arguments for such a distinction.

Evans describes his account of secondary qualities as a "dispositional route from subjective experience to objective property" (1982: 98). His main argument for a sensory or subjectivist account of secondary qualities is the supposed implausibility of objectivist accounts. (An objectivist account can be defined as one that denies that secondary qualities have to be understood in terms of how they affect sentient beings.) He contrasts his position with the attempt to make "the most direct possible leap" from subjective experience to objective property, describing this as an attempt to "make sense of the idea of a property of redness which is both an abiding property of the object, both perceived and unperceived, and yet 'exactly as we experience redness to be'" (*ibid.*: 98). This, he suggests, is impossible. Evans further characterizes objectivists as attempting to *extract* an objective property from our experiences (*ibid.*: 99). He argues that it would be impossible to extract the idea of an objective property from "colour as we see it" (*ibid.*: 99). And he backs up his suggestion that an objectivist account of colour is absurd by suggesting that it cannot respond adequately to the question of whether a colour property can exist in the dark. His dispositional route, by contrast, is supposed to avoid these difficulties.

There are, however, some difficulties with Evans's approach. First, there is no need for any but the most committed of empiricists to think of colour concepts as having to be *extracted* from experience (any more than any concept has to be). The apparent conflict between thinking of redness as both an abiding property and as what we experience it to be seems to stem from this assumption or one of two others. It might equally stem from the now discredited seventeenth-century idea that mental states make contact with the world by *resembling* worldly properties: what is generally called a "resemblance theory of intentionality". Or it might stem from the idea that the concept of red as it features in red experience characterizes an *inner* experience, an idea that McDowell rightly rejects (see below). Without those questionable assumptions, the argument against objectivism fails. Finally, colours can obviously exist in the dark although that is not a good condition for their detection.

These comments follow Peter Hacker's defence of an objective account of so called "secondary" qualities. In *Appearance and Reality* (1987), he argues that there is no important distinction between primary and secondary qualities. Secondary qualities such as colour are defined by appeal to colour samples and not by appeal to our experiences when looking at coloured objects. The connection between colours and experiences plays no definitional or clarificatory role. (He further argues that the dependence as described by Evans is quite obscure.) Secondary qualities are thus similar to supposed primary qualities such as length, which are also defined by appeal to public samples. While it is true that there are differences with regard to the systems of concepts into which judgements with samples are woven and that so called "secondary" qualities are generally tied to only one sensory modality, these differences are not sufficient to frame a metaphysically significant distinction of kind.

Aside from Hacker's specific objections to Evans (and by implication to some of McDowell's account), there is a more general Wittgenstein-inspired concern about the definition of sensory properties. It runs counter to a general Wittgensteinian hostility to placing definitional reliance on the inner experience. In this context, it looks at first as though McDowell is conceding too much to an empiricist audience. But, while Evans seems to be relying on an empiricist notion of concept *extraction*, McDowell distances himself from this view in *Mind and World*. Furthermore, although he thinks that one can only have an understanding of secondary qualities if one has an understanding of how they are experienced by a subject (e.g. a relation between being red and looking red) he does not construe looking red as a matter of inner experience.

> It is one thing to gloss being red in terms of being such as to look red, and quite another to gloss it in terms of being such as to induce a certain "inner experience" in us. Note that "red" in "looking red" expresses a concept of "outer experience" no less than does "red" in "being red", in fact the very same concept. (Sellars insists on this point in "Empiricism and the philosophy of mind".) (McDowell 1994: 31 n.7)

That said, however, once a connection between secondary qualities and inner experience is rejected, it is unclear what role the connection between being red and appearing red should play. It appears to run counter to the emphasis McDowell generally places, following Sellars, on veridical experience over mere appearance. As I shall describe in Chapters 4 and 5, on McDowell's favoured account, appearances are defined parasitically in terms of veridical experiences. In Section II, I shall return to the importance of the distinction between primary and secondary qualities given McDowell's more general post-Kantian account of nature.

McDowell's criticism of Mackie

McDowell provides the following account of Mackie's argument for an error theory of secondary qualities:

> On Mackie's account . . . to take experiencing something as red at face value, as a non-misleading awareness of a property that really confronts one, is to attribute to the object a property which is "thoroughly objective", in the sense that it does not need to be understood in terms of experiences that the object is disposed to give rise

to; but which nevertheless resembles redness as it figures in our experience . . . This use of the notion of resemblance corresponds to one key element in Locke's exposition of the concept of a primary quality. In these Lockean terms Mackie's view amounts to accusing a naïve perceptual consciousness of taking secondary qualities for primary qualities.　　　　　　(McDowell 1998b: 134–5)

Mackie thinks that it is merely an empirical fact that there are no primary qualities to which our colour concepts apply. McDowell argues, by contrast, that the very idea of such putative primary qualities is incoherent.

Starting with, say, redness as it (putatively neutrally) figures in our experience, we are asked to form the notion of a feature of objects that resembles that, but is adequately conceivable otherwise than in terms of how its possessors would look.

(McDowell 1998b: 135).

This is impossible because it requires adopting a notion of resemblance while giving up the notion of resemblance in phenomenal respects because that has to be explained in secondary quality terms (looking red to a subject).

McDowell's argument takes the form of a *reductio* and thus is independent of the success of the distinction between primary and secondary qualities to which both he and Mackie subscribe. Given Mackie's way of setting out the problem, the error that secondary quality experience is supposed to embody is in fact inconceivable. It is not just empirically false to say that colour concepts are primary, as, according to Mackie, their phenomenology seems to imply; they could not even be so conceived. So the argument for an error theory of secondary qualities fails.

Turning now to moral judgements, Mackie provides a parallel argument for an error theory of values and McDowell offers a parallel objection. If Mackie were right that experience of values was like experience of primary qualities, then, McDowell concedes, that would indeed involve an error. But it would not be an understandable empirical error.

For it seems impossible – at least on reflection – to take seriously the idea of something that is like a primary quality in being simply *there*, independently of human sensibility, but is nevertheless intrinsically . . . such as to elicit some "attitude" or state of will from someone who becomes aware of it.　　　(McDowell 1998b: 132)

More specifically, he goes on to argue that the perception of primary, non-subjective, qualities does not provide any resources for accounting for the role of *reason* or deliberation in judgements about values. Moral judgement rationalizes certain sorts of actions. So to model sensitivity to moral values on primary properties would require postulating a faculty "about which all that can be said is that it makes us aware of objective rational connections" (*ibid.*: 133).

Nevertheless, McDowell *does* want to locate the normative structure of moral requirements in a world "out there". His rejection of a primary quality model of moral judgement does not reinstate Mackie's neo-Humean view of nature or Blackburn's projectivism. Instead it construes values or secondary qualities as subjective in the sense of depending on the experience of a subject but not subjective in the sense of illusory or mere appearance (*ibid.*: 136). The key idea is that *the subjectivity of a property in the former sense does not undermine its reality.*

Secondary qualities are thus supposed to serve as a model for a property that is part of the fabric of the world but that nevertheless has to be understood through its effect on subjects. I shall later outline Wright's objections to this comparison between secondary qualities and values, but it is worth noting here Dancy's objection. He suggests that while the analogy with secondary qualities like colour is supposed to clarify how values can be both part of the world yet only understood in relation to the will, it does not succeed (1993: 156–63). The problem is that "Seeing colour as a disposition falsifies our normal colour experience, which does not seem to be the experience of a disposition. Colour, at least as we experience it, is stubbornly non-dispositional" (*ibid.*: 158). Dancy concedes that it might be possible to construe values as dispositions. If so, they would be dispositions to extract an appropriate or merited response from a moral subject. But, he argues, it is not possible to construe colours in that way. In the case of colours, the disposition to bring about effects seems instead to exist in virtue of the abiding colour property rather than the other way round. Thus there is no longer an explanation of how colours are both essentially phenomenal – tied to subjects' experiences – and in the world. And thus the analogy with secondary qualities will no longer help us place values in the world while retaining their motivational or will-related character. (Values might continue to seem essentially motivational if we construe them as dispositions, but no longer seem so clearly world-constituting).

Again, I think that this tension is simply not as great as it appears because of McDowell's emphasis on the claim that the world as a whole is "constitutively apt for conceptualization" and not an extra-conceptual world of things-in-themselves. In other words, the role of the analogy with secondary qualities – contrasted with primary qualities – is lessened. Both primary and secondary qualities are tied to the forms of conceptualization that make up the space of reasons. This claim will become clearer, however, in Section II, where I outline McDowell's deployment of a Kantian philosophy of nature in general to shed light on his moral philosophy.

One further related potential obstacle to a form of value or moral realism, already hinted at in the discussion of Mackie, is this. Moral realism requires that the output of one's sensitivity to moral facts is itself enough to play a motivational role in action. But a common assumption in the philosophy of action is that actions are sufficiently explained only by citing a *combination* of a cognitive state and a motivational state (a belief *and* a desire). McDowell's response to this obstacle is to question that assumption. He says that it is merely a piece of scientism to assume that the world cannot contain features whose perception includes motivational factors. Thus he aims to defend a form of moral *cognitivism*: one cognizes moral demands. I shall return to this point in Section III. But in line with the doubts expressed above about the distinction between primary and secondary qualities on which McDowell relies, the argument does not seem so clear-cut. I can flag an idea that will be discussed in Section II: if a proper understanding of *primary* qualities takes them to be a part of a world that is constitutively apt for conceptualization – and the world is thus to be partially re-enchanted or meaning-involving – then they cannot be taken to be radically independent of human experience either.

With these preliminaries in place, McDowell raises this question: can properties that are subjective in the sense of depending on the experience of a subject form part of the fabric of the world? Or, by contrast, is "the world fully describable in terms of properties that can be understood without essential reference to their effects on sentient beings" (McDowell 1998b: 114)? An argument that subjective properties *cannot* form part of the world requires a substantial philosophical account of what is genuinely part of the world. The best worked out such account, McDowell suggests, is Bernard Williams's discussion of the absolute conception in his *Descartes: The Project of Pure Enquiry* (1978). For that reason, I shall now detour to describe that absolute conception, and then outline McDowell's arguments that it begs the question against subjective properties.

John McDowell

Bernard Williams's absolute conception

Williams develops an account of the absolute conception in order to explain more fully an everyday understanding of knowledge. This involves the idea that knowledge (or just true belief) is accountable to an independent world. "Knowledge is of what is there anyway" (Williams 1978: 64). The absolute conception is supposed by Williams to constitute a filling out of what it is that knowledge is accountable to. It is part of an explanation of the objectivity of knowledge.

Williams's way of substantiating the absolute conception starts with the following thought. If two people have different but true beliefs, then it must be possible in principle to give an account of how their beliefs about the world relate both to one another and to the world (since all genuine truths are consistent). Perhaps their different beliefs stem from the fact that they are looking at different things. In which case, it must be possible to give an account of where they are and how their beliefs came to be formed as a result, partly, of their location. This common account both relates and contrasts their beliefs and the independent world.

The account itself is, however, a *representation* of a part of the world (containing two people, their locations and their beliefs). Thus if we can form a proper conception of that representation, this new conception must be of a representation of part of the world *distinct* from the world itself. Drawing this distinction requires forming a representation of the first account that relates it to, and contrasts it with, the world. It seems that a proper understanding of how knowledge is responsible to the world requires forming a representation of the first representation. This process iterates.

Postulating two different inquirers is, in fact, unnecessary for the thought experiment. The new representation can itself be the subject of a yet broader account of how it itself relates to, but is distinct from, the world it represents, and how it relates to other true representations of the world that could be given. Clearly this process can be iterated to include the relation between one representation and all other possible representations. The conclusion that Williams draws is that only if one can form such an *absolute* conception of the world, which includes how all possible true representations are related to it, can one have a proper conception of any individual item of knowledge, since that must include the contrast between representation and the world. Reflection on individual pieces of knowledge escalates into the absolute conception. Williams writes:

For if *A* or *B* or some other party comes in this way to understand these representations and their relation to the world, this will be because he has given them a place in some more inclusive representation; but this will still itself be a representation, involving its own beliefs, conceptualizations, perceptual experiences and assumptions about the laws of nature. If this is knowledge, then we must be able to form the conception, once more, of how this would be related to some other representation which might, equally, claim to be knowledge; indeed we must be able to form that conception with regard to every other representation which might make that claim. If we cannot form that conception, then it seems that we do not have any adequate conception of the reality which is there "anyway", the object of any representation which is knowledge; but that conception appeared at the beginning as basic to the notion of knowledge itself. That conception we might call the absolute conception of reality. If knowledge is possible at all, it now seems, the absolute conception must be possible too.

(Williams 1978: 65)

So far the argument has suggested that to have a proper understanding of knowledge, or true representations of the world, requires an understanding of the contrast between representations and the world. This in turn escalates into a conception of how true representations can be systematically related to one another and to the world. But this is still an abstract specification of the conception: a conception of the conception. Williams's idea is developed in response to a dilemma that the absolute conception raises. This concerns how the content of the absolute conception can itself be filled out.

Without some additional substantiation, there is a risk that the phrase remains empty, meaning vacuously "what true representations represent" (*ibid.*: 65). But if so, then, according to Williams, it will be impossible to understand the contrast between a representation and the independent reality it stands distinct from. On the other hand, any specific account of reality that we may be tempted to offer – perhaps in terms of objects, properties, fields of force, and so on – runs the risk of being merely another of our *representations* reflecting our local perspective and thus not a characterization of an independent reality after all. It runs the risk of being false.

Williams's own suggestion for evading both horns of this dilemma is to invoke the progress of science. This allows the non-local characterization of the absolute conception as that which is progressively revealed by science. (This is a kind of meta-conception, a conception of a conception.) It will include the findings of physics, chemistry and biology – or whatever sciences succeed them – concerning the fabric of the world in a narrow sense but also human sciences (cf. *ibid.*: 245). These will play a role in explaining both how it is possible to acquire the knowledge of the world we have obtained and also how it was possible to form the *false* beliefs that have littered the history of science since these are also, in a broader sense, part of world history.

One way of interpreting the history of science is to conclude that some of the features that human beings have previously taken to form part of the world – in the narrower sense – turn out to have been instead merely local features of our *perspective* on the world. Thus while it was once assumed that the world really was coloured, we now "realize" that colour is an artefact of the way in which humans and some other animals perceive the world. We can thus now entertain the thought that a combination of, perhaps, physics, neurophysiology and psychology will, in the future, describe not just how light and bodies interact but also how we see in colour, how we once projected this experience onto the world and how we later realized that this was wrong and came to develop the account of the world and ourselves that we are now contemplating.

On Williams's picture, the difference between primary and secondary qualities is this. Primary qualities are those that will be required by a future physics to describe the behaviour of the fundamental fabric of the world. Secondary qualities are those that are features merely of our local perspective on the world, of how the world appears to us with our particular sense organs. The progress of science is in part characterized by an increasing ability to describe the world in a way that prescinds from our specific sensory experiences and describes it instead as though from no particular perspective: a "view from nowhere" in Nagel's phrase (1986). Secondary qualities will still feature in scientific accounts but only as items to be explained in the history of science. They will be part of the broader world history, which includes our history, but not part of a narrower natural history of the world as it really is. Thus any account couched instead in secondary quality terms is not fully objective (in a sense that differs from McDowell's) because secondary qualities are not proper parts of the world.

McDowell's criticism of the absolute conception

I shall turn now to McDowell's criticism of this picture and the picture of nature it motivates. McDowell's starting assumption is that there is a fundamental distinction between primary and secondary qualities (see above). Secondary qualities, unlike primary qualities, have to be characterized by appeal to experiences. But despite conceding that there is a distinction between sensory and non-sensory qualities, McDowell argues that there is no reason to doubt that secondary qualities play a role as part of the fabric of the world.

Recall the dilemma that the absolute conception faces. To underpin the objectivity of representations it must mean more than merely: "whatever our representations represent". But on the other it cannot be substantiated by merely invoking one of our local representations of the world. That will collapse the necessary contrast between our parochial representations and what they are of.

Williams invokes science to escape this dilemma. We have a conception of the conception science will eventually give us articulated in non-local absolute concepts. Part of the moral of this account is that secondary qualities drop out from the account of properties of the world (in the narrow sense) and feature merely as aspects of our local perspective on the world to be explained (since they are part of the world history in the broader sense). Secondary qualities cannot form part of the fabric of the world and thus are not properly objective or real.

McDowell criticizes Williams's absolute conception in two ways. The first comes in Section 5 of his "Aesthetic Value" (1983). Here he disputes the idea that invoking the progress of science can be of any help with the dilemma Williams considers. The problem is that giving an account of science – so as to form an idea of the (absolute) conception – falls prey to the same sort of dilemma that trying to characterize the world (of which our representations are representations) directly. In the latter case the problem is that if one simply says that the world that our representations are of is *thus and so*, one merely uses another of our representations, and thus fails to describe the *absolute* conception. But if one says that the world is just whatever our representations are of, one falls into vacuity. According to McDowell, science faces a similar problem. If one describes science in a concrete way, spelling out specific methods, one is simply using features of our local perspective on science. But if one says "it is whatever gives us access to the world", one again falls into vacuity.

McDowell goes on to suggest that there is no need to worry about the second horn of the dilemma in the way Williams does, and thus no need to invoke the progress of science as a way of avoiding it. One can, instead, accept that one's conception of the world is one's own and that any further elaboration of how one has the beliefs about the world that one does will be an extension of one's own story, and not an account given from a perspective of cosmic exile. Just because we cannot step outside our beliefs or representations and describe their relation to the world – as though from an Archimedean point – does not undermine their objectivity. We can still non-vacuously characterize the world sufficiently to say that our beliefs are accountable to it. Of course, however, we do this by using more of our representations.

McDowell's second major criticism (in Section 4 of "Aesthetic Value") runs as follows. On Williams's picture we aspire to moving from our local perspective towards a "view from nowhere". But while the absolute conception is supposed to *contrast* with our local perspective, it also has to *include* it since even our local representations need explanation. But how can secondary or *sensory* qualities be described and explained except by *adopting* the relevant perspective? Knowing what it is that is to be explained requires adopting the perspective from which, *ex hypothesi*, they make sense. Thus there is a tension in the goals of the "view from nowhere" implicit in the absolute conception.

In the case of qualities like colour and taste, this argument turns on the idea that unless one has a grasp of what it is like to experience them, to enjoy the relevant quale or subjective experience, then one cannot have a conception of them. That is McDowell's account of "sensory properties". In the case of more obviously value-laden judgements and attitudes, such as judgements that things are funny, there is less temptation towards a reification of what is involved (e.g. humour qualia). But it seems no less plain that it would be a hopeless task to attempt to explain, from the disengaged and alienated perspective of the "view from nowhere", what it was to find something funny.

If the absolute conception cannot fulfil its role of demarcating those properties that constitute the fabric of the world and those that do not, then it cannot contribute to an argument that judgements of secondary qualities or values do not respond to genuine natural features of the world. McDowell does not advance an argument to show that these can be world-constituting properties but he undermines the best argument against that view. That task accomplished, our pre-philosophical view that moral judgements answer to a world of moral properties can be reinstated. Values are not wholly independent of us but they can form part of the world's fabric. McDowell writes: "Values are not brutely there – not there independently of our sensibility – any more than colours are: though, as with colours, this does not prevent us from supposing that they are there independently of any apparent experience of them" (1998b: 146).

The arguments discussed in this section have been based on a distinction between primary and secondary qualities with secondary qualities interpreted as dependent on us, as not *brutely* out there, although still out there independently of individual judgements. In Section II, I shall describe McDowell's discussion of the lessons for moral realism to be learnt from Aristotle and Kant. But before doing that I shall conclude this section by looking at a rival distinction between primary and secondary qualities. I shall argue that it does not impact on McDowell's main claims about the reality of moral properties.

Wright's argument against the analogy of colour and value

Whereas the philosophers discussed in this section broadly agree that there is a useful analogy to be drawn between secondary qualities and moral values, Wright has argued that this is not the case. His argument starts from a different but related account of the connection between secondary qualities and the subjects' experiences or judgements. This is explained by what he calls the "order of determination test". The idea is that this test gives different results for secondary qualities, such as colour, and for moral values. (The test is what underpins his more recent account of intentions discussed in Chapter 1.)

The order of determination test serves there to distinguish between primary qualities that inhere in the world independently of, and prior to, judgement, and secondary qualities whose extensions are fixed by judgement. In the latter case, judgement plays a *constructive* role. Ongoing human judgement constructs the extension of a secondary concept – the items the concept applies to – rather than such judgement being accountable to that extension, thought of as something that is already determined. The idea is as follows. There is a biconditional that holds between the instantiation of secondary quality concepts and the judgements that they obtain: x is R iff x would be seen as R by normally functioning observers in normal circumstances. Like the Euthyphro dilemma – is the pious loved by the gods because it is pious, or is it pious because they love it? – this can be read in two contrasting ways. Read right to left, it states that the judgements track or reflect the fact that the concept applies. Read left to right, it states that it is in virtue of the judgements being made that the concept applies. That that is the case does not undermine the *truth* of the application of the concept. But the explanation of that truth is different. The concept applies because of the practice of judgement rather than the fundamental constitution of the world.

Wright's order of determination test requires that four conditions are met. These are individually necessary for a judgement to be constructive and, according to Wright, jointly sufficient (Wright 1989: 247–9, 1992: 108–39). Although it is not necessary to spell these out in detail here, they are, in brief:

- a priority condition: the truth of the biconditional must allow a priori knowledge;
- non-triviality condition: the background conditions must avoid trivial "whatever it takes" specification;
- independence condition: the satisfaction of the background conditions must be logically independent of facts about the extension of the concept judged to apply;
- and extremal condition: there must be no better explanation of the biconditional than extension determination.

If these are satisfied then the conditional is supposed to be extension-determining. The reason is this. If one can spell out, a priori, substantial conditions under which judgements of a certain kind will turn out to be true, then, if there is no better explanation, the best explanation of this fact is that these judgements themselves serve as the standard of correctness. The extensions of the concepts judged are determined or constructed by the judgements.

Applied to secondary qualities, the idea is that one can state, a priori, substantial conditions for making judgements of colour, for example. Normal observers with normal visual systems in normal afternoon lighting will make correct judgements about colours. The best explanation for this general a priori truth is that judgements of this sort serve to fix the colours. This is all there is to being a particular colour.

For primary qualities, by contrast, the test gives a different result. Because there is no way to characterize ideal conditions for the perceptual judgement of, for example, shape that meets the four conditions, shape cannot be thought of as answering to such perceptual judgements. To give a sense of the problem, Wright points out that visual judgement of squareness requires that one changes one's perspective on the figure in question so as to distinguish genuine squares from other quadrilaterals. But the shape of the figure must remain stable during this change and that cannot be specified without violating the second or third condition. Furthermore, it is not a priori that shape can be successfully determined.

> For, bluntly, it is not *a priori* true, but merely a deep fact of experience, that our (best) judgements of approximate shape, made on the basis of predominantly visual observations, usually "pan out" when appraised in accordance with more refined operational techniques ...   (Wright 1988: 20)

Wright argues that when this test is applied to moral judgement, such judgements fail it. That is, moral judgements track rather than fix moral properties. The reason for this is that the circumstances that have to be spelled out for successful moral judgement (akin to conditions on normal lighting and normal observers in the case of colour) have to include the stipulation that the judger is a "morally-suitable subject" (*ibid.*: 23). Thus the third general condition is not met. Wright concludes that there is thus a disanalogy between moral properties and secondary qualities. (He goes on to cast doubt on a full analogy with primary qualities as well, partly because moral properties do not have the diversity of interactive role of primary qualities.)

Although Wright's order of determination test provides a suggestive way of thinking about the source of the objectivity of secondary qualities, it need not provide an objection to McDowell's Evans-influenced characterization of them. The point is that, whatever its precise significance, it is clear that McDowell does not intend the connection between secondary qualities and experience to play a reductive role. McDowell does not argue that it is in virtue of experiences had or judgements made that secondary qualities have the extensions they do. That would suggest that it was possible to give an account of the norms governing the correct use of "red", for example, without presupposing its content. Wright's account of secondary qualities dovetails with his constructivist account of rule-following and meaning. As I described in Chapter 1, McDowell rejects that view as one that cannot account for the phenomenology of meaning.[2]

---

2. Indeed, what is puzzling about Wright's test is the account he can give of concepts that fail it. What, according to him, accounts for the extension of concepts that are not determined by judgements?

This is not to defend the connection between secondary quality concepts and experiences that McDowell stresses. But in Section II, I hope to show that McDowell's general post-Kantian sketch of a philosophy of nature undermines the need for a contrast between primary and secondary qualities drawn in this way. One element of that picture, traced back to Kant, is the idea that the world of both primary and secondary qualities is constitutively fitted to our concepts. Put roughly, McDowell's post-Kantianism undermines the contrast in kind between primary and secondary qualities and suggests that all are secondary qualities in the sense of being constitutively apt for conceptualization within the rational space of reasons.

II The grounds of moral judgement and a moral outlook: Aristotle and Kant

The suggestion that the world contains moral values – even though they are appreciable only to one particular kind of subject – dovetails with McDowell's approach to the apparent need of a philosophical justification for moral judgements. McDowell defends an Aristotelian confidence in the fact that there really are genuine moral requirements placed on our reasoning that can be taken for granted. In this section I shall examine his account of why this confidence has been lost and thus why, in the light of this loss, it seems that moral judgement has to be justified in other terms. It will transpire that McDowell's account of the only partial independence of the moral world fits his defence of a generally post-Kantian account of the whole of the world. The central paper I shall discuss in this section is "Two Sorts of Naturalism" (1995b).

McDowell summarizes the aim of his interpretation of Aristotle as follows:

> We find it difficult not to want a foundation, but that is because of a location in the history of thought that separates us from Aristotle. To understand his naturalism correctly, we need to achieve a willed immunity to some of the influence of our intellectual inheritance, an influence of which Aristotle himself was simply innocent. That way, we can stop supposing the rationality of virtue needs a foundation outside the formed evaluative outlook of a virtuous person.   (1998b: 174)

This follows a discussion of what McDowell takes to be an erroneous reading of Aristotle in which Aristotle's naturalism is interpreted in a different way:

> There is an Aristotelian notion of what is necessary as that without which good cannot be attained. It can be tempting to suppose that when Aristotle relates human virtue to nature he is, in effect, exploiting that notion in order to validate the appeal of ethical considerations to reason. The idea is that the appeal is validated on the ground that the virtues are necessary in that sense, with the necessity founded in independent facts, underwritten by nature, about what it is for a human life to go well. But I think any such reading of Aristotle's intentions is quite wrong.   (*Ibid*.: 167–8)

Much turns on what *nature* is taken to include. On this wrong reading, an Aristotelian picture of the role of virtuous action, in underpinning human happiness or flourishing, provides a "theory-neutral" justification for attention to the virtues. On the assumption that human flourishing can be described in terms that do not themselves presuppose moral value or virtue, and on the assumption that acting virtuously promotes human flourishing, then there can be a justification for the real import of virtuous action. Such action is a means to the end of human flourishing, which can itself be conceptualized in independent, virtue-free, terms.

But, McDowell contends, Aristotle had no such justificatory or reductionist aim. Virtuous actions are worth performing for their own sake and not as a means to another end. A virtuous action's appeal consists, without mediation, in its being noble. But the evaluation of what is noble presupposes a moral standpoint and thus cannot serve as a neutral justification for it. This is also suggested by the fact that Aristotle "addresses his ethical lectures only to people who have been properly brought up" (*ibid*.: 174). In other words, he does not attempt to provide an independent way into a moral standpoint and does not attempt to justify one to potential outsiders.

In part, Aristotle's confidence is a form of chauvinism, McDowell suggests. He simply is not alive to the possibility of other moral views. But another key factor, noted in the first quotation in this section, is his historical location. Since Aristotle's time, the rise of modern science has transformed our view of the world or nature. The importance of this, according to McDowell, is that "It is a commonplace that modern science has given us a disenchanted conception of the natural world" (*ibid*.: 174). This contrasts with a medieval view of the world as filled with meaning, a book of nature with lessons for us. But, McDowell argues, this new view of the world has had a damaging effect on our thinking about judgements that cannot fit into this "disenchanted", meaning-free, view.

Given the success of science in telling us about the natural world, and given its methodological presupposition that nature is devoid of meaning, then it can seem – although this does not in fact follow – that whatever meaning or intelligible order is apparently found in the world is really the product of operations of the mind projected onto it. This is the assumption that drives neo-Humean accounts of moral judgement. Given this assumption, whatever standard of correctness a form of reasoning can answer to – on the assumption it is not in wholesale error – will have to be constructed from features of the world or nature described in a disenchanted manner. Hence the project of trying to "ground the rationality of ethics in something like what it is for the life of the species to go well" (*ibid.*: 177).[3]

McDowell suggests that the assumption that what is admittedly a successful methodological strategy for natural science is also a metaphysical insight can be put into the context of the interplay of Kant and Hume, to which I shall now turn.

The place of moral judgements in a post-Kantian view of nature

McDowell suggests that attention to the relation between the views of Kant and Hume can help make the idea that moral properties can form part of the real world seem less strange. He presents the following brief sketch. Hume argued that there is no meaning or intelligible order in the world and that what appears to be there is really the result of the projection onto the world of a subject's thoughts. But those thoughts or mental transactions can themselves be described, in principle, in equally meaningless terms as mere mechanisms. This gives rise to a sceptical view of such a meaningful order.

According to McDowell, Kant realized that the world cannot be, as Hume seems to think, "an ineffable lump, devoid of structure" (Mc-

---

3. The only other options seem to be either to convict, with Mackie, moral thinking as a systematic error or to construe moral reasons as supernatural and answering to standards of correctness that have nothing to do with our worldly nature, a form of rampant Platonism. McDowell rejects both views. The rejection of the latter helps explain his "particularism", discussed in Section III.

Dowell 1998b: 178). Instead "an acceptable world-picture consists of articulable, conceptually structured representations. Their acceptability resides in their knowably mirroring the world; that is, representing it as it is" (*ibid.*: 178). But if so, McDowell argues, "we cannot suppose (with Hume) that intelligible structure has completely emigrated from the world ... we have to suppose that the world has an intelligible structures matching the structure in the space of *logos*" (*ibid.*: 178). It cannot, after all, be independent of the space of meaningful thought. Unlike Rorty, McDowell is happy with the idea that true judgements mirror the world.

> But mirroring cannot be *both* faithful, so that it adds nothing in the way of intelligible order, *and* such that in moving from what is mirrored to what does the mirroring, one moves from what is brutely alien to the space of *logos* to what is internal to it.
>
> (*Ibid.*: 179)

This claim is important to McDowell's thinking in *Mind and World*, in which he borrows Sellars's phrase "the space of reasons", to stand for the space of *logos*. The space of reasons stands for the rational and normative structure that governs the use of concepts. (As examples of relations between items in that space, McDowell himself gives "implication or probabilification" (1994: 7).) According to McDowell, the world itself cannot lie outside the space of reasons. That is, to be a world at all is to possess the kind of intelligible structure charted in the space of reasons. The difficulty is then to hold on to this claim without subscribing to a form of idealism.

In "Two Sorts of Naturalism" (1995b), McDowell suggests that Kant combines the genuine insight that the world has to possess an intelligible structure mirroring our concepts with a bad metaphysical picture. That the world has such a structure is explained as a result of its joint constitution by both material from human subjectivity – material that belongs in the space of reasons – and a world of things-in-themselves that is fully independent of human subjectivity. Of course, on Kant's picture, this joint constitution happens, so to speak, transcendentally. Nevertheless, it means that the empirical world, the world of appearance, is not, as we pre-philosophically take it to be, fully independent of us. This leads to an unconvincing idealism.[4]

---

4. McDowell provides a different and more charitable reading of Kant in the Woodbridge Lectures (1998e), where he distinguishes more carefully the transcendental from the transcendent. I shall ignore this correction here.

McDowell suggests that one response to the threat of idealism in this version of a Kantian picture involves an attempt to *detranscendentalize* the picture while retaining the assumption that an objective world has to be thought of as intelligible in terms outside the space of reasons. In other words, while not construed as involving things-in-themselves, the world is taken to be devoid of meaning. This disenchanted world, which is the stuff of natural science, is taken to play the role of Kant's "in-itself" in being fully independent of human conceptualization. Meaning – and moral, aesthetic and many other non-scientific properties – is projected onto it by human minds.

There is a tension in this neo-Humean response. On the fully Kantian account of the construction of an intelligible empirical world through the interaction of the transcendental subject with the in-itself, *all* meaning and order is the result of a projection, albeit a transcendental one. On the detranscendentalized account, the disenchanted world is assumed to possess an intelligible order already. All *other* meaning is projected, this time through empirically describable processes. The tension comes from the fact that the disenchanted world is also taken – as is Kant's realm of the "in-itself" – as standing fully outside the space of reasons and human subjectivity. McDowell's brief "mirroring" argument sketched out above is that these two claims are incompatible.

Putting that worry aside, on the neo-Humean picture, whatever truth can attach to an area of judgement, such as moral judgement, must be thought of as accountable to the mind-independent world. That mind-independent world is identified with the disenchanted or meaning-free world of natural science. (Again, the alternatives are rejecting the form of judgement as constituting a systematic error or construing it as answering only to *supernatural* standards.) It is this assumption that gives the task of justifying moral judgements some urgency, for example, using concepts that have their use in describing a disenchanted world.[5] Thus the key to regaining Aristotle's lack of concern for this justificatory project is, McDowell suggests, rejecting this reaction to Kant. But what other response is available?

McDowell's suggestion is that it is possible to have much of the Kantian picture without the world of things-in-themselves.

---

5. This is not Kant's view. As I shall describe at the start of Section III, he takes moral judgement as answering not to the world but instead to a formal code imposed on our thinking from outside anything natural, i.e. supernatural.

We should not conceive the disenchanted natural world as a satisfying detranscendentalized surrogate for the "in itself". Since it is a world, the natural world is not constitutively independent of the structure of subjectivity. It is a mistake to conceive objectivity in terms of complete independence from subjectivity. We miss the point if, retaining the hankering that that idea expresses, we nod in the direction of Kant's lesson that the "in itself" is nothing to us, but think we can fasten onto the disenchanted natural world as the next best thing . . . The real lesson is that we ought to exorcize the hankering. (McDowell 1998b: 180)

Elsewhere, he offers another brief summary, which explicitly links his own thinking to the tradition of German Idealism: ·

Kant – to resort to a thumbnail caricature – established that the world . . . cannot be constitutively independent of the space of concepts, the space where subjectivity has its being. Kant himself preserved a residual role for the idea of something more brutely alien to the realm of thought than that, something that co-operates with mind in the transcendental constitution of the world. But Kant's successors saw (in one way or another) that the fundamental thesis, that the world cannot be constitutively independent of the space of concepts, does not require this residual recognition of an "in itself". This tradition is generally known as "German Idealism" . . . (but) need not be idealistic in any obvious sense. (*Ibid.*: 306)

The moral of this metaphysical picture is quite general. It applies to the world of physical as well as moral facts. McDowell suggests that, across the board, the world is not independent of us and our concepts. This is a general condition for it being intelligible. At the same time, he insists that this is not to subscribe to a form of idealism. But it is this thought that is illustrated by the comment (quoted in Chapter 1):

When we say "'Diamonds are hard' is true if and only if diamonds are hard", we are just as much involved on the right-hand side as the reflections on rule-following tell us we are. There is a standing temptation to miss this obvious truth, and to suppose that the right-hand side somehow presents us with a possible fact, pictured as an unconceptualised configuration of things in themselves. (*Ibid.*: 255)

I shall return to consider this very general post-Kantian framework and whether it really can escape a form of idealism in discussing *Mind and World* in Chapter 6. But, to go back to moral judgements, the general framework of Kant's account of how intelligible order is injected into the natural world implies a particular view of how intelligible moral order – in the form of significant, meaningful action – is injected into a world of mere movements. Just as the empirical world – the domain of theoretical reason – results from the injection of meaning into the realm of things-in-themselves, so, on McDowell's interpretation of Kant, the moral world – the domain of practical reason – results from the further injection of meaning into the empirical world. Both processes take place transcendentally. The neo-Humean view rejects the first aspect and replaces it with a view of what is really real, as given in meaning-free natural scientific terms. But moral order is injected into the world in something akin to Kant's idea.

McDowell rejects both these views. He repeats the diagnosis offered in the case of the non-moral world. He suggests that we should recognize Kant's insight but reject his way of responding to it. To be a world at all is to be structured in a way that is right for conceptualization and is thus not to be independent of our subjectivity. But we should reject Kant's account of the construction of the empirical world from something more independent: the in-itself. Similarly in the case of neo-Humean accounts of the moral world, we should reject a view of the world that is limited to the disenchanted description that emerges from the natural sciences. This means that McDowell can embrace a world of moral facts that moral judgements aim to get right. There is no need to attempt to justify moral thinking as serving a further purpose that can be described in disenchanted natural scientific terms.

Naturalism in moral philosophy

In what sense, then, is this a *naturalistic* account of moral judgement? On McDowell's interpretation of Kant's philosophy (both theoretical and practical), meaning or intelligibility is injected into the world from outside it. Thus, to take the case I am now interested in, the intelligibility presupposed by moral judgement is thought of as having its origins outside the world. It is not naturalistic. But by rejecting the hankering after a world that is independent of the structure of our concepts, McDowell has a different account of the origins of that intelligibility. Rather than having to be injected into the world – whether construed as ultimately dependent on Kant's realm of the "in-itself" or on a scientistic model of a disenchanted world – meaning and order is there already. So McDowell can argue that moral judgements aim to get right features of the world. His can properly be called a naturalistic account, once naturalism is rescued from its scientistic overtones.

Naturalism enters the picture in a second, complementary way. The ability to form moral judgements in the face of the moral facts – once one's eyes have been opened by suitable education – is taken to be part of our nature as human beings. It is part of our *second nature*. So our judgements answer to the moral nature of things and our ability to frame such judgements is a natural capacity we have, once trained. "The practical intellect's coming to be as it ought to be is the acquisition of a second nature, involving the moulding of motivational and evaluative propensities: a process that takes place in nature" (McDowell 1998b: 185). Although this is not made explicit, these two aspects are further united through a claim that was central to Section I. McDowell argues that the subject matter of moral judgements are more like secondary than primary qualities in that a proper understanding of them requires an understanding of a subject's experience. In the moral case, an understanding of moral properties requires a grasp of the role they play in our thinking, which includes their *motivational* powers. It is thus no accident that as well as describing the worldly component as natural, he also describes our moral reactions as natural too.

There are two further key differences between the standards that govern empirical or natural scientific judgements and moral judgements. First, in the former, but not the latter, the facts themselves play a *causal* role in our finding out about them. And, secondly, that causal role allows for an explanation of *convergence* on the results of particular judgements. Neither of these apply to moral judgements. But causation, McDowell argues, is not a neutral arbiter for the status of an area of reason. Although it fits into a view of the world described by natural science, it would be a further unjustified move to use it to argue against the involvement of the world of judgements that lie outside the natural sciences.

By bringing together a broadly post-Kantian philosophy of nature with Aristotle's confident moral realism, McDowell is able to defend a picture of nature that is much broader than conventional contemporary philosophical naturalism. There is no attempt to reduce properties to those found in physics as a metaphysical gold standard of what is really real.

In Section I, I described McDowell's arguments against the claim that values could not be part of the natural world. These turned on a distinction between primary and secondary qualities, with the latter interpreted as subjective or sensory qualities. The conclusion was that there was no reason to believe that the world only contains properties whose conception does *not* require a particular kind of mind or sensibility. I expressed some concern about the definition of secondary qualities as subjective. But it should now be clearer that, in the context of McDowell's more general post-Kantianism, the contrast between primary and secondary qualities is not as sharp as it might at first seem. Furthermore, the general emphasis on the idea that the world is "not brutely there – not there independently of our sensibility" could be taken to refer not so much to sensory experiences or qualia as to the rational structure of the space of concepts or reasons. So interpreted, the arguments of these two sections can be brought into line and the spectre of an overly empiricist account of secondary qualities rejected.

Before turning to McDowell's arguments against a generalist codification of moral judgement, I shall briefly describe a criticism of McDowell's moral cognitivism raised by Blackburn. The argument turns on the example of cuteness:

> Cuteness, our man says, elicits and justifies various affective reactions. It is hard to specify them except as perceptions of cuteness, but perceiving cuteness in women, when all goes right elicits and justifies reactions along the lines of admiration and arousal in men, or envy or admiration, from women. Indeed, there is a thick evaluative practice, together with procedures for regulating dissent, involved. Those who talk of cuteness are all "regular" (virtuous) guys, but there is to-and-fro over whether some features are incompatible with cuteness, such as intelligence, age, or big feet. But that is how it is in ethics. And, he may add, if it comes to votes, maybe a majority of people see it like him and his friends. (Blackburn 2000: 101)

Blackburn continues:

> Now it is *morally* vital that we proceed by splitting the input from the output in such a case. By refusing to split we fail to open an

essential specifically *normative* dimension of criticism . . . What is wrong with them is along these lines: they react to an infantile, unthreatening appearance or self-preservation in women, or overt indications of willingness to be subservient to men, with admiration or desire (the men) or envy and emulation (the women) . . . Children and pets are quintessentially cute. Applied to women, this, I say, is a bad thing. Once we can separate input from output enough to see that this is what is going on, the talk of . . . a special perception available only to those who have been acculturated, simply sounds hollow: disguises for a conservative and ultimately self-serving complacency. (*Ibid.*: 101)

Blackburn's idea is that McDowell's account of moral perception lacks properly critical resources. If all that can be said is that the world contains features for those subjects with the appropriate perceptive faculties to see them, that can only be understood by adopting the relevant perspective on the world, then it seems that no resources are available simply to deny the existence of the property. I do not think that this is a decisive point, however, for two reasons:

- McDowell's position does not lack critical resources. Although he suggests a perceptual metaphor for moral judgement, such judgement is still subject to reason, playing a critical role for perception. In *Mind and World*, McDowell discusses the way in which the concepts passively drawn on in experience also play a role in articulating a worldview (see Chapter 6). Through these connections, reason has a standing obligation to reflect on the status of concepts deployed in both active judgement and experience. Thus cuteness, as a proposed aspect of an understanding of the world, can be assessed from the broader context into which judgements of supposed cuteness fit. But granting reason that role does not require that we are able to identify a value-free basis for moral judgement.
- The example of cuteness does indeed seem to display the sort of dependence on a particular context or perspective that McDowell suggests is involved in adopting a moral perspective, even on Blackburn's supposedly descriptive analysis. If that analysis were correct – an "infantile, unthreatening appearance or self-preservation in women, or overt indications of willingness to be subservient to men" – it seems unlikely that the appearances involved could form a pattern recognizable to someone outside particular human evaluative practices.

III The uncodifiability of moral judgement

In this section, I shall examine briefly McDowell's claim that moral judgements are uncodifiable. This view has been described as "particularism" (Dancy 1993; Hooker & Little 2000). By placing my account of this element of McDowell's moral philosophy at the end of this chapter, I hope to have minimized the suggestion that it is the radical heart of a revisionary philosophical view. Although others, such as Dancy, who subscribe to a particularist account of moral judgement do indeed seem to intend by it such a radical revisionary view, it does not play that role in McDowell's philosophy.

The key influences on McDowell to be discussed in this section are Wittgenstein and Aristotle, rather than Kant and Aristotle. Thus the account he gives of moral judgement and virtuous action described here floats, to some extent, free of the Kantian picture noted above. The idea, in a nutshell, is that the result of a moral upbringing is initiation into an area of practical rationality by which one is equipped with a set of moral concepts that can be applied to both recognize the demands of situations and guide one's actions. But this area of the space of reasons cannot be codified into a kind of mathematics of moral principles. It thus becomes part of one's second nature to see the world as containing moral demands on one's actions.

As I have already described so far in this chapter, McDowell defends a form of moral cognitivism. Possession of virtue is a form of knowledge because it requires getting things *right*. Taking the example of the demands that kindness might make on a moral agent in a range of situations, McDowell argues that a kind person has a *reliable sensitivity* to those demands. Such sensitivity is a form of perceptual knowledge. Furthermore, since a potentially kind action would only in fact count as moral or virtuous if it were carried out for that reason alone – no further, perhaps self-serving motive can also be operative – sensitivity to the demands must alone explain the action.

> But the concept of the virtue is the concept of a state whose possession accounts for the actions that manifest it. Since that explanatory role is filled by the sensitivity, the sensitivity turns out to be what the virtue is. (McDowell 1998b: 52)

There is a kind of holism about the knowledge involved here. Since the demands of fairness, for example, might be trumped on occasion by those of kindness, "no one virtue can be fully possessed except by a possessor of all of them" (*ibid*.: 53). Virtue is thus a single complex sensitivity that is instilled as part of a moral outlook.

One feature of this account is, as has been briefly noted already, that McDowell thinks that moral actions are explained by a cognitive state alone; they are the result of a perception of the moral demands of the case. This breaks with the tradition in which any action is explained by a combination of a cognitive state and a motivational or orectic (driven by appetite) state. The traditional picture – exemplified in a "practical syllogism" – explains action by deploying a pair of mental states that can be expressed by a pair of sentences. It is a *practical* syllogism because the conclusion of the syllogism or argument is an action rather than a proposition. The first mental state – corresponding to the major premise – describes a general goal. The second mental state – the minor premise – expresses a belief and thus describes a fact. For example: I desire to feed the cat; I believe that I can only feed the cat by visiting the kitchen; thus I visit the kitchen.

The first premise – the desire – is not a matter for cognition. This fits a further metaphysical assumption:

> Cognition and volition are distinct: the world – the proper sphere of cognitive capacities – is in itself an object of purely theoretical contemplation, capable of moving one to action only in conjunction with an extra factor – a state of will – contributed by oneself.
>
> (*Ibid*.: 57)

A consequence of McDowell's one-factor cognitivist model appears to be that if two people act differently in response to a situation then they cannot have the same cognition or perception of it. By contrast, on the two-factor model of action explanation, they might agree in their cognitive states or beliefs but differ in their goals or desires. In fact, McDowell suggests a less radical Aristotelian idea. A moral agent may not do the right thing even though he or she has the right perception, but his or her perception is clouded by desires to act otherwise. But this modification does not reintroduce a two-factor model in the case of successful moral action.

McDowell makes three points to make this approach less counterintuitive:

- Following Aristotle, in properly virtuous action the reason for acting does not merely outweigh other potential reasons for acting otherwise. Instead, it *silences* them. Two people who act

93

similarly may not both achieve a state in which the reason for acting silences all other reasons.

- Virtuous action involves seeing, in the situation, specific features that call for a specific response. Two people viewing the same situation may not share the same perception of what feature in the situation is relevant for framing an appropriate judgement or action in response.

- It is merely a product of scientism to assume that the world cannot contain features whose perception includes motivational factors. That the distinction between theoretical contemplation and volition matches what is in the world and what is in us is merely an assumption.

The third of these points was discussed in Section I. McDowell argues that even properties or features whose understanding requires an understanding of our response to them can form part of the fabric of the world. The world contains more than would feature in the core of an absolute conception of it. The first point is really an instance of the second. In the rest of this section, I shall concentrate on how appreciation of what is the relevant feature of a situation can form part of a knowledge of virtue.

McDowell suggests that one reason for hostility to a cognitivist account of moral judgement is an assumption that if virtue is a form of knowledge then it must be codifiable. His response to this has two components. The first is to disarm a general assumption about the usual shape of understanding or rationality through an appeal to Wittgenstein's discussion of rule-following. The second is to appeal to an unprejudiced view of morality in which it is simply apparent that no system of moral principles would deliver the "right" result in all cases.

To take the second component first, having summarized how a non-cognitive view can deploy the practical syllogism in explanation of virtuous action, preserving a cognitive view only of the minor premise, he says:

> This picture fits only if the virtuous person's views about how, in general, one should behave are susceptible of codification, in principles apt for serving as major premises in syllogisms of the sort envisaged. But to an unprejudiced eye it should seem quite implausible that any reasonably adult moral outlook admits of any such codification. As Aristotle consistently says, the best generalisations about how one should behave hold only for the most part. (McDowell 1998b: 57–8)

This is the *only* argument McDowell deploys for particularism. He does not argue, for example, as Dancy does, that considerations that contribute prima facie to the moral justification for an action in one case might count against it in others (Dancy 1993: 97). He does not oppose what is often called "Rossian generalism": a view that ascribes importance to generalizations but denies that there is a calculus of their relative weights (Hooker & Little 2000: 3). There is no suggestion of a radical moral philosophy.

Nevertheless, McDowell suggests that Aristotle's obvious truth is missed because of a prejudice about the nature of rationality. Unpacking this prejudice includes a return to the subject of Chapter 1: Wittgenstein's account of rule-following. But it is worth noting now how implausible it would be to ascribe to McDowell a self-consciously revisionary view. The suggestion instead is that the observation that our moral judgement cannot be codified into an exceptionless set of principles is meant to be a pre-philosophical claim that is only resisted because of an implicit but mistaken philosophical theory.

Consider Wittgenstein's example of the "add 2" series. McDowell suggests that we tend to think of competence in continuing such a series as resulting from a psychological mechanism, an internal state, which reliably delivers the right result at each point. The misleading thought is this: postulating a psychological mechanism could explain why just the *right* numbers – out of the multitude of wrong numbers – are given for an infinite series. This picture can also be augmented, especially in mathematical cases, with the idea that the mechanism tracks or follows objective, perhaps supernatural, rails that are already out there, independently of us. Our continuing a series is merely going over, in bolder pencil, moves already made.

With this assumption in place, then, it seems that understanding any genuine concept can be codified by giving the principle or formula "that specifies the conditions under which the concept, in the use of it that one has mastered, is correctly applied" (McDowell 1998b: 62). This is a mistaken view that leads in turn to the assumption that all genuinely cognitive judgements must be governed by an explicit rule.

> Now it is only this misconception of the deductive paradigm that leads us to suppose that the operations of any specific conception of rationality in a particular area – any specific conception of what counts as doing the same thing – must be deductively explicable; that is, that there must be a formulable universal principle

suited to serve as major premise in syllogistic explanations of the
sort I considered above.   (*Ibid.*: 62)

Thus it seems that anything that fails to pass this test is not a case of
genuine concept application or conceptual judgement. So if moral
judgement is a candidate for rule-governed or conceptualized cognition, it should, it seems, be codifiable. If it is not codifiable then it is not
cognition either.

This line of argument rests on a mistake, however. It goes wrong in
the assumption that it is necessary, or even helpful, to postulate a psychological mechanism to explain an ability to follow a rule. Postulating
such a state of mind is idle because it cannot ground the kind of expectation that either we, or other people, will continue in the same (successful) way. Consider the case of determining which rule someone else
is following. As Wittgenstein shows – on McDowell's interpretation –
if inferring from their finite past to their future practice were not reliable in itself, postulating the intervening mechanism would not help
either. Past practice, once described as mere *inductive* evidence for a
mechanism, could be evidence for any number of diverging mechanisms. And there are similar problems in the first-person case because
one's own state of mind has to be interpreted correctly to determine
one's own correct future application of a rule. In both cases, the felt
need for an *interpretation* leads to a vicious regress. In the third-per-
son case, past practice has to be interpreted as following a particular
rule. In the first-person case, mental states, signs or processes have to
be interpreted as determining a rule.

As I outlined in Chapter 1, a key move to avoid this problem turns
on rejecting the view of theory-neutral evidence for another person's
grasp of a rule. As long as one adopts the same perspective, then one
can see the rule that is exemplified in the person's practice. That we
are able to adopt the same perspective depends on the fact that we
share many contingent features of human nature, including interests, feelings and perceptions of similarity that make up our "whirl of
organism" (Cavell 1969: 52).

With this philosophical corrective in place, McDowell can consider
what should be said about hard cases: disagreements about the application of a concept that resists resolution by argument. In the grip of
the prejudice that Wittgenstein exposes, one might assume that
either there is a piece of knowledge that could in principle be articulated or this is not a case of conceptual judgement. But since the
proper understanding of even codifiable judgement shows that what
is primitive is a notion of going on in the same way, which cannot be

explained as the result of a mechanism, the contrast between the two cases is diminished.[6]

The model of uncodified conceptual judgement, McDowell suggests, is this:

> We are inclined to be impressed by the sparseness of the teaching that leaves someone capable of autonomously going on in the same way. All that happens is that the pupil is told, or shown, what to do in a few instances, with some surrounding talk about why that is the thing to do; the surrounding talk, *ex hypothesi* ... falls short of including actual enunciation of a universal principle, mechanical application of which would constitute correct behaviour in the practice in question. Yet pupils do acquire a capacity to go on, without further advice, to novel instances. Impressed by the sparseness of the teaching, we find this remarkable. (McDowell 1998b: 64)

If there is no universal principle then it can seem miraculous that finite teaching enables students to go on in the same way. But this is a misleading contrast because if there is a universal principle, it would be equally miraculous how they grasp the *right* principle from finite teaching.

The moral of this recapitulation of Wittgenstein's discussion of rules in this case is this. Given that discussion, even in the case of judgements for which a universal principle can be written down, the ability to apply the principle depends on our basic responses to it. Justifications for particular responses to a rule come to an end. Fortunately, because humans share the same basic reactions, responses, routes of salience and so on, they typically come to an end in agreement. But this makes the idea of uncodifiable rules innocuous. Given that, to an unprejudiced eye, it should appear that moral judgements cannot be codified, that appearance can properly be taken at face value.

How, then, should the practical syllogism be applied in the case of the explanation of virtuous action? Recall that a non-cognitivist account of moral judgement can accommodate the practical syllogism in the following way. Cognition proper feeds into the minor premise

---

6. One way of putting this point – although not McDowell's – is to suggest an equivalence between a hard case for uncodifiable judgement and what could be said if someone were to question how to apply the series "add 2" at the point at which, in Wittgenstein's phrase, justifications have come to an end.

while the major premise displays something motivational or willed. But if moral requirements cannot be codified as single complex principles, what can be salvaged from this approach?

McDowell points out that Aristotle suggests that the motivational factor in moral action is "the virtuous person's conception of the sort of life a human being should lead" (*ibid.*: 66–7). McDowell's explanation of this is as follows. Consider a specific act of kindness to a friend, say, visiting them out of concern for their wellbeing. While the motivation of concern or desire for the wellbeing of friends, and a belief that a visit will help bring this about would serve as a core explanation for the act, those factors alone would not show that it had been done out of kindness. (Perhaps one has selfish reasons to be concerned with the wellbeing of friends.) It is only if the act is done as part of a general conception of how one should live that it is virtuous. In virtuous action that general conception underpins why, in a situation in which a number of different concerns could have been operative, just the one which was acted on was selected. The conception of how to live cannot, however, be definitively written down as a recipe for how any situation is to be viewed. It is instead exemplified in the selection of which features are important. In other words, it is exemplified in the cognition that is expressed in the minor premise of the practical syllogism. McDowell writes:

> [T]he conception of how to live must be capable of actually entering our understanding of the action, explaining why it was this concern rather than any other that was drawn into operation.
>
> How does it enter? If the conception of how to live involved a ranking of concerns, or perhaps a set of rankings each relativized to some type of situation, the explanation of why one concern was operative rather than another would be straightforward. But uncodifiability rules out laying down such general rankings in advance of all the predicaments with which life may confront one.
>
> What I have described as selecting the right concern might equally be described in terms of the minor premise of the core explanation. If there is more than one concern that might impinge on the situation, there is more than one fact about the situation that the agent might, say, dwell on, in such a way as to summon an appropriate concern into operation. It is by virtue of his seeing this particular fact rather than that one as the salient fact about the situation that he is moved to act by this concern rather than that one. (1998b: 68)

The conception of how one should live and the perception of what in a given case are the relevant features for moral judgement go hand in hand. McDowell concedes that even for virtuous action a core explanation can be framed with identifiable pure components corresponding to volition and cognition. But the context in which that action is virtuous requires a selection of what the relevant cognitive element is. And this selection cannot be analysed into purely cognitive and volitional elements in the way the non-cognitivist insists.

The idea that moral judgements require a particular standpoint, and that they cannot be understood from a sideways-on position, serves as a model for McDowell's view of how meanings and other features of the space of reasons come into view. Likewise, the idea that acquiring that standpoint is a natural accomplishment, a feature of our second nature, plays an important role in understanding how reason and nature can be reconciled. Indeed, in *Mind and World*, McDowell introduces second nature through the example of Aristotle's account of moral judgement. With these two ideas in place, in the next chapters I shall turn to the heart of the account of how the world can come into view as itself within the space of reasons.

Chapter 3

Formal theories of meaning and theories of sense

In this chapter I shall describe the background to, and the main themes of, McDowell's investigation of a Davidsonian "truth theory" of meaning. Such a theory of meaning aims to articulate the structure of natural language by drawing on the logical machinery of Tarski's semantic conception of truth. Its aim, in a sense to be clarified below, is to shed light on the nature of linguistic meaning.

Two major themes will emerge. One is McDowell's thinking that a theory of meaning cannot hope to explain meaning using meaning-free notions. The best approach to a theory of meaning is *not* to attempt to adopt a perspective *outside* language to try to explain the connection between language or mind and the world. The best reading of a Davidsonian theory of meaning is *modest*. It would contribute to our understanding of language mastery in particular, and being minded in general, but only by presupposing linguistic notions, that is, from *within* that world of meaning:

> [A] modest theory of meaning, by design, starts in the midst of content; so it cannot contribute to this task of representing content as an achievement . . . What is needed is an understanding of how content, explicitly conceived as inaccessible except "from inside", can be comprehended as a precipitate of simpler modes of activity and awareness than those in which it figures.
>
> (McDowell 1998a: 105)

The second theme is that of reflection on a Davidsonian theory providing a way of interpreting the Fregean distinction between sense and reference; and that distinction should play a role in our understanding of the relation of mind and world, as I shall describe more fully in Chapter 6. McDowell advocates a minimalist reading of the distinction dovetailed to his interpretation of Davidson.

At the end of the chapter, however, I shall suggest that while McDowell thus places the best possible interpretation on the role of Davidsonian theories, in so doing he undermines their value as theories of meaning in any reputable philosophical endeavour. There is, in other words, some difficulty in advocating such a theory of meaning within the context of a broadly therapeutic conception of philosophy.

The structure of the chapter is as follows. In the first two sections I set out Davidson's influential approach to the philosophy of language. Section I sketches Davidson's general approach to the philosophy of language through his idea of radical interpretation. This encapsulates the idea that the philosophy of language should adopt a third person approach. More specifically, light is shed on the nature of meaning by looking at the conditions of possibility of interpretation of an alien language from scratch. Second II outlines the formal structure of a Davidsonian theory of meaning using Tarski's logical machinery. This is the way Davidson suggests that the output from radical interpretation should be represented.

The remaining three sections outline McDowell's discussion of both the formal structure and the implicit background constraints imposed on it by radical interpretation. Section III considers the kind of insight that such a formal theory of meaning is supposed to give by examining the relation of truth and meaning. Section IV contrasts Dummett's and McDowell's interpretation of the aim of the theory: is it full-blooded or modest? Finally, Section V describes and assesses McDowell's suggestion that an austere Davidsonian theory can still sustain a distinction between sense and reference. The key lesson I shall draw is that McDowell thinks that a theory of meaning cannot represent meaning "as an achievement" (1998a: 105): it cannot describe meaning in meaning-free terms. Instead it is a codification of the nature of meaning for those already possessing a language. The distinction between sense and reference is then itself drawn from within this perspective.

I   Davidson and the philosophy of language of the field linguist

In order to outline Davidson's approach to the formal theory of meaning I need first to put it in the context of the second major element of his philosophy of content: the philosophy of language of the field linguist. This is developed from his fundamental assumption that there are no facts about meaning that are inaccessible from a third person perspective. Consequently, by investigating the conditions of possibility of radical interpretation, Davidson aims to uncover the metaphysics of meaning. I shall outline this approach and then, in Section II, describe how it connects with Tarski's work on truth.

Davidson's philosophy of language of the field linguist is based on the thought experiment of radical interpretation. In order to clarify what we understand when we understand our home language, Davidson considers the conditions of possibility of the radical interpretation of a foreign language. Radical interpretation is supposed to be interpretation from scratch (Davidson 1993: 77). It is a philosophical abstraction from the kind of interpretation undertaken by a field linguist having first contact with an alien tribe. Such interpretation, it is assumed, cannot presuppose bilingual speakers or dictionaries. It precedes those resources. Furthermore, according to Davidson, it cannot make substantial use of the content of the mental states of speakers. Whatever the connection between mental content and linguistic meaning, radical interpretation must earn access to, and cannot simply assume, facts about both. The intentional contents to which Grice appeals in the analysis of linguistic interchange, for example, cannot be identified prior to interpretation of the agent's language. Thus they cannot be appealed to in radical interpretation.

Interpretation must, instead, rely only on the evidence of correlations between utterances and the circumstances that prompt them: "[The radical interpreter] interprets sentences held true (which is not to be distinguished from attributing beliefs) according to the events and objects in the outside world that cause the sentence to be held true" (Davidson 1986a: 317).

Davidson's account of radical *interpretation* is a development from W. V. Quine's account of radical *translation*. But one key difference is its characterization of the evidence available:

> The crucial point on which I am with Quine might be put: all the evidence for or against a theory of truth (interpretation, translation) comes in the form of facts about what events or situations in the world cause, or would cause, speakers to assent to, or dissent from, each sentence in the speaker's repertoire. We probably differ on some details. Quine describes the events or situations in terms of patterns of stimulation, while I prefer a description in terms more like those of the sentence being studied; Quine would give

more weight to a grading of sentences in terms of observationality than I would; and where he likes assent and dissent because they suggest a behaviouristic test, I despair of behaviourism and accept frankly intensional attitudes toward sentences, such as holding true.   (Davidson 1984: 230)

Davidson takes the evidence available to radical interpretation to be worldly facts and events in the speakers' environments, together with the occasion of their utterances.

Davidson's methodological claim for the philosophy of content is that one can clarify the nature of both linguistic meaning and mental content more generally by examining how it is determined in radical interpretation. "What a fully informed interpreter could learn about what a speaker means is all there is to learn; the same goes for what the speaker believes" (Davidson 1986a: 315). Because it is intended to serve this philosophical purpose, Davidson concentrates on clear instances of radical interpretation – interpretation by field linguists – rather than the "interpretation" that, he claims, takes place in daily life: "All understanding of the speech of another involves radical interpretation. But it will help keep assumptions from going unnoticed to focus on cases where interpretation is most clearly called for: interpretation in one idiom of talk in another" (Davidson 1984: 125–6). Nevertheless, Davidson also thinks that everyday understanding of language involves radical interpretation. That claim puts some strain on the initial characterization of radical interpretation as interpretation from scratch because it undermines the contrast that such a description presupposes. If everyday "interpretation" is also really from scratch, what example could there be of interpretation that was not? But while Davidson makes this claim in part to defend his radical thesis that communal language plays no explanatory role in human understanding, it can also be seen as a reminder of the purpose of considering radical interpretation: that is, to shed light on what is understood when we understand speech and action generally. (The radical claim is defended in Davidson (1986b).)

Seen in this light, Davidson's account of radical interpretation serves as an example of reconstructive epistemology. It does not matter that our everyday understanding of other speakers does not proceed using the tools that Davidson describes. One might argue that everyday understanding works on the implicit assumption that others speak the same language as oneself. But radical interpretation does not aim at phenomenological accuracy. Similarly, it would not matter if real field linguists made use of interpretative heuristics less minimal than those Davidson describes. An example of that might be the assumption that any newly encountered human language has a good chance of being related to some previously encountered language. Such a principle would be useful if it turned out that all human languages sprang from a common source. Since radical interpretation is really a piece of reconstructive epistemology, it concerns the ultimate *justification* of ascriptions of content whatever the actual process of reasoning that gives rise to them. It concerns the evidence that could be used to justify both the possible heuristic suggested above and also our everyday methods of understanding. Radical interpretation is supposed to explain what the assumption that other speakers speak the same language amounts to. (According to Davidson, one of its consequences is that such talk of shared languages is of no philosophical significance.) It is precisely because it plays a clarificatory – via a justificatory – role that radical interpretation is characterized in the austere terms that it is.

The early Davidson sometimes suggests that progress can be made only if the evidence used in radical interpretation is not described in question-begging semantic terms:

> [U]ninterpreted utterances seem the appropriate evidential base for a theory of meaning. If an acceptable theory could be supported by such evidence, that would constitute conceptual progress, for the theory would be specifically semantical in nature, while the evidence would be described in non-semantical terms.
>
> (Davidson 1984: 142)

What reason does Davidson have for thinking that the evidence for a theory of meaning should itself be described in non-semantic terms? Two sorts of consideration suggest two related motivations. From the perspective of providing a general philosophical account of the nature of meaning, the motivation might run like this. If a philosophical account is to shed light on meaning by connecting it – albeit holistically – to the evidence that determines it, then that evidence should not be described in content-laden terms. If it is, no light will have been shed on what meaning is, since facts about meaning will have been presupposed in the description of evidence.

The other consideration depends more specifically on Davidson's chosen approach to the general philosophical account of meaning. Light is shed on meaning in general by reflecting on how radical interpretation is possible. But what final justification is there for ascribing meanings to other people? One method an interpreter could adopt for testing her interpretations – which Davidson assumes will form part of an interpretative theory or "theory of meaning" – would be to see whether in individual cases her interpretations agreed with those given by dictionaries or bilingual speakers. But in *radical* interpretation no such resources can be assumed, since they merely postpone the question of how ascriptions of meaning can be justified. In this context, it may seem that the evidence that is available must be characterized in non-semantic terms:

> In radical interpretation, however, the [interpretative] theory is supposed to supply an understanding of particular utterances that is not given in advance, so the ultimate evidence for the theory cannot be correct sample interpretations. To deal with the general case, the evidence must be of a sort that would be available to someone who does not already know how to interpret utterances the theory is designed to cover: *it must be evidence that can be stated without essential use of such linguistic concepts* as meaning, interpretation, synonymy, and the like.
>
> (*Ibid.*: 128, emphasis added)

If either or both of these arguments were compelling, then Davidson's approach to the philosophy of content would run counter to that of Wittgenstein and thus McDowell's own Wittgenstein-inspired views. One of the morals of Wittgenstein's discussion is, as I have described in Chapter 1, that no analysis of meaning can be given that turns on the interpretation of otherwise meaningless noises or movements. I shall shortly argue, however, that whatever Davidson's view of the matter, the thought experiment of radical interpretation can be pruned of any commitment to the description, in non-semantic terms, of the evidence that supports interpretation. Briefly:

- The results of radical interpretation can still be supported or criticized by appeal to evidence, even if that evidence cannot be described (*qua* evidence) in non-semantic terms. The evidence can still be used to test interpretation because of the systematicity and holism implicit in radical interpretation. Just because it is described in semantic terms does not undermine its independence of the theory for which it is evidence. Construing an utterance as a particular assertion will have consequences for how similar-sounding utterances are thought of.
- It is wrong to assume that radical interpretation only sheds light on meaning if the connection between meaning and evidence is explicitly represented in the results of that interpretation. The

nature and limits of possible evidence can play an implicit role. Davidson's key claim is that there are no facts about meaning that are *inaccessible* to the radical interpreter. But this connection between meaning and interpretation need not be directly encoded in the results of radical interpretation. Thus there is no need to require that the input can be characterized in non-semantic terms.

In fact, Davidson himself realizes that his project cannot escape all intentional notions and in later accounts he drops the requirements about its non-semantic nature:

> My way of trying to give an account of language and meaning makes essential use of such concepts as those of beliefs and intention, and I do not believe it is possible to reduce these notions to anything more scientific or behaviouristic. What I have tried to do is give an account of meaning (interpretation) that makes no essential use of unexplained *linguistic* concepts. (Even this is a little stronger than what I think is possible.) It will ruin no plan of mine if in saying what an interpreter knows it is necessary to use a so-called intensional notion – one that consorts with belief and intention and the like. (*Ibid*.: 175–6)

It may seem that Davidson is suggesting that linguistic meaning can be analysed in terms of mental content: that is something like Gricean intention-based semantics. But that is not the strategy he follows. The distinction between the narrowly semantic and the more broadly intentional marks his preferred strategy for coping with a general difficulty for radical interpretation.

Davidson thinks that, ultimately, facts about mental content have to be determined in the same way as facts about linguistic meaning. Meanings and contents are interdependent. This presents a principled difficulty for radical interpretation:

> A speaker who holds a sentence to be true on an occasion does so in part because of what he means, or would mean, by an utterance of that sentence, and in part because of what he believes. If all we have to go on is the fact of honest utterance, we cannot infer the belief without knowing the meaning, and have no chance of inferring the meaning without the belief. (*Ibid*.: 142)

Thus the interpreter faces the task of unravelling two sets of unknowns – facts about meaning and facts about beliefs – with only one sort of evidence: linguistic actions that depend on both meaning and belief. How can the interpreter, to change the metaphor, break into this interdependent set of facts?

Davidson's solution has two stages. First, he takes the evidential basis of radical interpretation to be the prompted assent of a speaker, which he characterizes as "the causal relation between assenting to a sentence and the cause of such assent" (Davidson 1986a: 315). It is possible to know that a speaker assents to a sentence without knowing what the sentence means and thus what belief is expressed by it (or vice versa). Characterizing a speaker as holding a particular sentence true is an intentional interpretation of what is going on – the speaker is described by relation to a propositional content – but it does not *presuppose* a semantic analysis of the sentence. That will be derived later.

The second step is to restrain the degrees of freedom of possible beliefs in order to interpret linguistic meaning. The interpreter must impose his or her own standards of truth and coherence on ascriptions of beliefs and meanings. There must be a presumption that any utterance or belief held true really is true. Further, in a significant range of cases, the interpreter must assume that the object of an utterance, and the belief the utterance expresses, is the cause of the utterance and belief. (As Davidson remarks in a passage quoted above, the relevant cause is a worldly state of affairs rather than, as Quine suggests, proximal stimulation at the boundary of the body.) This complex of related assumptions governing the rationality imputed – generally labelled the principle of charity – enables interpretation to get off the ground. If utterances are assumed by the interpreter to be generally true and to concern the worldly states of affairs that prompt them, then they can be correlated with those observed states of affairs. Their meaning can thus be determined. Given an overall interpretation, exceptional false beliefs can then be identified.

These a priori constraints on interpretation operate in a general manner but allow exceptions. Thus even the basic datum that a speaker holds a particular utterance true can be revised in the light of the subsequent interpretation of their other beliefs and meanings. The epistemology of interpretation is fallible and holistic. So the appeal to evidence should not be regarded as a foundational or reductive account of meaning. The earlier prescription that evidence should be describable in theory-free non-semantic terms (while still being represented as evidence) does not fit easily with the holism that Davidson more generally emphasizes.

Davidson's basic strategy can now be summarized as follows. On the assumption that radical interpretation has access to all the facts about content, content can be explicated by examining the conditions of possibility of radical interpretation. Thus Davidson assumes that content can be captured by a third person perspective and that it can be fully analysed through its connection to the action of agents in the world. In the weakest sense of the term, Davidson can be seen, in his philosophy of content at least, as promoting a form of philosophical behaviourism providing that this is not interpreted in its Quinean and reductive sense. Meaning is explicated through its role in human behaviour.

II Davidson and Tarski

I shall now turn to Davidson's suggestion of how the output of radical interpretation should be codified as a formal theory of meaning. This will require a brief account of the connection between Davidson's and Tarski's work on truth. But, in fact, the broader philosophical issues explored below will not turn on the details of that analysis.

Davidson introduces the idea of a theory of meaning without giving a clear idea of its purpose. He makes two comments on the subject. One is that knowledge of such a theory would *suffice* for understanding (Davidson 1984: 125). The other is that it is a *necessary* condition for languages to be learnable that a constructive or compositional account of the language could be given (*ibid.*: 3). But, even taken together, these do not explain how provision of a theory of meaning helps the philosophical enterprise of clarifying linguistic and mental content. (Davidson does not say explicitly, for example, that speakers have implicit knowledge of a theory of meaning that *explains* their ability.) This issue of just what the theory is supposed to be a theory of, and what (if any) its explanatory role is, is an important one. As I shall describe, it is one of the key foci of McDowell's debate with Dummett.

Davidson gives a clearer account of his motivation for the particular structure of the theory he advocates. In particular, he is more explicit in his reasons why such a theory should be *extensional*. Theories of meaning of the form "*s* means *m*", where *m* refers to a meaning of a word or sentence, have proved to be of little use in showing how the meaning of parts of a sentence structurally determine the meaning of the whole. Things can be improved by modifying the theory's structure to be "*s* means that *p*", where *p* stands for a sentence. But this still leaves the problem that "wrestling with the logic of the apparently non-extensional 'means that' we will encounter problems as hard as, or perhaps identical with, the problems our theory is out to solve" (*ibid*.: 22). The solution is to realize that what matters for such a theory is not the nature of the connection between *s* and *p* but that the right *s* and *p* are connected:

> The theory will have done its work if it provides, for every sentence *s* in the language under study, a matching sentence (to replace "*p*") that, in some way yet to be made clear, "gives the meaning" of *s*. One obvious candidate for matching sentence is just *s* itself, if the object language is contained in the meta-language; otherwise a translation of *s* in the meta-language. As a final bold step, let us try treating the position occupied by "*p*" extensionally: to implement this, sweep away the obscure "means that", provide the sentence that replaces "*p*" with a proper sentential connective, and supply the description that replaces "*s*" with its own predicate. The plausible result is
>
> (*T*)   *s* is *T* if and only if *p*.   (*Ibid*.: 23)

Further reflection suggests that, if this is to serve as an interpretation, the appropriate predicate for *T* is truth. We want the sentence *s* to be *true* if and only if *p*.[1]

The proposed theoretical schema has the further advantage (and motivation) that it dovetails with Tarski's account of truth. Tarski's account is pressed into service to show how the meanings of sentences are constructed from the meanings of words (which are themselves abstracted from the meanings of sentences). Davidson's use of Tarski inverts its normal explanatory priority. Tarski assumes that facts about meaning can be presupposed in the task of giving an extensional definition of truth in a language. By contrast, Davidson suggests that truth is a suitably primitive, transparent and unitary notion to shed light on meaning (Davidson 1984: 134). With this change of emphasis, Davidson can then borrow Tarski's technical machinery to articulate the structure of a given language. I shall now outline Tarski's semantic conception of truth.

There continues to be considerable disagreement about the philosophical significance of Tarski's work on truth, and of just what (if

---

1. McDowell gives a strikingly similar account of the role of truth in a meaning theory in "Meaning, Communication and Knowledge" (1998a: 31–4, §2).

any) light it sheds on the nature of truth (cf. Davidson 1990; McDowell 1978; 1998a: 132–54). But it is uncontentious that Tarski provides a logical model of how the truth-condition of any sentence of a formal (first-order) language can be derived from a more basic set of axioms. One way of thinking about Tarski's semantic conception of truth is to consider two much simpler models than the one that is useful for Davidson. So consider truth theories for each of the following:

- a language with a finite number of sentences;
- a language with a finite number of whole atomic sentences and truth-functional connectives that can be used to build an unlimited number of more complex, molecular sentences;
- a language whose building blocks are sub-sentential predicates, truth-functional connectives and quantifiers: Frege's first-order logic.

Take the first of these languages. At its simplest, a Tarskian truth theory could be given for a language with a finite number of atomic whole sentences with no connectives for building further molecular sentences. The aim of a Tarskian truth theory is to specify the truth-conditions of any sentence in the language. In this case, the truth theory would simply be a *list* of instances of the T schema: s is T if and only if p. Each sentence named on the left-hand side of an instance of the T schema would be paired with a sentence in English, for example, that stated the condition under which it was true. Since the aim of a Tarskian theory is to spell out truth-conditions, we can help ourselves to the fact that the sentence on the right-hand side *translates* or *interprets* the named sentence on the left. Armed with the list, and given any from the finite number of atomic sentences, one could look up the condition under which it was true.

Note that each instance of the T schema is written in a *metalanguage*. It contains the name of an *object language* sentence – usually achieved just by putting inverted commas round a sentence – and a condition spelling out its truth-condition, in the form of a sentence of the metalanguage. The object language sentence is thus named or *mentioned* and the sentence of the metalanguage spelling out its worldly truth-condition is *used* to give its truth-condition.

Now consider the second of the languages. A further degree of complexity is introduced by adding truth-functional connectives to the object language. A simple list will no longer serve as a truth theory because there is no limit to the number of complex sentences that can be formed simply by conjoining, for example, one atomic sentence with others, or even perhaps different tokens of the same sentence type. The resultant complex sentence can then be further conjoined with other atomic or complex sentences. Note that the truth-condition of the final result will still be determined by a complex function of the truth-conditions of the component atomic sentences, and thus derivable from them. But since the process of conjoining sentences can, in principle, be repeated without limit, a general method of spelling out the truth-conditions of arbitrary sentences of the object language will have to be *recursive*. It will have to be repeatedly applicable so that the output of one operation can feed in as the input to the next application until the constituent atomic sentences are reached. So a Tarskian truth theory for this language will have to contain both a list of the atomic sentences with a specification of each of their truth-conditions and some general rules specifying how the truth-condition of a complex sentence, say, "*A* and *B*" is a function of "*A*" and "*B*" (where *A* and *B* may themselves be complex sentences needing further analysis). The last element is given by the truth-table for each of the connectives. So "*A* and *B*" is true iff "*A*" is true and "*B*" is true. "*A* or *B*" is true iff "*A*" is true or "*B*" is true.

For a simple language with the form of propositional or sentential logic, a Tarskian truth theory is still quite simple. It contains axioms giving the truth-conditions of the basic or atomic sentences of its object language and iterable rules specifying the truth-conditions of complex combinations of atomic sentences using connectives. Given the specification of the truth-conditions of the basic sentences, and given general rules for the truth-conditions of complex sentences that can be built up from them, the truth-conditions of arbitrarily complex sentences can be calculated. Given a complex sentence, one can analyse it as a function of the truth-conditions of its component parts, which can in turn be decomposed eventually to reach atomic sentences whose truth-conditions are listed.

The third kind of language introduces a yet further level of complexity. In this case, the component parts of whole sentences need not themselves be whole sentences. Frege's predicate logic (the logic of one-, two- or many-place predicates and relations together with the universal and existential quantifiers) is just such an example. Because predicate logic allows for whole ("closed") sentences to be built up from sub-sentential units ("open sentences"), which are thus themselves neither true nor false, a truth theory for it requires, in addition to what has gone before, the technical notion of *satisfaction*. The open sentence

Fx, unbound by any quantifier, is neither true nor false. It says something like: " ... is *F*". Suppose "*F*" is replaced by "red". Then " ... is red" is neither true nor false by itself. But Tarski suggests we can say that it is *satisfied* by some object providing that object is red. Similarly, the open sentence "*x* loves *y*" is satisfied by an ordered pair of objects if the first loves the second.

Given this intuitive idea of the satisfaction of predicates by objects (in fact by ordered sequences of objects to cope with multi-place relations), Tarski then goes on to define separately the conditions under which *existentially* and *universally* quantified closed sentences are satisfied by sequences of objects. Finally, he defines the conditions under which any closed sentence is true in terms of satisfaction. It turns out that a closed sentence is true if it is satisfied by *all* sequences of objects.

Tarski needs to ensure that the definition of truth in terms of satisfaction has the right consequences for the truth of universally and existentially quantified sentences. Thus in the case of a universally quantified sentence, it should be true if and only if everything is as it says. Taking the example of $(\forall x_4)(x_4$ is round), where the subscripts allow for many variables in a sentence, Richard Kirkham puts the point in this way:

> Tarski ensures this by setting two conditions that must be met for a sequence S, to satisfy a universally quantified sentence such as "$(\forall x_4)(x_4$ is round)":
>
> 1. S must satisfy the open sentence that would be created by deleting the quantifier. So in this case it must satisfy "x_4 is round". Thus whatever object S has in the fourth place must be round.
> 2. This same sentence must also be satisfied by every sequence that is just like S except that it has a different object in the fourth place. (Kirkham 1992: 156)

Since

> [F]or every object in the world, there is some sequence just like S except that it has just that object in the fourth place. So, since condition (2) tells us that *all* of these sequences must satisfy "x_4 is round", the condition says, in effect, that everything in the world other than the object in the fourth place of S must be round. Between them (1) and (2) are saying that *every* object must be round. (*Ibid.*: 156)

Thus "$(\forall x_4)(x_4$ is round)" is satisfied by sequence S if and only if every object is round. A consequence of this definition is that if S satisfies the sentence, then so does every other sequence because, again, those sequences satisfy the sentence only if every object is round.

The definition of the satisfaction of an existentially quantified sentence is given in the following related way.

> An expression of the form "$(\exists x_k)\varphi$" is satisfied by a sequence S if and only if some sequence differing from S in at most the kth place satisfies φ.
>
> But ... for every object there is some sequence just like S except that it has that object in the kth place. So the conclusion will be met when and only when something in the world φs. Notice here too that if one sequence satisfies the existential claim, they all do. (*Ibid.*: 157)

Thus both universally and existentially quantified sentences are satisfied by one sequence if and only if they are satisfied by every sequence. With these definitions in place, Tarski is able to stipulate that a sentence of either kind is true providing it is satisfied by every sequence.

Even this brief sketch of the general shape of a Tarskian truth theory for a language with the same logical structure as Fregean predicate logic should reveal in outline the modest philosophical role (if less modest technical role) of satisfaction. It serves as part of the internal workings of the theory, so that correct instances of the T schema can be derived for each whole (i.e. closed) sentence of the object language. The basic axioms of the theory concern the satisfaction of predicates by objects rather than truth of sentences. But although Tarski provides a definition of truth in terms of satisfaction, the primary purpose of a truth theory is to allow the derivation of instances of the T schema for complex sentences in the object language.

With this brief summary in place, Davidson's use of Tarski's theory of truth should now be clearer. The Tarskian machinery provides a model of how the truth-condition of any sentence in a language might be determined by a finite list of axioms (which give the meaning of individual words) and rules of combination (which give the grammar). Setting out a Tarskian truth theory for a language such as English articulates the structure of that language.

Of course, this use of Tarski's theory of truth depends on it being possible to regiment natural language in the same way as artificial or formal languages, and there are notorious obstacles to this project.[2] It also depends on finding a way to overcome the following result of inverting the explanatory priority of truth and meaning, and using merely an extensional connective in the theory.

As the quotation in Section I makes explicit (p. 110), at the heart of his meaning theory Davidson replaces the intensional connective "means that" with the extensional form "*s* is true if and only if *p*". Clearly, however, the fact that the truth-values of the left- and right-hand sides of this conditional agree does not in itself ensure that the right-hand side provides an *interpretation* of the sentence mentioned on the left-hand side. In Tarski's use of the *T* schema, it can simply be assumed or stipulated that the right-hand side provides an interpretation by being the same sentence as, or a translation of, the sentence mentioned on the left-hand side. (Tarski helps himself to facts about meaning to show how to determine the conditions under which a truth-predicate applies to sentences of the object language.) But Davidson has to earn the right to that claim. His suggestion is that instances of the *T* schema should not be thought of as interpretative in themselves (Davidson 1984: 61). Rather, it is the fact that each instance can be derived from an overall theory for the language that also allows the derivation of many other instances of the *T* schema with the correct matching of truth-values, that is interpretative. Only if the theory systematically correctly matches words on the left- and right-hand sides of *T* schema instances will it have a chance of generating all and only true instances. But if it does, that is very strong evidence for a match of meaning. Instances of the *T* schema play a role within the larger deductive structure of the meaning theory of a whole language.

I can now summarize Davidson's project of outlining a formal theory of meaning. On the twin assumptions that we have a clearer antecedent understanding of the concept of truth than we have of meaning and also that natural language has a structure that can be regimented, a formal theory of meaning that allows the derivation of instances of the *T* schema ("*s*" is true iff *p*) represents a language in a finite axiomatized theory.

So much, then, for the formal structure of a Davidsonian theory of meaning. What light does it shed on the nature of language or meaning? In the rest of this chapter, I shall examine McDowell's response to this question. Sections III and IV address it directly by examining the

---

2. Perhaps the most familiar, and one on which Davidson himself worked, is the analysis of reported speech. For recent discussion see Dodd (2000: 19–48).

connection between truth and meaning and then examining the debate between McDowell and Dummett. Section V examines McDowell's suggestion that even a theory as austere as a Davidsonian theory of meaning can sustain the distinction between sense and reference, which plays an important role in Chapter 4.

III What is the relation between truth and meaning?

In the opening words of two early papers "Truth-Conditions, Bivalence and Verificationism" (1976) and "On the Sense and Reference of a Proper Name" (1977), McDowell offers overviews of the role of a Davidsonian truth theory:

> An interesting way to raise questions about the relation between language and reality is to ask: how could we state a theory knowledge of which would suffice for understanding a language? Donald Davidson has argued that a central component in such a theory would be [a] theory of truth, in something like the style of Tarski, for the language in question.   (McDowell 1998a: 171)

> If there can be such a thing as a theory of meaning for a language, meaning cannot be anything but what any such theory is a theory of. Hence a clear and convincing description of the shape that a theory of meaning for any language would take, not itself uncritically employing the notion of meaning, ought to remove all perplexity about the nature of meaning in general.   (*Ibid.*: 3)

But what exactly is the role of a Davidsonian truth theory here? What is the kind of perplexity about meaning that such a theory can remove? A first clue to the modesty (in both a general and a technical sense) of McDowell's interpretation of the proposal can be gleaned by thinking about the following problem.

The connection between meaning and truth can be used to shed light on either. Given an understanding of truth, Davidson argues, we can derive an account of meaning:

> In Tarski's work, *T*-sentences are taken to be true because the right branch of the biconditional is assumed to be a translation of the sentence for which truth conditions are being given. But we cannot assume in advance that correct translation can be recognised without pre-empting the point of radical interpreta-

tions; in empirical applications, we must abandon the assumption. What I propose is to reverse the direction of explanation: assuming translation, Tarski was able to define truth; the present idea is to take truth as basic and to extract an account of translation or interpretation. The advantages, from the point of view of radical interpretation, are obvious. Truth is a single property which attaches, or fails to attach, to utterances, while each utterance has its own interpretation; and truth is more apt to connect with fairly simple attitudes of speakers. (Davidson 1984: 134)

But the same connection can be deployed in the opposite direction. As the quotation above makes clear, this alternative is Tarski's approach. It is also implicit in more minimalist approaches to truth such as disquotational or redundancy theories.

As Bernhard Weiss puts it: "Minimalists or deflationists about truth argue that our concept of truth is all but captured via (some version of) the disquotational schema, '*P*' is true iff *P*" (2002: 63). The underlying idea of such an approach is that there is no substantial explanatory property common to truths. Because "is true" is a predicate, there may be "no harm" in taking truth to be a property (Dodd 2000: 136). But there is no prospect of a successful philosophical project to show, for example, that all truths correspond to facts where "correspondence" and "fact" have independent analyses.

The most minimal such theory was put forward by Frank Ramsey. His "redundancy theory" proposed that since "is true" served simply as a device for disquotation in *T* schema instances, it could be eliminated without loss (Ramsey 1927). Truth is not, however, eliminable because of the need sometimes to make indirect or compendious assertions, for example, in cases where what is said is not known although it is known to be true. An example may be someone asserting that everything the Pope says is true. Because of cases like this, Weiss says that truth is "all but captured" in the disquotational schema. Nevertheless this need not commit us to thinking that there is anything more to truth than the transparent property expressed in the equivalence of asserting that *P* or asserting that "*P*" is true.[3]

A minimalist or deflationary account of truth thus deploys the *T* schema to shed light on the nature of truth on condition that one already has an understanding of the meaning of "*P*" and *P*. The explanatory direction is thus the opposite of Davidson's approach to meaning. Both directions of explanation require that one has

---

3. For elaboration see Horwich (1990).

independent purchase on either truth or meaning. So it appears that one should not be able to put forward both a Davidsonian theory of meaning and a minimalist theory of truth. Paul Horwich, for example, a minimalist on truth, supports an account of meaning based on descriptions of the *use* of words without formalization in the manner of Tarski. Davidson himself simply relies on a prior grasp of an unanalysed (or at least partially unanalysed) conception of truth. Dummett takes issue with Davidsonian approaches and argues that attempting to explain meaning in terms of truth is superficial until a substantial account of truth is given (Dummett 1993: 475–6). But his underlying assumption seems to be the same: that meaning can only be explicated given a substantial independent understanding of truth.

At first sight, however, McDowell appears to support both a broadly Davidsonian truth theory of meaning *and also* a minimalist theory of truth.

> The basis of the truth-conditional conception of meaning, as I see it, is the following thought: to specify what would be asserted, in the assertoric utterance of a sentence apt for such use, is to specify a condition under which the sentence (as thus uttered) would be true. The truth-conditional conception of meaning embodies a conception of truth that makes that thought truistic. *(I am inclined to think it is the only philosophically hygenic conception of truth there is.)* The truism captures what is right about the idea that "... is true", said of a sentence, functions as a device of disquotation, or, more generally, of cancellation of semantic ascent. (McDowell 1998a: 88–9, emphasis added)

> My truism might be held to capture the intuition that finds expression in the redundancy theory of truth. *(Ibid.*: 90)

This suggests that, whatever its role in an account of meaning, McDowell is also in sympathy with a minimalist account of truth. Are these sympathies in tension?

McDowell sets out the potential problem of adopting a minimalist theory of truth in the context of a Davidsonian truth theory of meaning in this way (*ibid.*: 4). If meaning is taken to be a problematic concept, and one to be sanitized by an explanation that relies on the concept of truth, then some substantial account of truth itself seems to be called for. There is need for an account of the nature of truth in general. Tarski shows how to define truth for a particular (formal) language, or "true-in-*L*" (where *L* names a language), but (arguably) does not show what different predicates of this form for different languages have in common. In "true-in-*L*", "true" is semantically inert (*ibid*.: 4). So it might be thought possible, in the context of a Davidsonian theory of meaning drawing on Tarski, that a retreat to a characterization of truth-for-a-particular-language would do. But if meaning in general is taken to need clarification this will not work, because the only content given to "true-in-*L*" will flow *from* an antecedent grasp of meaning rather than the other way round.

As I shall explain, McDowell sidesteps this sort of objection. His version of a Davidsonian theory of meaning puts no direct explanatory weight on the concept of truth. It "claims no particular conceptual illumination from the notion of truth as such" (*ibid*.: 43). Thus, there is no need for a substantial independent account of truth.

Repeating again some of what Davidson said, the idea is that a theory would work as a theory of sense or meaning providing it connected a suitable sentence *s* to be interpreted with an interpretation *p* in the form "*s . . . p*". Now, given that the aim of the theory is to give the meaning or sense of the sentence on the left-hand side and thus has to *mention* that sentence, *s* (or "*s*") is really the *name* of a sentence. Following Davidson's idea that the best way to do this is to apply a predicate (for example "*F*") to *s*, this leads to a formulation: "*s*" is *F* under some condition. If we want to use the condition described on the right-hand side to state the *content* (or meaning or sense) of the sentence, then *F* will turn out to be truth. (McDowell says that such a theory *would not be false* if the predicate were written "true".) However, we can understand the nature and purpose of a theory of meaning without understanding that *truth* will play this role. "The thesis should be, not that sense is what a theory of truth is a theory of, but rather that truth is what a theory of sense is a theory of" (*ibid*.: 8). McDowell's thought here is that the prior constraints that single out a theory as a theory of sense do not concern its internal structure except in so far as it reveals how the content of an utterance, using a sentence, is a function of its parts. The purpose of a theory of sense just is to make speech acts (and actions more broadly) intelligible.

It does this by providing descriptions of them under which they are reasonable, in part by connecting target sentences with the content of potential utterances that can be made with them. It merely "turns out" that the truth-predicate can play a useful role in the internal structure of a theory of sense of the sort McDowell envisages. But that is not what gives the theory of sense its purpose and content.

The fact that the used sentences specified the contents of sayings potentially effected by uttering the mentioned sentences would guarantee that the predicate could, if we liked, be written "true"; it would guarantee that the theory, with its theorems written that way, was a true theory of truth. But it would be the guaranteeing fact, and not the guaranteed fact, that suited the theory to serve as a theory of sense.   (*Ibid.*: 172–3)

McDowell puts this point elsewhere by saying that Davidson's suggestion is that a certain kind of truth theory can be treated as if it were a meaning theory, providing that it is arrived at (we could say justified) in a certain way. A specific subset of truth theories might be arrived at by making them pass tests stronger than those that are relevant merely for containing true instances of the T schema. If so, what the truth theory actually says is less important than the tests that it was made to pass. It is these that enable it, in addition to being true, also to be interpretative (cf. *ibid.*: 110).

One virtue of this modest account is that it does not fall prey to an objection made against Davidsonian truth theories of meaning. The objection runs like this. The connection at the heart of a Davidsonian theory of meaning is the extensional "if and only if". Thus, given a true theory of meaning for a language, one can derive an equally true theory by conjoining a spurious truth with the condition on the right-hand side of every instance of the T schema. None of the new biconditionals would be false, but they would no longer give the meaning of the sentences mentioned on their left-hand sides. They would not serve as a theory of meaning. Thus merely ensuring the truth of every instance of the T schema does not guarantee interpretation.

On McDowell's interpretation of the project, such cases can simply be ruled out as not meeting the interpretative condition of a theory of sense. The new theory would not make utterances of speakers form an intelligible structure. This, in turn, suggests a principled limit to the explanatory aim of the theory.

What I am proposing here, then, is not elucidation of the notion of sense in terms of other notions, still less any hope of reducing it to those others, but simply a description of its relation to those others; the hope being that a notion that is at first sight problematic may be rendered less so by an explicit account of its location, so to speak, in a conceptual space in which we normally find our way about without thinking.   (*Ibid.*: 7)

In this section I have summarized McDowell's view of the modest aims of a theory of meaning, given that it can be combined with a minimalist approach to truth. In Section IV, I shall examine a more specific sense in which it is modest.

IV Modest or full-blooded meaning theories?

The second reason for describing McDowell's interpretation of a Davidsonian truth theory of meaning as a modest theory derives from his argument with Dummett. Whereas Dummett argues that a Davidsonian theory of meaning should be *full-blooded*, McDowell argues in defence of *modesty*. In fact, the issues in this and the previous section are closely connected, and McDowell introduces his disagreement with Dummett in a familiar way.

Commenting that Dummett has argued that one cannot simultaneously support a redundancy theory of truth and also a truth-conditional conception of meaning, McDowell summarizes Dummett's reasoning as follows:

> [T]he redundancy theory gives a word for truth only *within* a language. That means that such a word "is of no use in giving an account of the language as from the outside" ... The idea is, then, that a proper account of a language must be "as from the outside" ...   (McDowell 1998a: 90)

On this reading, the requirement for full-bloodedness for a theory of meaning is the requirement that it does not simply presuppose key facts about content. Instead, it gives an account of the basic predicates and referring terms of a language rather than treating them as primitive. (As codified in a Tarskian theory of meaning, these are given in the satisfaction axioms.) Dummett equates the distinction between full-bloodedness and modesty as that between a theory that attributes "to a speaker who understands the name a knowledge of the condition which must be satisfied by any object for it to be the bearer of the name" and one that "will simply represent him as knowing, of the object for which the name in fact stands, that it is the bearer" (Dummett 1993: 21). Put this way, Dummett equates modesty with accommodating what he calls "bare knowledge" (*ibid.*: 24) of references. As we shall see, McDowell thinks that modest theories can still accommodate senses and he denies that bare knowledge of particulars is possible, but he does think that a modest theory need not state a *condition* an object has to satisfy for a name to apply to it.

A swift motivation for a full-blooded theory follows from a common first response to a Tarskian theory of truth (and thus also to a Davidsonian theory of meaning). Consider a famous instance of the *T* schema (a "snow bound triviality", in Davidson's memorable phrase (1984: 51)) in the context of a Tarskian theory of truth.

"Snow is white" is true iff snow is white.

Surely, runs the common objection, a theory that tells us only trivialities of this sort tells us nothing substantial of the relation between true sentences and the world and thus the nature of truth in general. After all, the right-hand side of the *T* sentence can only set out the condition under which the named sentence is true if we can take for granted the connection between the metalanguage and the world. Similarly, when this same mechanism is deployed within a theory of meaning, it can only tell us the meaning of the named sentence if we can take for granted the meaning of the *T* sentence as a whole, especially its specification of the condition on the right-hand side.

The usual first response to this objection – hinted at earlier in this chapter – is to distinguish between use and mention. The sentence on the left-hand side is *mentioned*; the phrase on the right-hand side is *used*. Thus the *T* sentence as a whole *does* say something substantial: it states the worldly condition under which the named or mentioned sentence on the left-hand side is true. The appearance of triviality is minimized in examples in which the named sentence is not simply a fragment of the metalanguage. Such cases promise to detail how the representational powers of, for example, French sentences are built up from their component parts. The detailing takes the form of a theory, perhaps stated in English, that articulates the compositional structure of French.

But even in such a case, the theory will terminate in axioms that simply list equivalences between French and English terms. These take the form of satisfaction axioms, such as: x satisfies "... est rouge" iff x is red. And it is this that provokes Dummett's concern. If the purpose of a theory of meaning is not merely to track the structure of one language in another (e.g. French in English), but to shed light on meaning or representational content in general, then it looks as though a question is being begged. No account is given of those axioms from a position that assumes no facts about meaning. Of course, as McDowell points out, this will only seem to be a lack if there is some possibility of not begging this question.

McDowell argues that Dummett's advocacy of full-bloodedness is a response to two perceived threats (McDowell 1998a: 93–5): psychologism and behaviourism.[4] I shall describe Dummett's rejections of psychologism and behaviourism in turn.

- Dummett rejects modesty because he takes it to involve a picture in which language merely *encodes* thoughts. A modest theory on this understanding would map utterances onto thoughts. But given that picture of the role of a theory of *language*, there would have be a further independent account of the content of *thought*. Without that further theory it seems that modesty leaves a vital part of the account of the content of utterances unaccounted for. Furthermore, the conception of language as a code makes understanding others a mere *hypothesis*. One would have to form a hypothesis about the thoughts underlying given utterances on the basis of evidence. That smacks unacceptably of *psychologism* to Dummett.[5]
- Dummett also rejects what may seem the obvious alternative: describing speech behaviour from "outside content" in such a way as to omit what is most important in an account of linguistic performance: its connection to minds. This would be a form of *behaviourism*.

On McDowell's account, full-bloodedness is an attempt to tread a middle ground between psychologistic hypothesis and mindless behaviourism. A full-blooded theory charts the tacit knowledge that guides a speaker's linguistic performance. It is thus both manifested in behaviour, so as to escape the charge of psychologism, and, at the same time, because it is a form of knowledge, its correct description can be acknowledged by the speaker. Thus there is no danger of falling into a mindless description of speech behaviour.

McDowell criticizes this picture on two key grounds:

- The attempt to articulate the implicit knowledge that guides a speaker without recourse to content-involving concepts fails. Dummett offers an account of the ability that corresponds, for example, to an understanding of the concept "square". In this, he

---

4. This account of Dummett resembles McDowell's diagnosis of Wright's misunderstanding of Wittgenstein, discussed in Chapter 1, except that he accuses Wright of failing to escape from a form of norm-free behaviourism.
5. As I described in Chapter 1, McDowell shares Dummett's hostility to hypothesis and psychologism in his account of the understanding of others when discussing Wittgenstein. He disagrees, however, that modesty is a form of psychologism.

makes use of the word "square" to describe this ability as being "able to discriminate between things that are square and those that are not" (Dummett 1993: 98, quoted in McDowell 1998a: 91). Now, although the account does not "display" the word in its role as the determinant of content – as in, for example, believing *that chess boards are square* – it does use the term "square". So if this account is supposed to *guide* the use of the word "square" it will presuppose the ability it sets out to explain. But to argue instead that it is supposed to guide not the use of the *word* but the grasp of the *concept* that the word expresses would be a form of the very psychologism, and the conception of language as a code, that Dummett rejects.

- The pattern of use that Dummett's example is supposed to capture cannot be captured from "outside content" for Wittgensteinian reasons. The connection between grasp of a concept and a description of appropriate behaviour is too loose unless the behaviour can be described as manifesting that concept. This is one of the consequences of the rule-following considerations, which was made generally clearer in the critical reception of Kripke's interpretation of Wittgenstein, and was discussed in Chapter 1. The norms of meaning cannot be derived from descriptions of the use of words that do not already help themselves to normative, rule-presupposing descriptions. Such word use or behaviour is otherwise "an equally good manifestation of an indefinite number of different pieces of such implicit knowledge" (McDowell 1998a: 96; see also 1998a: 114–18).

McDowell goes on to suggest, as a possible interpretation of "square", a disjunction of, say, square with other things. Equally, we could imagine "bent predicates", like Nelson Goodman's grue and bleen, where "grue" is defined as green before time *t* and blue afterwards, and "bleen" is blue before time *t* and green afterwards, for some value of *t* (Goodman 1983). Such bizarre possibilities are, of course, normally ruled out in practice. But it is unclear that they can be ruled out from Dummett's reconstruction of the project of theorizing about meaning from a position outside meaning. McDowell considers and dismisses three ways of narrowing down the range of interpretative possibilities:

- One might assume that the speaker is a speaker of English. But the *right* to that assumption is what is at issue here.
- One might hope that the fact that a speaker accepts an interpreter's gloss on what he or she is doing when the interpreter offers

an interpretation of the speaker's behaviour using the word "square" would suffice. But this would require that we already knew what the word "square" meant on the speaker's lips when they accepted this interpretation.

* One might rely on the greater simplicity of assuming that the behaviour is square-tracking behaviour rather than anything else. But that would make interpretation a hypothesis.

McDowell's diagnosis of the underlying problem here is that a full-blooded conception of a theory of meaning adopts an essentially behaviourist conception of language *use*. It is thus forced, against Dummett's explicit wishes, to locate the mental aspect of speech *behind* that behaviour (McDowell 1998a: 100). McDowell's alternative view of speech recapitulates a theme from his discussion of Wittgenstein. It is to see meaning *in* a tract of speech behaviour.

Dummett's account of a full-blooded theory of meaning is designed to be a middle course between the psychologistic idea that speech is a code for thoughts hidden behind it, and a merely behaviourist account of speech that banishes any mental element. Full-bloodedness is supposed to chart a mental element without recourse to mere hypothesis of just what thoughts lie behind speech. McDowell argues that it fails to be such a stable middle ground. Instead he suggests that modesty, when properly understood, occupies just this ground.

A modest theory shares with behaviourism a concentration on the surface of speech behaviour rather than what might lie behind it, and thus escapes the charge that communication rests on a mere hypothesis. But it shares with psychologism the assumption that there is more to meaningful speech than the thin and mindless descriptions provided by behaviourism. It does this by construing the behaviour as making manifest a grasp of rich, meaningful norms, even if only to someone already in possession of an understanding of meaning. Speakers of a language can both put their thoughts into language and hear the thoughts of others expressed in that language. McDowell suggests that modesty amounts to this sort of claim: "some table-tops are square can be heard or seen in the words 'Some table-tops are square', by people who would be able to put their own minds into those words if they had occasion to do so" (*ibid*.: 99).

In response, Dummett objects that: "On McDowell's account, there is nothing in virtue of which the words of a language have the meanings that they do; it is simply a brute fact that they have them" (Dummett 1987: 258). Ascriptions of meaning are "barely true". He goes on to contrast this with his own account in which "the words and sentences of a language mean what they do in virtue of their role in the enormously complex social practice in which the employment of the language consists" (*ibid.*: 259). But this mistakes the nature of modesty. As McDowell replies, modesty is consistent with this claim but only on the assumption that the patterning of linguistic behaviour is not described in content-free terms. It is instead described as, for example, "expressing the thought that something is agile" (McDowell 1998a: 114).

In his commentary on Dummett, Weiss concedes the force of many of McDowell's Wittgensteinian arguments against full-bloodedness. He concedes, with Dummett, that Wittgenstein has shown that the epistemology of rule-following is minimal: there is nothing *by which* we judge something to be a correct application of a word. But, again with Dummett, he wishes to resist what he calls the "metaphysical conclusion" of rule-following: that in cases where no actual judgement has been made, there is no sense to what would have been the correct application.[6] Weiss suggests that a description of a pattern of use provides a way of accepting epistemological minimalism while rejecting the supposed "metaphysical conclusion" of rule-following. If the goal of explaining what *guides* a speaker's use of, say, the word "square" is abandoned (for Wittgensteinian reasons), then Dummett's example of a description of its pattern of use without saying that the speaker *knows* that "square" applies to square things is still full-blooded because it does not presuppose facts about a speaker's mental content (Weiss 2002: 32–40).

But this is not a satisfactory option. The purpose of articulating the implicit knowledge that guides speakers was to steer a third way between psychologism and behaviourism: preserving a role for mind without making meaning a hypothesis. In describing the pattern of use of a word in a way that eschews a description of the content expressed, Weiss denudes it of its rational purpose and mindedness.

Akeel Bilgrami raises the following objection against McDowell's modest account of meaning.

> [McDowell] argues that we must think of understanding others as a form of direct perception of their meanings and he intends that analogy to be taken quite literally. By it, he means that we must think of understanding as simply perceiving in the bodily motions and sounds of others, their meaning and their thoughts ... which, I believe, does make the mistake of denying all theoretical status

---

6. This interpretation corresponds to "semantic anti-realism", which has been described and rejected as an interpretation of Wittgenstein in Chapter 1.

to "meaning". I ... take meaning to be a theoretical notion ...
constructed partly out of the relations in which their possessors'
sounds and bodily motions stand to their environments. (I contrast
theoretical posit not with common sense posit, but with the idea
that there is something directly perceived and which is not to be
viewed as a construction out of a theoretical procedure which
involves an essential appeal to an external element in the constitution of what is constructed.)   (Bilgrami 1992: 202–3)

[M]eaning and content are not a matter of direct perception.
They are theoretical notions.   (*Ibid.*: 207)

The objection is that if meaning can be directly perceived it cannot
be theoretical. Bilgrami offers three characterizations of a theoretical
account of meaning:

- Meaning is not directly observable and must instead be a matter
  of theoretical inference.
- It thus involves construction from non-meaningful, norm-free
  items: mere sounds and motions.
- It depends on relations between speakers and their environments.

The first two characterizations are false. The third is true, but it can
be made without concluding that meaning is theoretical.

Taking the third characterization first, if meaning is essentially
relational, it cannot be based on internal objects or mental representations. (This is McDowell's rejection of the master thesis, discussed
in Chapter 1.) Mental states prescribe the facts or events that would
satisfy them. If the claim that meaning is directly observational were
inconsistent with these comments then it would be right to say,
instead, that it must instead be a matter of theoretical inference.
Thus one (erroneous) motive for saying that meaning is theoretical is
the assumption that nothing that has the normative and relational
consequences of meaning could be directly observable. But that turns
on the idea that what is directly perceivable must be norm-free. And
that is just the claim that McDowell has undermined.

The second characterization of meaning provides evidence that
this is the presupposition of the objection. If the claim that meaning
is theoretical means that it results from theoretical construction
from norm-free input, then it must be false. As McDowell argues,
drawing on Wittgenstein, such a view leads to the regress of interpretations and meaning scepticism (see Chapter 1).

It is not, however, necessary to regard meaning as theoretical, in the sense of requiring construction from meaningless items such as bare sounds and bodily motions, to accept that it is theoretical in the sense that the ascription of meaning to utterances and content-laden mental states to people is always subject to correction. This point is, however, better put simply by saying that meanings and mental states are ascribed in the context of interpretative theories that make overall rational sense of agents. That holistic project places relational constraints on interpretative theory in accordance with the principle of charity, but it does not require construing the input to such theories as non-intentional.

A modest theory of meaning is thus closely connected to McDowell's interpretation of Wittgenstein and to his account of the space of reasons, discussed in Chapter 2, where I described McDowell's idea that we have a *second nature*. Once suitably educated, we can respond to the requirements of moral features of the world. Moral judgements are constrained by moral features, which are no less real than the world's physical features. Similarly, initiation into the tract of the space of reasons that concerns language enables a subject to hear in an utterance its meaning or content. A part of the world is opened to perception. But this is not to say that there is any other way of articulating the subject's ability aside from commanding a view on that area of the space of reasons.

I think, therefore, that the main moral of the debate with Dummett is not so much the best way of taking forwards the technical project of developing a formal theory of meaning, which is a project continuous with that of formal linguistics. Instead, it concerns the best philosophical approach to understanding the connection between facts about meaning and facts about nature. Facts about meaning are just as real or natural as, for example, Fodor's favoured facts about physics, but they are, nevertheless, irreducible to physical facts. The impossibility of anything other than a modest theory of meaning supports the latter aspect of that claim. The framework developed from a reading of Wittgenstein, Aristotle and Kant underpins the former. I shall return to the real interest in a formal theory of meaning at the end of this chapter.

V Is a theory of meaning really a theory of sense?

In the final section of this chapter I shall outline one further key claim that McDowell makes about a modest reading of a theory of meaning:

that it allows a distinction between sense and reference. This is significant because one of McDowell's important philosophical commitments is to the importance of a neo-Fregean approach to thought. In Chapter 4, I shall describe the connections between McDowell's anti-Cartesian picture of mind, singular thought and neo-Fregeanism. But to prepare the way I shall now turn to McDowell's reconciliation of Davidson and Frege. This will provide an overview of his approach to a theory of sense.

It may seem surprising that a modest theory of meaning can help with the distinction between sense and reference. It seems simply to state – in its satisfaction axioms – connections between words and things: references. Indeed, one of Dummett's charges against modesty is that it cannot be made to fit a Fregean conception of sense. This was hinted at in his contrasting account of full-blooded theories, as charting knowledge of a *condition* that an object has to satisfy for a name to apply to it. Such an approach fits, for example, Searle's "loose sense" model, in which understanding a name involves knowing a cluster of descriptions, most of which have to apply to an object for it to bear that name (Searle 1958). Unless a theory full-bloodedly charts such substantial knowledge, how can it be a theory of sense rather than just reference?

Fitting a Fregean conception of sense is, however, one of the motivations for McDowell's interest in theories of meaning, in accordance with Davidson's formulation. Outlining how a truth theory can serve as a theory of sense in something like Frege's understanding of that term is the aim of his "On the Sense and Reference of a Proper Name" (1977).

> A Tarskian truth-theory entails, for each indicative sentence of the language it deals with, a theorem specifying a necessary and sufficient condition for the sentence to be true. The theorems are derivable from axioms that assign semantic properties to sentence-constituents and determine the semantic upshot of modes of combination. Now Frege held that the senses of sentences can be determined by giving truth-conditions, and that the sense of a sentence-constituent is its contribution to the senses of sentences in which it may occur. The parallel is striking. It suggests that we might construe Davidson's proposal as a proposal about the nature of a theory of (Fregean) sense for a language.
>
> (McDowell 1998a: 171)

The challenge this suggestion raises is, however, that a Davidsonian theory appears to be too austere to be able to support the richness of a theory that deals with sense and reference (or perhaps senses in addition to referents). It seems clear that the axioms of a Davidsonian theory – the satisfaction axioms from a Tarskian theory – specify references (*Bedeutungen*) of names rather than senses (*ibid.*: 174). So how can a theory of references also be, in some regard, a theory of sense?

Recall that Frege introduced the distinction between sense and reference (*Sinn* and *Bedeutung*) in order to account for the possibility of informative identity statements. To take a familiar example, the discovery that Hesperus is Phosphorus, and thus that "Hesperus is Phosphorus" is true, was empirical. But if the role of the name "Hesperus" is simply as proxy for an object, and the role of the name "Phosphorus" is as proxy for an object, and if these two objects are in fact one and the same, then the informative identity statement should say the very same thing as the (comparatively) uninformative "Hesperus is Hesperus".

Frege's solution to this problem is to suggest that, in addition to their reference, names also have senses. Since "Hesperus" and "Phosphorus" have different senses, the senses of the whole sentences to which they contribute are different. Frege calls the senses of whole sentences "Thoughts". He introduces the senses of names as the "modes of presentation" of the reference. In a further example, in which two names turn out to be names of the very same mountain but seen from two different viewpoints, it seems that, in some cases at least, different modes of presentation may be associated with different spatial perspectives. So if a Davidsonian truth theory lists references, how can it support the notion of Fregean sense?

There are three elements to McDowell's answer:

1. The underlying motivation for a Davidsonian truth theory and Fregean theory of sense coincide.
2. A Davidsonian theory does articulate different senses for names even if it does not state them.
3. The distinction between sense and reference can be mapped onto a distinction between knowledge by description and knowledge by acquaintance.

Truth theories as theories of sense, 1

The first part of McDowell's resolution of the apparent tension builds on the account already given of his view of the fundamental role of both a Davidsonian meaning theory and a Fregean theory of sense. Theories of meaning or of sense serve to rationalize speech behaviour. They do this by placing meaningful descriptions on a range of potential speech acts. (McDowell says rather surprisingly, given modesty, that speech acts are "describable, antecedently, only as so much patterned emission of noise" (McDowell 1998a: 172). This is surprising because it suggests that the theory is stated from a perspective *outside* content.) A condition of adequacy of the descriptions the theories of meaning or sense specify is that it would have to be the case that:

> speakers' performances of the actions thus ascribed to them were, for the most part, intelligible under those descriptions, in the light of propositional attitudes; their possession of which, in turn, would have to be intelligible, in the light of their behaviour – including, of course, their linguistic behaviour – and their environment. (*Ibid.*: 172)

He goes on to say that the point of the theory of sense is understanding behaviour and thus *fathoming* people. *Sense* as a theoretical philosophical concept is given content in this project of interpreting or making *sense*, more colloquially, of one another. What is clear from the description is that McDowell closely ties the formal axiomatized theory to a broader interpretative project in much the same way that Davidson presses Tarskian truth theories into service to codify the results of his account of interpretation from scratch in radical interpretation. It is this that underpins McDowell's argument, summarized above, that, although truth theories are not necessarily interpretative, they are providing they are selected on the basis of their passing further, interpretation-based, tests. Although they do not explicitly state meaning equivalencies, they can be taken to provide them (cf. *ibid.*: 110). "[S]erving as a theory of sense is not the same as being one" (*ibid.*: 173).

This framework provides one part of the answer to the question of how a truth theory can be a theory of Fregean sense. McDowell suggests that the *point* of the Fregean notion is just to meet the same general constraint that a Davidsonian truth theory has to meet. It has to be generally interpretative, even if this fact is not explicitly stated *within* the theory. But although that may be the general motivation for thinking that the two approaches share the same aim, it does not yet show that a Davidsonian theory can be made out to be a theory of sense in anything like Frege's understanding of that term. This is where the second element of McDowell's answer comes into play.

Truth theories as theories of sense, 2

On Frege's account, the senses of the component parts of a sentence determine the sense of the whole sentence or the Thought that it can be used to express. But this is not an indication of support for a bottom-up approach to language. The senses of parts of a sentence – eventually the words – are *abstracted* from the senses of whole sentences. The senses of words are abstracted from their systematic contribution to the sense of sentences or Thoughts, which are taken as having explanatory priority. In the *Grundlagen*, Frege asserts what has come to be known as the context principle: "it is only in the context of a proposition that words have any meaning" (Frege 1950: 73). Another way of thinking of this approach is to think of it as giving priority to truth, not reference (cf. Luntley 1999: 18). Is there an echo of this approach in Davidsonian truth theories?

The closest equivalent in Davidson's Tarski-inspired structure to an account of the senses of words in a Fregean approach is the list of satisfaction axioms. The role these play is similar in one respect: they are selected on the basis of having the right deductive *consequences* at the level of whole-sentence instances of the T schema. A Davidsonian truth theory earns the additional right to the title of a meaning theory by having the right pairing of mentioned sentences and worldly conditions. Thus the satisfaction axioms are abstractions that aim to capture the systematic contribution words make to different sentences.

But this is still only a partial answer to the question: how can a theory as austere as a Davidsonian theory capture sense, given that satisfaction axioms state *references*? McDowell's answer turns on the difference between truth theories that are interpretative and those that are not. Consider a pair of clauses from a truth theory such as:

"Hesperus" stands for Hesperus.

"Phosphorus" stands for Phosphorus.

Since Hesperus is Phosphorus, the right-hand sides could be exchanged, or just one name – "Venus", say – could be used on the right-hand side with no loss of truth. If a theory containing the original clauses were a true truth theory for the language, then so would one containing either modified form. But that is not to say that both would be equally serviceable interpretative theories or theories of sense. The dire consequences of these changes for interpretation would show in the instances of the T schema – the theorems assigning truth-conditions to sentences – derived from them. "Bearing directly on the theorems, the requirement [of providing interpretation] bears indirectly on the deductive apparatus that generates them" (McDowell 1998a: 177).

This suggests that, despite the benefit of hindsight, no interpretation theory for a language containing both "Hesperus" and "Phosphorus" can streamline its ontology, even if this requires neologizing in English, say, names from the language in question. McDowell writes:

> Suppose a smoothly functioning hypothesis has it that the mountain that some of the interpreter's subjects call "Afla" is also called, by some of them, "Ateb". Suppose competence with both names coexists, in at least some cases, with ignorance that there is only one mountain involved. Suppose ... that the mountain is new to the interpreter, and that he proposes to take over means for referring to it, in expressing his new theory about it, from his subjects. Since he knows (let us suppose) that there is only one mountain involved, his own needs in geographical description (and so forth) would be met by taking over just one of their names. But a theory of their language that said of both names that, say, they stand for Afla would ... be incapable of making sense of some utterances. To leave room for the combination of competence and ignorance, an interpreter who follows the strategy of adopting names from his subjects needs, at least in his theory of their language, to use both of their names.
>
> (*Ibid.*: 188)

This focus, again, on the use to which a truth theory is put suggests that the kind of sensitivity to the rational structure of a speaker's utterances and beliefs that sense is supposed to capture is captured in a Davidsonian approach. In effect, McDowell concedes that a truth theory does not *state* the senses of expressions but adds: "Why should we hanker after a theory that does that mysterious thing, if a theory that does some utterly unmysterious thing instead can be made to serve the purpose" (*ibid.*: 173)? The distinction between a truth theory that captures the sense of linguistic terms – as part of a broader project of making rational sense of speakers – and one that, although true, does not do that, turns not on what is stated within the theory but on its ability to serve that broader function.

Truth theories as theories of sense, 3

McDowell's third suggestion for mapping a Davidsonian truth theory onto a Fregean theory of sense is less satisfactory. He sets it out in the following dense passage:

> If there is to be any affinity between my use of "sense" and Frege's "*Sinn*" I must keep room for a distinction between sense and reference. There must be contexts where "sense" is required and "reference" would not do. Now clauses of the sort that I have just exemplified specify, surely, *references* (*Bedeutungen*) of names, and it might be thought that the distinction had disappeared.
>
> That thought would be wrong. Frege's notion of sense belongs with a notion of understanding, and we can get at what is involved in understanding a language by a careful employment of the notion of knowledge ... Semantically simple expressions would be mentioned in axioms of [a theory of sense] ..., designed so that knowledge of the truths they express – in the context of knowledge of enough of the rest of the theory – would suffice for understanding utterances containing those expressions. The hypothetical knowledge involved here, then, is knowledge of truths ... The reference (*Bedeutung*) of a name, on the other hand, is, in Frege's usage, its bearer – an object. To know the reference of a name would be ... to know that object: acquaintance, perhaps, but in any case not knowledge of things ... It is not, then, the sort of knowledge that it would make sense to *state* in clauses of a theory. The grammatical distinction between knowledge of things and knowledge of truths guarantees a difference of role for "sense" and "reference". Without putting that difference at risk, we can claim that a clause that does no more than state – in a suitable way – what the reference of an expression is may nevertheless give – or as good as give – that expression's sense.
>
> (McDowell 1998a: 174–5)

The idea of knowledge of reference expressed in this passage is epistemic. Because we can say that we are acquainted with someone or something and thus "know" that person or thing, there is a role for knowledge of reference that cannot be stated. Consider "I am acquainted with the Lake District". This is distinct from the kind of knowledge of things underpinning an ability to answer the question: "What region of the United Kingdom is called the 'Lake District'?"

Knowledge in this second sense, knowledge of a truth, "could reasonably be held to be knowledge that, in the context of appropriate further knowledge not itself involving the name, would suffice for understanding utterances containing the name – that is, precisely, knowledge of its *sense*" (*ibid.*: 175).

The aim of this characterization of *reference* is, I assume, to capture an extensional locution like "Smith believes, of Jones, that he is his brother", which presupposes no mastery of the name "Jones", by contrast with the statement "Smith believes that Jones is his brother". But it seems unfortunate to approach reference through the idea of *unstatable* knowledge by acquaintance, especially given that the axioms of a truth theory are taken to state references. At the same time, however, McDowell wants, for good reason, not to characterize senses epistemically as routes to references. But I think the point has already been put more simply in the discussion of the second way of characterizing senses above.

Not all true truth theories are interpretative. Despite the extensional connective at the heart of a Davidsonian truth theory, there is more to an interpretative theory than its truth. It is this that underpins the connection between Davidson's strategy (at least as interpreted by McDowell) and Fregean sense. Effectively, the distinction between sense and reference is the distinction between a truth theory that is interpretative and one that, although true, is not. Of course this does not allow reconstruction of the idea that senses are epistemic intermediaries or routes to objects. But that is the price of McDowell's Wittgenstein-inspired objection to placing mental intermediaries between subjects and their world.

It is worth noting just how minimal McDowell's account of sense is, as so far articulated. Two further elements deserve particular note. The first concerns the apparent insubstantiality of what knowledge of senses comprises. The second concerns the kind of articulation of linguistic abilities that a modest theory provides.

The apparent insubstantiality of knowledge of senses

Dummett raises a general objection to a modest theory of meaning. (Originally he directed this against Davidson, but later decided that Davidson himself does not advocate modesty.) A theory of meaning must ascribe more to a speaker than just knowledge that "'Hesperus' stands for Hesperus" expresses a truth; the speaker must know the truth expressed. But, it seems, a modest theory, which does not provide a substantial account of what is known in knowing the meaning of a name, cannot account for this distinction.

As I have explained, McDowell's response to this objection is to point out that even a modest theory is constrained by its interpretative role. So the deployment within a modest theory of an axiom such as "'Hesperus' stands for Hesperus" only pulls its weight if it contributes to an interpretation of a speaker's ability:

> Such a clause would do no work in the description of a linguistic capacity actually possessed by a given speaker – knowledge of what it says would play no part in duplicating, by explicit employment of a theory, anything that he could do without reflection – unless he showed an ability to use the name, or respond intelligently (with understanding) to uses of the name on the part of others, in speech acts construable as being about the planet. (McDowell 1998a: 182)

The context that justified including such an axiom would involve tracts of speech behaviour that made it clear that "Hesperus" was being used to refer to that planet. Given this context, it is warranted to ascribe more than just knowledge that the axiom expresses a truth but instead knowledge of the truth expressed. This also provides an element of agreement between McDowell and Dummett in their joint rejection of the possibility of bare knowledge of particulars (cf. Dummett 1993: 23, 85). "There is considerable plausibility in the idea that, if we are able to find in a person any propositional attitudes at all about an object, we must be able to find in him some *beliefs* about it" (McDowell 1998a: 183).

Luntley suggests the following interpretation of the move that is made here. It "takes something to get into a state of knowledge", that is reported as knowing that "'Hesperus' stands for Hesperus" expresses a truth (Luntley 1999: 257). But it takes more to get into the state described as knowing that "Hesperus" stands for Hesperus. One account of the difference would be to state, as part of a full-blooded theory of meaning, knowledge of a condition that an object has to satisfy to be Hesperus. Knowing that condition would account for the different states of knowledge. But McDowell's modest theory contains an austere account of sense that denies that there is such statable knowledge. So what can make the difference? The answer is to follow Davidson in appealing to the broader structure of the theory of meaning. The theory has to capture overall the rational pattern of a subject's speech and action. If it does this, then the way in which the axioms state references captures the way in which the subject, for example, thinks of Hesperus. Thus the theory is a theory of sense rather than senses.

The fact that nothing further needs be said for the theory to count as a theory of sense is well made by Dodd:

> To give a name's sense is to specify *what must be known* by some-one who understands the name. And what must be known, if one is to count as understanding the name "Clark Kent", is that "Clark Kent" denotes Clark Kent. Clark Kent is the man one should have in mind when one uses the name. The claim that *how* one comes to single out Clark Kent should be constitutive of the sense one attaches to the name is a *non sequitur*. It is to conflate *what is understood* (that is, the ability possessed) by someone who understands the name with *how one comes to determine* an object as the name's bearer (how one comes to have the ability in question). (Dodd 2000: 54, original emphasis)

The articulation of linguistic abilities

McDowell's austere account has also been criticized by Bilgrami on the grounds that although it avoids messiness in the statement of the theory of meaning, how the theory contributes to an understanding of subjects is obscure and, in any case, messiness will return in the surrounding interpretative context (Bilgrami 1992: 156). Bilgrami advocates instead a modification of a Davidsonian theory in which the axioms of the theory include summaries of a subject's beliefs about objects. This disagreement is the result of two deeper disagreements. Bilgrami advocates what is, in effect, a descriptive theory of sense for proper names. And he thinks that a theory of meaning should dovetail with an account of singular thoughts that are not object dependent in the way McDowell insists, which I shall describe in Chapter 4.

Bilgrami's view turns on a descriptivist full-blooded version of the broadly Fregean project. In Chapter 4 I shall describe McDowell's objection to this approach. McDowell rejects the idea that thought and world make contact through a kind of blueprint. He attempts to combine the virtues of non-descriptive accounts of names (which have typically been developed on causal lines) with a Fregean model.

But the objection that McDowell's account of a Davidsonian theory avoids messiness only at the cost of either obscurity or messiness elsewhere appears misplaced. That turns on the assumption that it is part of the brief of a theory of meaning to *explain* the connection of thought and world rather than merely *display* it in perspicuous form.

A modest theory of meaning articulates the structure of a language. What is more it connects – as Dummett requires of a truth theory – with an account of the practical abilities that a speaker must have. But it does this in a very different way to a Dummettian full-blooded theory. McDowell gives the following example: "This man is engaging in behaviour construable as his saying that Hesperus is visible above the elm tree" (McDowell 1998a: 193). The behaviour of the speaker is described as *manifesting* a linguistic ability. But that description of the behaviour places it in a pattern or context only for a theorist who has *already* mastered the concepts that capture the speaker's meaning. This means that the pattern of use that a modest theory articulates is a pattern only relative to a prior grasp of meaningful notions. It is not pinned down to notions that belong "outside content" (*ibid.*: 193) or available from a sideways-on perspective, or a perspective of cosmic exile.

Having now sketched McDowell's minimalist interpretation of the role and nature of a Davidsonian theory of meaning, I can return to a question I flagged at the start of the chapter. What does outlining the shape of a Tarskian theory of meaning contribute to our understanding?

This question is prompted in part by the oblique way both McDowell and Davidson introduce the role of the theory of meaning. Neither say explicitly what the role of the theory is. Furthermore, what McDowell does say in favour of the modesty of a truth theory makes it clear that it does not shed light on content from outside. So it cannot explain how one can come to express thoughts in language although it can display the structure of language. The last comment is, however, incidental. No Davidsonian theory has yet been developed for a natural language and there are formidable obstacles still to be overcome (Horwich 1999: 22–3).

Does McDowell's account of meaning depend on the possibility of the provision of a formal theory of meaning? It would be surprising if it did because the construction of a formal theory would be an instance of substantial philosophical theory building. It would conflict with his general metaphilosophical approach, which is instead to diagnose the sources of philosophical bafflement and thus to explain problems away rather than to answer them on their own terms.

Fortunately, I think the answer to this question is "no". McDowell argues for the modesty of a formal theory of meaning largely on the the grounds of the impossibility of taking a stance from outside content. At the same time, he defends a formal theory on the grounds of not what it states but the context of interpretation. What insight the outline of a formal theory does give is inherited from Davidson's account of radical interpretation. This includes the account McDowell gives of sense. We can think of a theory of sense as a perspicuous representation of the thoughts and speech of subjects that makes overall sense of speech and action. Whether this can be formalized in a truth theory turns out to be of merely derivative interest.

Chapter 4

Singular thought and the Cartesian picture of mind

A theme common to Chapters 1–3 is this: McDowell's approach to rule-governed practice, to moral judgements and to grasp of meaning within a language has been to emphasize the impossibility of adopting a useful philosophical stance "outside" the area of judgement in question. There is no prospect of a fruitful analysis that starts outside a region of conceptual judgement and attempts, for example, to ground those judgements using a description of the world couched in independent concepts. To put the point less metaphorically, McDowell rejects any form of philosophical analysis that consists of providing a *reduction* of one set of concepts into another that is supposedly less philosophically perplexing.

In this chapter I shall examine another instance of this general theme. McDowell gives an account of singular or object-dependent thought that rejects the contemporary neo-Russellian assumption that such thoughts contain both conceptual elements and extra-conceptual worldly objects. Such an account describes thoughts simultaneously from within and without. Instead, he sketches a neo-Fregean account that describes such thoughts from within the perspective of Fregean sense. This will underpin the key claim that McDowell makes in *Mind and World*: that there is no outer boundary to the conceptual order. So even perceptual experience, which, in contrast with the beliefs those experiences give rise to, might seem to be a point of contact with an extra-conceptual world, is really, according to McDowell, always already conceptualized.

The reason for this preliminary focus on singular or object-dependent thoughts is that McDowell suggests that discussion of singular thought "can help with some venerable philosophical difficulties about the relation between thought and reality" (McDowell 1998a: 229).

There are three key ideas in McDowell's analysis, which are discussed in the three sections of this chapter. First, a proper understanding of singular thoughts can be reconciled with a Fregean theory of sense. Secondly, singular thought helps reveal the fallacious underpinnings of a Cartesian picture of the mind as an internal realm separated from the rest of the world. It is this separation that then seems to require a substantial philosophical account to bridge the gap and explain how world-directed thoughts are possible. Thirdly, correcting the Cartesian picture of mind suggests the need for a "disjunctive" account of perceptual experience. On this account, experience can be a form of direct openness to the world. (On the other hand, it can also be the other disjunct: mere appearance.) These three elements taken together help clarify the general project that I described in the Introduction: showing how the world lies within the space of reasons.

In Section I, I shall describe singular thoughts in more detail. In brief, they are thoughts that (arguably) depend not just for their truth (or falsity) but for their very content on the existence of the objects they are about. One sub-species of this class of thoughts comprises perceptually based thoughts expressed by sentences such as "That glass is half empty!" To pre-empt the Fregean approach that will be discussed, it is clear prima facie that singular thoughts have different senses to descriptive thoughts even if they share the same referent. Consider the thoughts "That glass is half empty" and "The only pint glass being used in the snug at the Somerville Arms is half empty". Both these thoughts might be true of the same object, but because a thinker could rationally believe one and not the other – for example, because they are ignorant of where they are sitting – they have different senses. One of the claims of a neo-Fregean analysis is that singular thoughts cannot be reduced to descriptive thoughts, no matter how complex they are.

Perceptually based thoughts are counter-instances to what McDowell calls a "blueprint theory" of the mind (McDowell 1998a: 186). On that theory, mind and world make contact through a *specification* or *description* that the world satisfies. A blueprint theory fits descriptive thoughts that can be linguistically specified independently of context. By contrast, in singular thoughts the mind makes contact with the world without a description. Instead, the object itself, singled out in this case through perception, plays the role of fixing the subject matter of the thought (in the example of the glass above, *what* is half empty).

At the same time as he stresses the importance of object-dependent thoughts, however, McDowell distances himself from most American work on singular thoughts. He argues that contextual factors are not extraneous to a theory of sense. In this he follows Evans's work in *The Varieties of Reference* (1982). Objects are not *barely* (that is non-conceptually) present together with other conceptual elements in thoughts. Instead, following Frege, thoughts as a whole are senses with nothing but senses as constituents. Thus objects play a role in thoughts through so-called *de re* modes of presentation. In this way they can play a role within fully conceptualized thoughts. The reason for taking this line is, in brief, that a theory of sense is a theory of understanding, and one could take different attitudes towards a "Russellian" thought in which objects were barely present. In disarming the opposing view of the role of context, McDowell draws a key distinction between thinking of concepts as part of the *content* of a thought and thinking of them as *vehicles* for carrying that content. The latter requires that conceptual content can be fully encoded in mental representations.

In Section II, I shall examine the use McDowell makes of singular thoughts to attack a Cartesian picture of mind. The discussion of singular thought is part of a more general criticism of Cartesian theories of mind that take thoughts to be freestanding mental entities. These are often combined with a "blueprint" theory of how mind and world make contact: thoughts are specifications that the world matches. But once mental entities are thought of as freestanding, McDowell suggests, their intentionality becomes mysterious and the mind goes "blank or blind" (McDowell 1998a: 243). Singular thoughts reveal instead that one's mental state is partly constituted by one's point of view on the environment. One consequence of this view, for example, is that instead of having to represent the world to ourselves to guide our actions, we let the world itself guide our actions.

In Section III, I shall describe McDowell's "disjunctive" account of perceptual experience. This contrasts with a "highest common factor" model in which both veridical and illusory experiences share a common ingredient: the real content of the experience. McDowell argues that such a model cannot explain how perceptual *knowledge* is ever possible because worldly facts, access to which constitutes the difference between perception and illusion, always lie outside the common experience. By contrast, McDowell argues that experience is either of a fact or a mere appearance of a fact (hence the label "disjunctive"). But if it is the former then the experience itself takes in, or is constituted essentially through relation to, the worldly fact. Having introduced the disjunctive account of experience in this chapter, I shall return to its supposed anti-sceptical properties in Chapter 5.

I Singular thought in the philosophy of content

Russellian singular propositions

The paper I shall concentrate on in this chapter is the very dense "Singular Thought and the Extent of Inner Space" (1986). In this section, I shall focus on lessons drawn in it for the philosophy of thought or content. (In Section II, I shall examine its anti-Cartesian picture of mind.) McDowell's discussion begins with Russell. As far as the philosophy of thought or content is concerned, what is striking about the aim of the paper is its reconciliation of Russell's and Frege's accounts of thought. As I shall explain, McDowell aims to point out the possibility of generalizing Russell's account of object-dependent propositions, freeing it from Russell's Cartesian epistemology, but then wrapping it in a Fregean theory of sense or thought. (I shall use "proposition" and "thought" to signal Russell's and Frege's accounts, respectively, although the final account that McDowell offers combines these influences.)

Russell claims that in order to think a thought about something, one needs to know what thing one is thinking about (although in what follows the idea that this is *knowledge* will play no role). Further, this condition can be satisfied – thought can latch on to the world – in one of two distinct ways: by *acquaintance* or by *description*. Matching this epistemological distinction is a semantic distinction between singular and descriptive propositions.

Descriptive propositions are the subject of Russell's famous semantic theory of descriptions. This is a codification of what sentences containing descriptions – whether explicitly or implicitly – can be used to assert. Since such sentences can express thoughts it is also a contribution to the philosophy of thought. The analysis solves two key problems: it provides a meaning for sentences (expressive of thoughts) that contain descriptions that are not satisfied by anything; and it explains how statements that identify the subject of two descriptive phrases, in fact satisfied by the same thing, can nevertheless be informative.

In both cases, if the meaning of the descriptive phrase was simply the thing it picked out in the world, these features of our everyday use would be mysterious. (The former would fail to say anything meaningful because it would not express a complete thought; the latter would be trivial.)

What is perhaps most significant about the theory of descriptions for philosophical analysis is that a sentence such as "The present king of France is bald" is not analysed as an instance of subject–predicate form. The underlying logical structure is taken to diverge from the most obvious interpretation of its surface form. It is analysed as making quite *general* claims. Thus "The present king of France is bald" is analysed as a conjunction of three general quantified sentences:

- There is at least one present king of France.
- There is at most one present king of France.
- Every present king of France is bald.

In this analysis, nothing stands for the apparent subject phrase "the present king of France"; there is no equivalent of that subject phrase in the three general claims. Russell suggests, further, that many other judgements that seem not to connect to their subjects via descriptions should also be analysed in the same way. Examples include sentences using historical names such as "Homer was bald". The motivation for this claim is tied to the severe restriction that Russell places on acquaintance, described below.

Returning to the idea that in thought one must know which object the thought is about, McDowell explains its application to *singular* propositions in the following way:

> The underlying idea is that to entertain a proposition one must know how one's thinking represents things as being. If the proposition is singular, one can satisfy that requirement only by knowing which object is represented, and how it is represented as being ... The notion of acquaintance with an object, now, is the notion of an immediate presence of object to mind.
>
> (McDowell 1998a: 231)

Propositions that connect to objects via acquaintance are those that contain "proper names" strictly understood (Russell 1917: 162). The key difference between propositions that link to the world via descriptions and those that contain genuinely referring expressions is that the latter are vulnerable to the vicissitudes of the empirical world in the following way: "logically proper names combine with predicates to express propositions which would not be available to be expressed at all if the objects referred to did not exist" (*ibid.*: 228).

As the most famous example (cited above) illustrates, a key motivation for the theory of descriptions is that it provides an analysis in which something is still thought, even though there is nothing that stands in the place of "the present king of France". By contrast, a singular thought depends on the existence of the object that a logically proper name stands for. A sentence containing a logically proper name that has no object fails to express a proposition. More loosely, it fails to express a thought. McDowell summarizes this dependence as follows:

> [W]hich configuration a mind can get itself into is partly determined by which objects exist in the world. One might have expected the topology of psychological space, so to speak, to be independent of the contingencies of worldly existence; Russell's thought is that we can intelligibly set that expectation aside, but only when the mind and the objects are related by what he calls "acquaintance".   (*Ibid.*: 230)

This gives a picture of the mind of the following sort. When entertaining a descriptive proposition, one's state of mind, the "topology" of mental space, is independent of whatever objects exist in the world (although whether one's thoughts are *true* or *false* will still depend on worldly states of affairs). When entertaining a singular proposition, by contrast, one's mental state depends on the objects with which one is acquainted. Given that one can be in error about everyday objects, this dependence suggests a radically anti-Cartesian possibility: one may be in error about the nature of one's own thoughts. One may think that one is entertaining a singular proposition when one is not, when the supposed thought fails.

Russell, however, places a severe restriction on the application of acquaintance in such a way that this anti-Cartesian possibility is ruled out. He argues that one can *only* be acquainted with one's sense data and oneself. Thus the only logically proper names are uses of "this" and "that" for sense data and "I" for oneself (no doubt those uses that Wittgenstein characterized as "I as subject" (Wittgenstein 1958: 66)). In these cases, there is no possibility of entertaining a singular proposition and merely being under an illusion that the logically proper name has a bearer. It is because this restriction is placed on singular propositions that the theory of descriptions is required to analyse sentences expressing such thoughts as "Homer was bald", which appear to contain direct referring devices but that might be subject to error. These are also analysed as implicitly containing general quantified claims.

McDowell suggests that Russell's idea of singular, or object-dependent, propositions can be widened by giving up Russell's Cartesian restriction on the objects available for acquaintance. If instead of placing philosophically motivated limits on this, one accepts at face value the idea that perception provides a form of acquaintance with everyday objects, a different conception of singular propositions or Thoughts (to use Fregean terminology) emerges. The following passage sets out a key aspect of McDowell's picture of the relation of mind and world:

> A typical visual experience of, say, a cat situates its object for the perceiver; in the first instance egocentrically, but, granting the perceiver a general capacity to locate himself, and the objects he can locate egocentrically, in a non-egocentrically conceived world, we can see how the experience's placing of the cat equips the perceiver with knowledge of where in the world it is (even if the only answer he can give to the question where it is is "There"). In view of the kind of object a cat is, there is nothing epistemologically problematic in suggesting that this locating perceptual knowledge of it suffices for knowledge of which object it is (again, even if the only answer the perceiver can give to the question is "That one"). So those visual experiences of objects that situate their objects can be made out to fit the account I suggested of the notion of acquaintance; abandoning Russell's sense-datum epistemology, we can say that such objects are immediately present to the mind ...
>
> (McDowell 1998a: 231)

Thoughts can latch on to the everyday world through direct perceptual contact with it. Objects can thus figure in thoughts by being seen. But there is another key aspect that McDowell also deploys: a Fregean conception of senses.

Neo-Fregean singular thoughts

A key difference between a Russellian account of object-dependent propositions and a neo-Fregean account of singular thoughts is this. On a Russellian account, in addition to a predicate (which can be thought of as a fragment of conceptualized content), such a proposition contains the subject matter of the proposition, namely the object itself. By contrast, Frege argues that thoughts are senses with nothing but senses as constituents. They are *fully* conceptualized. The motivation for this approach, described in Chapter 3, is that a theory of sense is required to shed light on the rational structure of an agent's speech and action.

As familiar examples suggest, it is possible for an agent rationally to have contradictory thoughts about the very same thing. The standard philosophical example is thoughts about the morning star and evening star, Phosphorus and Hesperus, which are both Venus. Thus a finer grain is needed in the attribution of thoughts than is available in a purely referential or extensional theory, and this is why senses are introduced. (If thoughts about Phosphorus and Hesperus were both described merely as thoughts about Venus then it would be impossible to account for differences of opinion about the morning and evening star.) Senses are individuated by what would make rational sense of speech and action. Evans describes the "intuitive criterion of identity" for senses or thoughts as follows:

> The thought associated with one sentence S as its sense must be different from the thought associated with another sentence S* as *its* sense, if it is possible for someone to understand both sentences at a given time while coherently taking different attitudes towards them, i.e. accepting (rejecting) one while rejecting (accepting), or being agnostic about, the other.
>
> (Evans 1982: 18–19)

A consequence of emphasizing the definition that thoughts are senses with nothing but senses as constituents is that it can seem to preclude a Fregean account of *singular* thought. The assumption is that Fregean senses should be modelled on Russell's account of descriptive thoughts.

As McDowell points out, Russell's restriction on what can feature in singular propositions makes it plausible that no one would ever be in a position to take different attitudes to singular propositions because, for example, no one could be ignorant of the identity of two logically proper names ("This!" and "This!") for the very same sense datum. Thus with that restriction there would be no need to postulate different senses. But on McDowell's extension of acquaintance to cover, for example, acquaintance with cats, this ignorance becomes a real possibility. Thus the kind of examples that motivate a distinction between sense and reference will also be found in such singular thoughts. Fortunately, a Fregean account of object-dependent singular senses is not, in fact, ruled out.

McDowell suggests that a common misreading of Frege is to assume that he anticipated the theory of descriptions. On this reading, senses are descriptive and thus Fregean thoughts can only make contact with the world through *general* specifications codified in the theory of descriptions.[1] With that assumption in place it seems futile to attempt to reconcile Russell's suggestive comments about acquaintance with the general machinery of Fregean theory. But, following Evans's work in *The Varieties of Reference* (1982), McDowell suggests that there is nothing contradictory about that.

> Russell's insight can perfectly well be formulated within this framework, by claiming that there are Fregean thought constituents (singular senses) that are object-dependent, generating an object-dependence in the thoughts in which they figure. Two or more singular senses can present the same object; so Fregean singular thoughts can be both object-dependent and just as finely individuated as perspicuous psychological description requires.
>
> (McDowell 1998a: 233)

This begins to give an account of object-dependent singular senses but does not yet diagnose resistance to the account. In another paper, "*De Re* Senses" (1984a), McDowell diagnoses the mistaken assumption that lies behind the objection to the very idea of such senses. The diagnosis – drawn from examining Tyler Burge's account of the distinction between *de re* and *de dicto* expressions – focuses on the role of concepts.

The basic idea is that if thoughts are Fregean in character then they must be conceptualized. But it is then assumed that for a thought to be fully conceptualized it must be fully linguistically codifiable, or encoded in internal mental representations. This would preclude Fregean singular thoughts.

Burge argues, or at least assumes, that if thought constituents are conceptual then they must be internally represented and *de re* thoughts are not. He says:

> The rough epistemic analogue of the linguistic notion of what is expressed by a semantically significant expression is the notion

---

1. Searle's account of proper names develops this account into a cluster of associated descriptions (Searle 1958).

of a concept. Traditionally speaking, concepts are a person's means of representing objects in thought ... From a semantical viewpoint, a *de dicto* belief is a belief in which the believer is related only to a completely expressed proposition (*dictum*). *The epistemic analogue is a belief that is fully conceptualised.*

(Burge 1977: 345–6 quoted in
McDowell 1998a: 217–18, original emphasis)

Burge here connects fully conceptualized thoughts with thoughts that can be fully *linguistically* codified: that is, thoughts that can be fully represented by inner mental representations. Since *de re* thoughts, by contrast with descriptive thoughts, depend for their identity on contextual features of the environment – they depend on the presence of objects picked out – they cannot be fully linguistically codified. They cannot be fully captured by inner representations because they depend on non-descriptive contextual links to worldly objects. Thus if concepts are identified with a means of *representation* of thoughts, then *de re* thoughts cannot be fully conceptual. Instead, the objects involved would, as Russell's picture has it, be *barely present* in the thought, alongside conceptual elements, but would themselves be extra-conceptual.

As McDowell points out, however, this argument depends on illicitly running together two ideas of concepts: as aspects of mental content and as the inner *vehicles* or *bearers* of that content. McDowell illustrates this distinction as that between what is *expressed* by words and what does the *expressing*: the words themselves (McDowell 1998a: 218). That illicit association can be rejected, and with it the argument against *de re* thoughts being part of a fully conceptualized thought. *De re* thoughts are not codifiable by inner mental representations and thus cannot be carried by vehicles of content. But that does *not* imply that they are *not* part of the conceptual order.

Note that McDowell accepts the equation of Fregean senses with concepts but with a proviso: "If we want to identify the conceptual realm with the realm of thought, the right gloss on 'conceptual' is not 'predicative' but 'belonging to the realm of Fregean sense'" (McDowell 1994: 107). That singular senses are part of the conceptual order – understood as part of the Fregean realm of sense – is indicated by general Fregean arguments for the possibility of taking different attitudes to the same thing. If concepts are thought of as contents not vehicles, there is no difficulty here.

Recent neo-Fregean and neo-Russellian theories: one versus two components

There is an ongoing debate between neo-Fregean and neo-Russellian theories of object-dependent thought. Without attempting to summarize that debate, it is worth noting one aspect of it that impacts on the picture of mind that emerges from consideration of singular thoughts. As I have described, McDowell, following Evans, argues that singular thoughts should be understood as an extension of Fregean (or neo-Fregean) theory. Thus they are construed as senses, albeit object-dependent senses, with only senses as constituents. This commits McDowell to a *one-component* picture of singular thoughts, rather than a *two-component* picture. I shall outline the difference between these approaches and sketch an objection to the two-component approach.

A two-component account of thought develops naturally from Putnam's famous twin earth thought experiment. Putnam imagines a place, twin earth, which is identical to earth except for the fact that water on earth is replaced by a substance of different chemical structure on twin earth, although it is in all qualitative aspects identical. On the assumption that we consider earth and twin earth before the development of atomic theory, Oscar on earth and his corresponding twin on twin earth might associate the same descriptive content with the word "water". Nevertheless, what makes their "water thoughts" (thoughts they would express by saying "water . . .") true or false is different in the two cases and thus the thoughts are different. Given that Oscar and twin-Oscar might be physically identical – aside from practical details about the water content of human beings – these differences in belief do not depend on differences in the physical make-up of their thinkers. Thus, according to Putnam, "Cut the pie any way you like, 'meanings' just ain't in the head!" (Putnam 1975: 227).

A two-component response to this proposes that thoughts are composed from both internal elements (which can be determined by what is "in the head") and external contextual elements. The former, the narrow contents, are what both Oscar and twin-Oscar have in common. In David Kaplan's terminology, the narrow content is the *character*; John Perry develops a similar analysis using the term *role* (Kaplan 1979; Perry 1977, 1979). In the case of utterances, character is identified with the meaning of the sentence used. It is also what is entertained by, or in the mind of, a speaker.

In a particular context – for example on earth or on twin earth – the narrow content determines the truth-conditions of the thought as a whole: the wide content. In different contexts, the same narrow content can determine different truth-conditions and thus different thoughts. (This is the force of Putnam's thought experiment.)

One of the motivations for a two-component account is this. Because the narrow content of a thought is determined by what lies in the head, it can play a role in causal explanation of action. By contrast, contextual factors outside the head do not fit this model of action explanation. Thus wide content appears to be causally irrelevant.

Furthermore, the division of content into two forms fits with one interpretation of Putnam's thought experiment. When Oscar and twin Oscar reach for a glass of clear colourless fluid with the words "Water will quench my thirst", it looks as though their actions are the same. If so, they call for the same type of explanation. That is provided for by the fact that they share the same narrow contents. In fact, this argument is not decisive. As Christopher Peacocke suggests, one can equally claim that because the actions involve different substances they are indeed different and call for different explanations (Peacocke 1993).

A two-component theory is neo-Russellian. A full analysis of a thought or an utterance contains both mental elements and worldly features in combination. As an example, Perry gives the following neo-Russellian account by rejecting Frege's claim that the sense of a sentence is a thought. He takes, instead, the sense of a context-dependent singular term to be what is shared between different contexts: its "role". Only in a context does such a "sense" determine a reference. Thoughts are then construed as combinations of the incomplete sense of the predicative part of a sentence and the referent of the demonstrative in a context, however that is picked out.

> We can take the sense of a sentence containing a demonstrative to be a role, rather than a Fregean complete sense, and thoughts to be ... individuated by object and incomplete sense, rather than Fregean thoughts. Though senses considered as roles, and thoughts considered as information, cannot be identified, each does its job in a way that meshes with the other. To have a thought we need an object and an incomplete sense. The demonstrative in context gives us the one, the rest of the sentence the other. The role of the entire sentence will lead us to Truth by leading us to a true thought, that is just in case the object falls under the concept determined as reference by the incomplete sense. (Perry 1977: 493)

This view contrasts with McDowell's neo-Fregean, one-component view. As I shall describe further in Section II, McDowell insists that worldly features are not "constituents of" thoughts, even though they "figure in" them (McDowell 1998a: 237). Thoughts are senses and contain only further senses as constituents. They do not contain extraconceptual objects alongside conceptual elements. Objects *figure in* thoughts as *de re* senses.

François Recanati has argued, however, that there is not as much difference between neo-Russellian and neo-Fregean approaches as might first appear (Recanati 1993: 193–208). Recanati's two-components are described slightly differently from the account above. He suggests that a complete thought can be decomposed into an objective truth-conditional content and the mode of presentation under which it is thought (*ibid.*: 194). In other words, the objective component itself appears to possess truth-conditions. These in turn are not themselves sensitive to sense. This is because he thinks of truth-conditions extensionally rather than intensionally. In other words "Hesperus has risen" and "Phosphorus has risen" have the same "objective truth-conditions" (Recanati 1993: 195). In order, then, to rationalize action, the objective truth-condition has to be thought of in a particular way and it is this that makes up the whole thought.[2]

Recanati goes on to compare how the different kinds of analysis cope with different features of thought and suggests that they are similar. For example, both can accommodate the fact that differences in sense need not result in differences in objective truth-condition. A neo-Fregean can accept a difference between the full thought and its objective truth-conditions without accepting that a full thought is somehow *made up from* those objective conditions and the way they are thought of. Similarly, while a neo-Russellian argues that narrow content or character is needed to explain what is common between indexical thoughts uttered by different speakers, a neo-Fregean can accommodate this point by talking of *types* of senses. Roughly speaking, in these cases, the neo-Fregean takes elements of thought to be abstractions from a single whole while the neo-Russellian takes the whole to be built out of the component parts.

Nevertheless, because Recanati assumes that, although singular thoughts constitutively depend on a worldly object, as McDowell insists, they should be thought of as decomposable into two ingredients

---

2. As I described in Chapter 3, McDowell's invocation of a Davidsonian truth-conditional approach to meaning, by contrast, ensures that the truth-conditions linked to an utterance are themselves sensitive to its sense.

– a truth-conditional content and a mode of presentation – his favoured account is clearly a two-component analysis. On Recanati's account, in the case of the referring component of an object-dependent thought, there is both an object (as in Russellian theory) and a mode of presentation (as in Fregean theory). I shall shortly sketch two objections to this approach.

Bilgrami subscribes to a similar division of labour in the case of singular thoughts, even though he insists on the unity of content; that is he rejects a division of content into wide and narrow forms (Bilgrami 1992). Influenced by Davidson, Bilgrami defends a form of externalism about mental content. That is, his form of externalism is inconsistent with the Cartesian idea that our thought contents would be unaffected were we deceived by an evil genie. A subject's mental states depend on external factors; they are externally constituted. But this relation is general rather than particular.

> A *general* characterization of the doctrine of externalism is that the contents of an agent's beliefs are not independent of the world external to the agent. It is a denial of the view that intentionality is fully characterizable independent of the external world, or to put it in terms of Descartes's First Meditation, it denies the view that an agent's intentional contents would be just what they are even if it turned out that there was no external world. (Bilgrami 1992: 2)

Bilgrami's externalism depends on the totality of relations between a subject and the world charted in something like Davidson's radical interpretation. But he rejects the idea of genuinely object-dependent thoughts because, like defenders of narrow content, he wants to give the same explanation of actions that depend on genuine singular thought and actions that depend on hallucination. (As described above, the alternative view is that these are different actions and thus, *contra* Bilgrami, require distinct explanations.)

Bilgrami takes singular or demonstrative thoughts to play a particular role in the explanation of action because of their special reflexivity. Thus they cannot be captured by any descriptive account. But he argues that that role does not require that there are genuinely object-dependent thoughts.

> What makes something have the role of a demonstrative thought? Not the fact that an external object is involved, because if the agent is hallucinating it is *not* involved. Rather, the fact that in his psychological economy there is an element of reflexivity, even

though there is no external object. And in particular cases, that is perfectly possible. That is, it is perfectly possible, in particular cases, that the reflexive element essential to demonstrative indexicals can exist, without there being an object there. Demonstratives, in those particular cases, can continue to play the psychological role which is peculiar to them and which comes from their special reflexivity. (*Ibid.*: 163)

The suggestion is that if an agent can correctly be interpreted as having the capacity for singular thoughts, on the basis of their speech and actions, that need not require such thoughts to be genuinely object-dependent. That general capacity requires that there are causal and sensory relations to the external world, but it does not require such a connection for every genuine singular thought. Although there is a general relation between singular thoughts and the presence of objects, singular thoughts are not individually object-dependent.

There is no need to demand that each singular thought must be object-dependent in the Russellian way. Hence I conclude, contra Evans, that since this ineliminably reflexive psychological role can exist even if, on occasion, there is no object present ... it can be shared by hallucinator and veridical perceiver. (*Ibid.*: 163)

Bilgrami explicitly attacks the division of content into wide and narrow forms (*ibid.*: 15–63). He argues, instead, that there is only one notion of content that is both externally constituted (like conventional wide content) and explanatory of action (like conventional narrow content). Assessing his theory is not the aim of this book. But his account of singular thought appears, nevertheless, to rely on a two-component theory in this respect. Singular thoughts, whether veridical or illusory, depend on demonstrative concepts. In veridical singular thoughts, an object is present to the subject while a general demonstrative concept is entertained. But whereas on a McDowellian theory the nature of a subject's perspective on the world is described using context-specific senses, on Bilgrami's account it has to be described using general concepts that are not context specific.

One *difference* from most other two-component theories stems from the fact that, for Bilgrami, concepts merely stand to terms as contents stand to sentences: thus concepts are *aspects* not *vehicles* of content. Nevertheless, because such concepts are general, differences in specific *de re* senses need to be explained in general terms. For this reason the first of the two criticisms of two-component theories set out below will still apply to Bilgrami.

John McDowell

Objections to a two-component view

The main challenge for a two-component analysis is twofold. First, since narrow content carries the burden that in a neo-Fregean account is carried by sense, the rational structure of thought has to be captured using transitions between mental representations. Although this seems plausible in the case of thoughts that can be fully linguistically codified, such as descriptive thoughts, it is implausible in the case of singular thoughts. The problem is that thoughts expressed using the same indexical terms are different if they pick out different items. But on a two-component picture, that difference lies outside the narrow content.

This objection has been developed into an account of dynamic thoughts by a number of philosophers following Evans. McDowell gives the following sketch.

> [I]f one "keeps track of" a day as it recedes into the past, thinking of it successively as *today, yesterday, the day before yesterday*, and so on, that enables one to hold on to thoughts about it – thoughts that preserve their identity through the necessary changes in how they might be expressed. These "dynamic thoughts" are not Russellian propositions; not just any mode of presentation of the day in question would demand the appropriate capacity to keep track of it, so a dynamic thought is not determined by the sheer identity of its object. (McDowell 1998a: 217)

Dynamic thoughts also apply in the case of spatial navigation. The problem then for a two-component theorist such as Perry – and in this case, I think, Bilgrami too – is to explain the transitions between linguistic expressions that count as expressing the same underlying thought. Luntley puts this objection as follows:

> Perry's task is to define the rules for the modulation of belief states (the linguistic expressions of belief) that capture the constancy of content through time and/or spatial movement. Such rules need to pick out sequences of belief states that hang together rationally. Perry's problem is that there would appear to be no general rules for collecting together sequences of such states that do not appeal to the very idea of belief content that he is trying to define. The reason for this is that bare rules of applied linguistic usage covering modulation of tense or modulation of demonstrative expression from "this" to "that", or vice versa must not be so coarse grained that they end up attributing to us an idealised rationality ... (Luntley 1999: 316–17)

They must not simply codify correct transitions between tensed statements in minutes or between spatial demonstratives "this" and "that" in metres because speakers may be insensitive to this but without lack of rationality. We can, in other words, track a moving cat using the expressions "this cat" and "that cat" without an idealized ability to estimate distances. "There must, however, be some such modulation, or else our beliefs would never survive beyond the moment of their first articulation, and we could then make no rational sense of our behaviour through time or spatial movement" (*ibid.*: 317). Thus the problem that dynamic thoughts raise for a two-component theory is to explain a subject's perspective on the world, expressed in different utterances that nevertheless express the same thought, without appeal to features of the external world actually present. A broadly McDowellian account, by contrast, can help itself to the idea of a subject's self-conscious navigation through a world of objects without needing to map that world onto a prior set of (possibly inner) concepts.

Secondly, there is a more general question about how the internal element of thought – the narrow content – can have *any* form of intentionality. By starting with internal mental representations, a two-component view has to do substantial philosophical work to explain how they can be about anything. (This criticism does not, however, apply to Bilgrami.) I will discuss this point which turns on the interrelation of the philosophy of thought and of mind, in Section II.

One of the arguments for a two-component theory, including Bilgrami's account, is the problem of explaining perceptual error for a genuine *de re* theorist. That topic lies outside the scope of this book. But it is worth noting that there are options available. In the case of mistaken identity, a *de re* theorist has no particular problem. That cat has been mistaken for a rabbit, for example. In some contexts, cats just do look like rabbits. But in the case of hallucination, such as Macbeth's, there is nothing to be mistaken for a dagger. What then is being thought?

The obvious answer is that the subject is thinking a (false) descriptive thought. It may, as Luntley suggests, be a descriptive thought that contains an embedded reference to a place (*ibid.*: 340). Either way, this has an anti-Cartesian consequence; a speaker can be in error about the kind of thought that they are thinking. They may think that they are thinking a singular object-dependent thought when in fact they are thinking a descriptive thought of some sort. But the assumption that the topology of mental space is infallibly knowable is one of the targets I shall consider below.

II Singular thought and the philosophy of mind

The connection between the account of the philosophy of thought or content and an anti-Cartesian picture of mind and its relation to the world is suggested in the following passage:

> In a fully Cartesian picture, the inner life takes place in an autonomous realm, transparent to the introspective awareness of its subject; the access of subjectivity to the rest of the world becomes correspondingly problematic, in a way that has familiar manifestations in the mainstream of post-Cartesian epistemology. If we let there be quasi-Russellian singular propositions about, say, ordinary perceptible objects among the contents of inner space, we can no longer be regarding inner space as a locus of configurations that are self-standing, not beholden to external conditions; and there is now no question of a gulf, which it might be the task of philosophy to try to bridge, or declare unbridgeable, between the realm of subjectivity and the world of ordinary objects. We can make this vivid by saying, in a Russellian vein, that objects themselves can *figure in* thoughts that are among the contents of the mind ... firmly distinguishing "figure in" from "be a constituent of" as a natural way of insisting on object dependence.   (McDowell 1998a: 236–7)

I shall return to the distinction between objects *figuring in* and being *constituents of* thoughts in Chapter 6. For now it suffices to note that this distinction marks the difference between a Fregean account of singular thoughts, in which objects figure in thoughts as part of the realm of *sense*, and a Russellian account, in which the objects themselves are constituents of thoughts – more properly *propositions* – as part of the realm of *reference*. To repeat, in the latter case no simple account can be given of how there might be rational disagreement over thoughts about the same *res*.[3] The first part of the passage reveals a significant view of the mind, which underpins much of McDowell's account in *Mind and World*.

---

3. Latter-day neo-Russellians attempt – without success – to cope with this by packing more into the conceptual element of the analysis of singular thoughts while retaining the assumption that the *res* is barely present and itself outside the conceptual order.

Singular thoughts and the master thesis

The comment that, given an account of singular thoughts we can no longer regard "inner space as a locus of configurations that are self-standing, not beholden to external conditions" (McDowell 1998a: 237) extends a claim from Chapter 1. One of the morals of the discussion of Wittgenstein was this. The sceptical argument against meaning, which derives a vicious regress of interpretations from the assumption that understanding a rule must be a form of interpretation, is itself motivated by a further master thesis about the nature of mind.

That master thesis is that understanding is a state that merely *can be* interpreted as having a particular content or bearing on the world. (Wittgenstein draws on this misunderstanding when he talks of the temptation to say that meaning is the *last interpretation*.) This in turn follows from the conception of understanding as a freestanding entity on the model of a signpost that just "stands there" and thus has to be connected with a practical ability by a further interpretation. The same model is often also applied to other intentional states, such as hopes, expectations, intentions and the like.

As described in Chapter 1, McDowell denies that understanding can be thought of as a freestanding state, an inner signpost. Intentional states are instead *essentially* directed. This claim is made less stark by connecting it to claims about the practical abilities that are the baseline for explanation or justification both in everyday practice and also in philosophy. By denying the master thesis, McDowell undercuts the assumption that meaning must depend on an interpretation, and thus he undercuts the argument for scepticism about meaning.

That same general lesson is applied in the discussion of singular thoughts and experience. It is a feature of the Cartesian picture that the mind is populated with mental items that are freestanding and independent of the outer world. But singular thoughts resist assimilation to that picture. And this fact promises, McDowell suggests, a way of escaping one of the key problems of a Cartesian legacy: its vulnerability to scepticism about the external world.

> The point of the conception of singular thought that I have been recommending is that it treats the Cartesian fear of loss [of the world] in a different, and fully satisfying way: not trying to bridge a gulf between intentionality and objects, nor by a cavalier refusal to worry about the problem, while leaving what poses

it undisturbed, but by fundamentally undermining the picture of mind that generates the Cartesian divide.

(McDowell 1998a: 259)

I shall return shortly to the consequences for scepticism of McDowell's anti-Cartesian picture. But first, what exactly is the relation between the diagnosis of Kripkean rule-scepticism and the role of singular thoughts in McDowell's attack on Cartesianism? Concentrating on McDowell's "Putnam on Mind and Meaning" (1992a), Alex Miller argues that there is no easy connection.

McDowell gives the following sketch of the conclusion of Putnam's famous twin earth argument in his "The Meaning of Meaning" (Putnam 1975). The extensions of natural kind words like "water" depend on scientifically discoverable facts about the substances that are actually connected to the correct use of those words.

Now it seems plausible that the extension of a word as a speaker uses it should be a function of its meaning; otherwise we lose some links that seem to be simply common sense – not part of some potentially contentious philosophical theory – between what words mean on speakers' lips, what those speakers say when they utter those words, and how things have to be for what they say to be true. If we keep those links, Putnam's thesis about extension carries over to meaning: that a speaker means what she does by "water" must be constituted at least in part by her physical and social environment. As Putnam memorably puts it: "Cut the pie any way you like, 'meanings' just ain't in the *head!*"

(McDowell 1998a: 275–6)

But given the first assumption about how the extension of natural kind words is fixed, there is an alternative interpretation available.

Meanings are in the mind, but, as the argument establishes, they cannot be in the head; therefore, we ought to conclude, the mind is not in the head. Rather than arguing, as Putnam does, that the assumption that extension is determined by meaning will not cohere with the assumption that knowledge of meanings is wholly a matter of how things are in a subject's mind, we should insist on making the two assumptions cohere, and conceive the mind in whatever way that requires. (*Ibid.*: 276)

On this alternative, instead of conceding that meanings have an extracranial worldly dependence but denying, therefore, that they can come to mind, McDowell suggests that we should also concede that *mental states* have an extracranial worldly dependence. He then goes on to attempt to diagnose the source of resistance to this idea. The first step is this:

> Putnam's argument works against the theory that he sets up as its target, just because the theory is stipulated to include the claim that the mind is in the head. Another way of putting that claim is to say that states of mind, in some strict or proper sense, are what Putnam calls "psychological states in the narrow sense": that is, states whose attribution to a subject entails nothing about her environment. (*Ibid.*: 277)

Thus McDowell rejects the claim that states of mind are *narrow* in Putnam's sense. This fits the account of object-dependent singular thought discussed in this chapter.

Miller, however, argues that the rejection of this narrow conception of psychological states needs more than is provided by McDowell's diagnosis of the master thesis lying behind interpretational theories of meaning and mental content (Miller 2004). There is a distinction, in other words, between arguing that mental states have content essentially – do not need to be *interpreted* to be about anything – and arguing that there are context-dependent thoughts, thoughts whose content *depends* on an essential connection to the world.

> And there is certainly no straightforward entailment from
> (*) The psychological state which constitutes my thought that someone is drinking water in the next room has its representational content essentially
> to
> (**) It is essential to my thinking the thought that someone is drinking water in the next room that there is (or has been) some water in my environment. (Miller 2004: 137–8)

Surely Miller is correct about the lack of implication. Suppose that there were descriptive thoughts whose content could be specified using the theory of descriptions and suppose that none of the predicates deployed in the analysis required contextual relations to fix their content. Nevertheless, if Kripkean scepticism were to be avoided, a proper account of entertaining such thoughts would still have to reject the master thesis. Thinking such thoughts could not consist in being in a state that merely *could be* so interpreted. But, *ex hypothesi*, these thoughts would have no contextual dependence.

Nevertheless, the example suggests a plausible McDowellian response to Miller by applying McDowell's criticism of Burge above (p. 150). The master thesis fits an approach that takes the theory of descriptions as not only an analysis of the *content* of a kind of thought but also as an indication of the shape of the *vehicles* of thoughts of that type that are supposed to explain having thoughts. Descriptive thoughts, on Burge's and many others' accounts, are carried by internal representations. Thoughts that can be fully linguistically codifiable are assumed to be coded in mental representations. But if so they fit the master thesis in that they are states that merely *can be* interpreted thus and so. By rejecting the master thesis, McDowell rejects any *explanation* of content in which it is carried by inner vehicles.

Although rejecting the master thesis does not *imply* that there is a class of object-dependent thoughts, it does remove a key motivation for denying them. That motivation is to assume that content-laden mental states are explained through inner representations. If that were generally true, then there could not be genuinely object-dependent singular thoughts. By attacking that assumption, McDowell can make space for such singular thoughts.

McDowell does not, and does not need to, *argue* for the *existence* of singular thoughts. To the extent that there are any such arguments, the arguments that there are genuinely singular thoughts are based on the failure of descriptive accounts to analyse and thus explain away apparent singular thoughts (e.g. Luntley 1999: 312ff.) and the failure of explanations of mental content in terms of inner representations.

McDowell describes the form of explanation he rejects in the following way:

> In Putnam's argument, mental representations are representations in the sense in which, say, drawings or sentences are representations. A representation is an item whose intrinsic nature is characterisable independently of its representational properties: a symbol ... But from the fact that thinking, say, that one hears the sound of water dripping is *representing* that one hears the sound of water dripping, it does not follow that thinking that one hears the sound of water dripping must in itself consist in the presence in the mind of a symbol: something into which the significance that one hears the sound of water dripping can be read, as it can be read into the sign-design "I hear the sound of water dripping", although in both cases the symbol's bearing the significance is extraneous to its intrinsic nature ...

> What never comes into view is this possibility: that being, say,
> struck by a thought is not, in itself, the presence in the mind of an
> item with a non-representational intrinsic nature . . .
>
> (McDowell 1998a: 286)

This passage contains a rejection of the master thesis. But without
that assumption there is nothing mysterious about conceptualized
singular thoughts coming before the mind without an inner vehicle.
That is the gap in Putnam's thinking that McDowell aims to fill.

Cartesian approaches to mind

I shall now return to the connection between a Cartesian picture of
mind and scepticism. Working through how concentration on singular thought might free us from Cartesian worries turns on appreciat-
ing what, according to McDowell, is characteristic about the kind of
scepticism that Descartes popularized. Cartesian scepticism and the
Cartesian account of mind are interdependent. Picking up the discussion of perceptually based thoughts, McDowell starts by considering
a Cartesian account of perceptual experience. There are two key
ingredients that give rise to scepticism:

- construing the mental (at least in the case of perceptual experiences) as itself comprising a realm of facts, or truths, about
  appearances;
- construing these facts about the mental (at least in the case of
  perceptual experiences) as knowable to their subject infallibly
  without any epistemic risk; ruling out any facts about the mental
  that do not enjoy this infallibility.

The first of these is summarized like this:

> Descartes extends the range of truth and knowability to the
> appearances on the basis of which we naively think we know
> about the ordinary world. In effect Descartes recognises how
> things seem to a subject as a case of how things are . . .
>
> (McDowell 1998a: 239)

The suggestion here is that as well as there being truths about how
the world is, and there being appearances or experiences of the world,
there are also truths about those appearances or experiences. This
approach to appearances provides a kind of consolation once an
argument for scepticism about the external world has been given. One

can at least take refuge in the idea that one can instead know inner truths, what it is like for the world to *appear* to be thus and so, even if one cannot know whether it *is* thus and so. But this is not enough to make scepticism about the external world plausible in the first place. A further ingredient is needed to split off the inner from the outer realm.

McDowell suggests that the second assumption that underpins Cartesian scepticism is this:

> Simply accommodating subjectivity within the scope of truth and knowability seems, in any case, too innocent to account for the view of philosophy's problems that Descartes initiates. We need something more contentious: a picture of subjectivity as a region of reality whose layout is transparent – accessible through and through – to the capacity for knowledge that is newly recognised when appearances are brought within the range of truth and knowability ... there are no facts about the inner realm besides what is infallibly accessible to the newly recognised capacity to acquire knowledge. (*Ibid.*: 240–41)

This assumption threatens us with what McDowell calls "the loss of the world". If inner truths can be known infallibly then they themselves cannot be world-involving. So consider a subject for whom the world appears to be thus and so. If the full mental facts are infallibly known, then the subject can know that it *appears* that the world is thus and so. But it is a further fact, not constitutive of the subject's mental state itself – the state of being subject to such an appearance – that the world actually *is* thus and so. It cannot be constitutive of that mental state because it is not the sort of thing that can be infallibly known. On the Cartesian picture, the mental is a "self-contained subjective realm, in which things are as they are independently of external reality (if any)" (*ibid.*: 242). Thus whether the world really *is,* as its appearance to the subject would have it, is "wholly located in the outer realm". And thus "subjectivity is confined to a tract of reality whose layout would be exactly as it is however things stood outside it, and the common-sense notion of a vantage point on the external world is now fundamentally problematic" (*ibid.*: 241).

In other words, McDowell aims to show how Cartesian scepticism is the result of a picture of the mind that separates mental states and the world. This division leads to a *loss of the world* rather than merely doubts about the possibility of *knowledge* of the world, because even when beliefs are true, on this picture, the mind *never* reaches as far as the world.

In Section III, I shall examine the epistemological consequences of the account of experience that fits the Cartesian picture and McDowell's "disjunctive" alternative. (This discussion will be further developed in Chapter 5.) In the rest of this section I will consider more generally the Cartesian picture of the mental as a form of inner space and McDowell's objections to it.

The picture of mental states as freestanding internal states is not confined to Descartes' immaterialist account of the mind. It is also shared by many contemporary approaches to the philosophy of mind, such as functionalism and Davidson's anomalous monism. These identify mental states with physical, neurological states and thus the inner space of the mind is literally inner: lying within the confines of the skin. (Functionalism identifies mental states with functional states but most functionalists assume that these are at least token-identical with physical states.)

McDowell suggests that contemporary forms of materialism share a key motivating assumption with Descartes: that mental states play a causal role in the explanation of action. The attempt to fit everyday psychological explanations into the pattern of natural scientific explanation typically, and apparently plausibly, involves construing mental states as independent causal intermediaries between perception and action. This, McDowell suggests, motivates Descartes's construal of mind as a separate realm of freestanding entities. But it also applies to much contemporary philosophy of mind.

Most materialist approaches to the philosophy of mind do not explicitly attempt to account for mental content or intentionality. The mental-state type most frequently cited for functional analysis, for example, is pain. Nevertheless there is an influential family of approaches to intentionality generally known as "representationalism", which fits the Cartesian image by populating the mind with freestanding mental representations. A clear recent statement of one version of this approach is given by Fodor in his language of thought hypothesis (LOT):

> Practically everybody thinks that the *objects* of intentional states are in some way complex: for example, that what you believe when you believe that ... P & Q is ... something composite, whose elements are – as it might be – the proposition that P and the proposition that Q.
>
> But the (putative) complexity of the *intentional object* of a mental state does not, of course, entail the complexity of the

mental state itself. It's here that LOT ventures beyond mere Intentional Realism ... LOT claims that *mental states* – and not just their propositional objects – *typically have constituent structure.* (Fodor 1987: 136)

And in a recent review of Fodor's work the general picture is put like this:

Thoughts are vehicled [i.e. carried by or encoded in] in sentences of an internal language of thought whose syntactic structure matches the logical form of their content. Transitions between thoughts are a function solely of their syntactic properties. Only when understood in these terms, maintains Fodor, can thoughts be causally efficacious and intentional realism preserved.

(Bermúdez 2001: 549)

But with this general picture in place, serious problems arise for all such approaches, whether forms of Cartesian immaterialism or modern materialism: "once we picture subjectivity as self-contained, it is hard to see how its states and episodes can be anything but blind" (McDowell 1998a: 244). It is mysterious how freestanding inner states can be about anything and can possess intentionality. One substantial objection to this approach was discussed in Chapter 1. With the master thesis that the mind is populated by items that just stand there like signposts, there is a real problem explaining how they can be reconnected normatively to items in the world. Approaches that bind such items to objects or facts through an *interpretation* seem destined either simply to beg the question about the content of the interpretation or fail to sustain the necessarily normative connection between mind and world.

Contemporary philosophers working within this tradition are aware of this challenge and have devised a number of mechanisms to connect internal states with the world in order to animate them without the illicit appeal to interpretation. A common strategy therefore is to appeal to a causal mechanism (e.g. Fodor 1987, Papineau 1987, Sterelny 1990). The idea is that inner states possess the content they do in virtue of causal connections between them and worldly states. This in turn is motivated by the observation that effects often cause information about their causes, exemplified in the idea that smoke *means* fire.

In a book summarizing representationalist approaches to content, Kim Sterelny says:

> Thoughts are inner representations; thinking is the processing of
> inner, mental representations. These representations have a
> double aspect ... [T]heir role within the mind depends on their
> individualist, perhaps their syntactic, properties ... [and] they
> are representations in virtue of relations with the world. Mental
> states represent in virtue of causal relations of some kind with
> what they represent.   (Sterelny 1990: 39)

Since one of the key conditions of adequacy of an analysis is capturing
the normativity of thought, the test of which representationalists are
most aware is accounting for the possibility of false thought. This is
known as the "disjunction problem", because the problem turns on
preventing an analysis of the content encoded by an inner item –
given in terms of the causes of the tokenings of that inner state –
collapsing into a disjunction of all its possible causes and thus ruling
out cases of error (where, for example, one erroneously thinks *cow* in
the presence of a horse). Without a solution to the disjunction
problem, a causal theory of content cannot account for false thought
and thus for the normativity of thought in general. It is thus a necessary, although not a sufficient, condition for a causal analysis of
intentionality.

Solutions to the disjunction problem attempt to specify – in non-
question-begging ways – which are the content-constituting causal
connections between inner mental states and worldly items and
which connections merely underpin errors. Two influential strategies are Fodor's asymmetric dependence theory and teleosemantics.

- *Fodor's asymmetric dependence theory* (see Chapter 1) invokes a
  higher-order dependence between the laws that connect worldly
  objects and internal representations. Roughly, the laws that
  underpin the erroneous tokening of the cow representation in the
  face of a poorly seen horse depend on the generally reliable
  tokening of "cow thoughts" in the face of clearly visible cows, but
  not vice versa.
- *Teleosemantics*, defended in different forms by, for example,
  Millikan and Papineau (Millikan 1984; Papineau 1987), invokes
  evolutionary selective history to further characterize the causal
  relations, either by specifying ideal circumstances that underwrite causal connections that are constitutive of the content of
  representations (Papineau) or by characterizing the proper or
  biological function of the representation (Millikan). The idea is
  that the function of the representation can be spelled out using

evolutionary theory without regard to its content. The content will thus be explicated through the proper function. The distinction between correctness and incorrectness in the tokening of a mental representation can be defined by reference to its functioning in accord with its biological function.

There are, however, grounds for doubting whether any attempt to provide a satisfactory response to the disjunction problem can escape the kind of challenge that Wittgenstein highlights in his description of the regress of interpretations (as discussed in Chapter 1) (see especially Godfrey-Smith 1989; Peacocke 1992; Thornton 1998). But McDowell raises a different sort of challenge, which reflects instead an objection to the whole structure of explanation of intentionality put forward.

McDowell's objection turns on the idea that accounts of intentionality that depend on a composite picture of freestanding internal states and causal relations to the external world have the wrong structure to account for the phenomenon of a subject having a *perspective* on the world:

> Representational bearing on the external world figures in a mode of description of those states and events that takes into account not only their intrinsic nature but also their relations to the outside world. Light enters into the picture, so to speak, only when we widen our field of view so as to take in more simply the layout of the interior ...
>
> What makes this unsatisfying, however, is the way in which the internal component of the composite picture, and not the compositely conceived whole, irresistibly attracts the attributes that intuitively characterise the domain of subjectivity. Consider, for instance, the idea of what is accessible to introspection. If introspection is to be distinguishable from knowledge at large, it cannot be allowed access to the external circumstances that, according to this position, partly determine the full composite truth about the mind; so its scope must be restricted to the internal component (remarkably enough, in view of the darkness within) ... [Similarly] Frege's notion of a mode of presentation is supposed to have its use in characterising the configurations of the interior (remarkably enough, in view of the fact that they are in themselves blind). But a mode of presentation should be the way something is presented to a subject of thought ...
>
> Quite generally, nothing could be recognisable as a characterisation of the domain of subjectivity if it did not accord a special

status to the perspective of the subject. But we create the appearance of introducing light into the composite picture precisely by allowing that picture to take in all kinds of facts that are *not* conceived in terms of the subject's point of view. So if the composite picture contains anything corresponding to the intuitive notion of the domain of subjectivity, it is the dark interior. The difficulty is palpable: how can we be expected to acknowledge that our subjective way of being in the world is properly captured by this picture, when it portrays the domain of our subjectivity – our cognitive world – in such a way that, considered from its own point of view, that world has to be considered as letting in no light from outside? (McDowell 1998a: 250–51)

McDowell's main concern here is this. Once an account of intentionality starts with freestanding inner states and attempts to animate them using contingent causal connections to items in the outside world, then it cannot explain how a subject can have a perspective on the world. In the passage above two subsidiary arguments are deployed.

One problem is this. According to the family of theories being criticized, the intentionality of internal mental representations is supposed to be underpinned by causal connections. But if the metaphorical inner space of the mind is equated with the literal inner space of the brain and nervous system, then those causal connections lie outside the mind. McDowell suggests that giving an account of subjective aspects of a mind such as the mind's access to itself in introspection will have to be characterized using only the resources available having subtracted the causal relations that lie outside the mind. But without those relations, what is left has no world-involving character or intentionality. Hence the phrase "darkness within" (*ibid.*).

This general point is given a more specific focus by thinking of how differences of Fregean sense are to be explained. Taking the case of two senses with the same reference (such as thoughts about Hesperus and Phosphorus), McDowell points out that the difference between them cannot be explained by the causal relations outside the body, relations that are shared and are part of the world of reference. Instead, on the criticized picture, the difference will have to turn on internal aspects. Again, however, these are not themselves world involving, which dims the prospect of accounting for senses.[4]

---

4. I noted a related difficulty at the end of Section I. By dividing content into two forms, a two-component theory of thought has the challenge of explaining rational differences between thoughts using only the resources of internal linguistic codification.

Furthermore, the very idea of a sense is supposed to be the way objects are thought about or presented to a subject. It seems impossible to capture this property using internal elements that have no essential relation to the outer world. If senses are equated with internal vehicles of content then there is a separation of the sense from that which it is supposed to present. The presenting sense appears to be an opaque intermediary between subject and world, and not a form of access to that world.

McDowell denies that there is a separation between an inner mental space and an outer world. He suggests a number of different metaphors instead, including openness to the world and interpenetration of mind and world. But these suggestions are merely metaphors. The key lesson of the discussion of a Cartesian model is that the mind should not be thought of in spatial terms at all.

The general lesson from this discussion for the overarching project, highlighted in the introduction, of showing how the world can lie within the space of reasons is this. One of the sources of the problematic dualism of mind and world is a Cartesian picture of inner space. With that picture in place, then it appears that there is a need for a substantial piece of philosophical theory to reconnect mental and worldly items or, in other words, an explanation of intentionality. But that picture rests on assumptions that can be exposed and rejected. Furthermore, as I described in Chapter 1, the assumption that the mind is populated with freestanding items feeds the felt need of a form of rampant Platonism. Only an inner item understood on the lines of rampant Platonism could take a rational subject by the throat and force a particular interpretation on them. So by rejecting the Cartesian picture of mind, McDowell can recommend a therapeutic form of merely naturalized Platonism. Thus proper attention to singular thoughts leads to a proper understanding of much broader areas of philosophy.

Despite the focus on the very possibility of representational bearing on the world, McDowell puts much of the discussion of Cartesianism in epistemological terms. In the final section, I shall begin to outline the form of epistemological externalism McDowell recommends. It follows from the idea that experiences are not internal states of a subject but are instead a form of direct openness to an outer world. This discussion will continue in Chapter 5.

III The disjunctive account of experience and openness to the world

In Sections I and II, I explored McDowell's discussion of the role of singular thoughts in forming a coherent picture of the relation of mind and world. A proper understanding of singular thoughts reveals, he argues, that mental states as a whole cannot be constitutively independent of the world. Singular thoughts constitute important counter-instances to the Cartesian picture of the mind as an autonomous realm of freestanding items. At the same time, however, the fact that thoughts can depend on essential relations to worldly items does not justify a rejection of Fregean sense in these cases. Singular thoughts involve singular senses that are individuated in such a way to contribute to an understanding of the rational structure of subjects' speech and action.

In this section I shall consider a natural extension of the anti-Cartesian point. If mental states were freestanding and autonomous then perceptual experiences would need in some way to be tied to the world that they are pre-philosophically (and correctly) taken to reveal. One such approach is a causal theory of perception, which takes for granted the idea that in perception and hallucination alike there is a common experiential state – the state of things looking as though something is the case – and then uses causal relations to provide a necessary condition for successful perception.

Summarizing the causal approach, William Child gives the following distillation of claims by Paul Snowdon (1981), who criticizes the approach, and Grice (1961), who supports it:

(1) If S sees o then:
(a) there is a state of affairs reportable by a sentence of the form "It looks to S as if . . .", and,
(b) o is causally responsible for this state of affairs.
(2) Conditions (a) and (b) are imposed by our ordinary concept of vision.

(Child 1992: 298)

The idea is this. The causal condition makes the difference between:

- it looking to someone as though there is an object in front of them and this actually being a case of perception; and
- it looking to someone as though there is an object in front of them but this not actually being a case of perception.

171

The *truth* of the judgement formed on the basis of how things appear would not be enough to rule out cases where the appearance is coincidental and not produced by the object in question. The causal condition plays a role analogous to that of justification or warrant in the analysis of knowledge.

The hope of a causal analysis is that it sheds light on the reliability of perception as a way of finding out about the world. Following in a Kantian tradition, Strawson, for example states that:

> The thought of my fleeting perception as a *perception* of a continuously and independently existing thing implicitly contains the thought that if the thing had not been there, I should not even have *seemed* to perceive it. It really should be obvious that with the distinction between independently existing objects and perceptual awareness of objects we already have the general notion of causal dependence of the latter on the former ...
>
> (Strawson 1979: 51, original emphasis)

Such a causal analysis takes the form of an 'inference to the best explanation' (Snowdon 1981: 182). The causal dependence of the inner experience on a worldly object is the best explanation of the general reliability of perception for knowledge. Nevertheless, there are powerful McDowellian arguments against this analysis of perception.

Recall from Section II that one of the features of a Cartesian account of mind, according to McDowell, is that the mind is a region of reality about which there are no facts except those that could be infallibly known to a subject. This picture is a development of a traditional view to the effect that there are truths about appearances as well as truths about the world. But Descartes's further modification limits the constitution of the mental to a circumscribed *transparent* inner realm. This means that the distinction between veridical perception and qualitatively identical hallucination cannot itself be a feature of the mental. It must lie *beyond* experience: "Such differences must now be wholly located in the outer realm; they must reside in facts external to a state of affairs that is common to the two disjuncts and exhausts the relevant region of the inner realm" (McDowell 1998a: 241). This observation leads to two general objections to this picture of experience and a causal analysis of perception. One is an epistemological argument, which I shall mention below but discuss at greater length in Chapter 5. The other has already been touched on in Section II: freestanding inner states would be *blind*.

Beginning with the second objection: a causal analysis of the *reliability* of perception thus comes too late in the overall analysis of perception. If there were already reason to interpret non-relational freestanding inner states as representative of the world, then it might be necessary to establish their reliability as a method of finding out about the world. A substantial philosophical account might then reconnect the mental realm with the world and head off a threat of scepticism based on the worry that such states might not be in harmony with reality.[5] But such a causal vindication would be more like the discovery that the states were reliable symptoms or indications of some worldly state – such as the connection between goose bumps and cold – rather than showing how the states had representational content.

The epistemological objection runs as follows. If the difference between genuine perception and illusion depends on the presence of facts that do not lie outside experience (which is common between the two cases) then perceptual knowledge is never possible. Even in the case of veridical perception, a subject's experience stops short of the facts. Thus it is a matter of accident whether or not perceptual beliefs are true or not.

McDowell's diagnosis, however, is that the felt need for a causal vindication of perception flows only from the adoption of an implausible philosophical theory: the master thesis that the mind is populated by intrinsically non-relational items. If that assumption is rejected, and with it the assumption that there is no more to mental states than can be surveyed infallibly by their subject, then experience can be construed in a way that does not stop short of the Cartesian "outer" world.

In rejecting the Cartesian picture, McDowell can argue that experience is a form of direct openness to the world. Thus, when all goes well, an experience is just access to a fact. Of course, things may not go well. In that case, experience is a *mere* appearance. But there is no mental element common to both cases. This gives rise to a disjunctive account of experience:

> Short of the fully Cartesian picture, the infallibly knowable fact – its seeming to one that things are thus and so – can be taken disjunctively, as constituted either by the fact that things are

---

5. Child's causal account does not fit this mould. He does not take causation to link an inner item with a worldly item. But for just this reason, it is not clear what role causation is required to play (Child 1992).

manifestly thus and so or by the fact that that merely seems to be the case. On this account, the idea of things being thus and so figures straightforwardly in our understanding of the infallibly knowable appearance; there is no problem about how experience can be understood to have representational directedness towards external reality. (McDowell 1998a: 242)

Because experience is understood not as an internal mental entity to be injected with representational bearing on the world but as simply access to that world, there is no gap between experience and the world to be bridged. This line of thought is similar to Davidson's argument against "epistemic intermediaries". Considering the connection between our judgements and the world he says:

Introducing intermediate steps or entities into the causal chain, like sensations or observations, serves only to make the epistemological problem more obvious. For if the intermediaries are merely causes, they don't justify the beliefs they cause, while if they deliver information, they may be lying. The moral is obvious. Since we can't swear intermediaries to truthfulness, we should allow no intermediaries between our beliefs and their objects in the world. Of course there are causal intermediaries. What we must guard against are epistemic intermediaries.

(Davidson 1986a: 312)

There is a clear difference (to which I shall return in Chapter 6) between Davidson's and McDowell's views on the importance of experience for beliefs. On McDowell's account, experience plays a crucial role in accounting for the rational friction between our beliefs and the world. Davidson, by contrast, claims that only beliefs can stand in a rational relation to other beliefs. But, although important, this disagreement masks an underlying agreement. McDowell's project in *Mind and World* is to explain how experiences are themselves part of the space of reasons by arguing that they are always already conceptualized. Effectively, this is to make experiences more like beliefs, which McDowell and Davidson would agree are always already conceptualized. The more explicit area of agreement between Davidson and McDowell is their rejection of experiences as inner states that ground beliefs. Of such *inner* states – neurological and other stages in the causal chain from world to mind – both can agree that they play a causal role but not a rational role.

By rejecting the assumption that there is a highest common factor that explains the character of both veridical experience and a corresponding hallucination of perceptual illusion, McDowell is able to reconnect mental states to the world:

> Of facts to the effect that things seem thus and so to one, we might say, some are cases of things being thus and so within the reach of one's subjective access to the external world, whereas others are mere appearances. In a given case the answer to the question "Which?" would state a further fact about the disposition of things in the inner realm (a disposition less specifically mapped by saying merely that things seem to one to be thus and so); since this further fact is not independent of the outer realm, we are compelled to picture the inner and outer realms as interpenetrating, not separated from one another by the characteristically Cartesian divide. (McDowell 1998a: 241)

The idea here, which moves towards the epistemological discussion I shall assess in Chapter 5, is that the "outside" world contributes to the mental states of subjects. This was highlighted in the case of singular thought. But experience in general is understood on the same model.

The clear advantage of a disjunctive account is its promise to sidestep the question of the intentionality of experience. Having an experience is just having the world in view. It is not a freestanding inner state that copies or represents that world. But there is a phenomenological objection to be overcome. Surely there must be a highest common factor between experience and a corresponding hallucination of perceptual illusion to explain why one can be mistaken for the other? Surely that implies that there is a common element whose existence is not dependent on the state of the world, given that it can also be entertained in the case of illusions? McDowell's response is to deny that the phenomenology implies that there is a common explanatory element. Although it is true that things *seem* the same in veridical and illusory cases, this does not imply that there *is* a common element that *explains* that sameness of seeming. He writes:

> The uncontentiously legitimate category of things that are the same across the different cases is the category of how things seem to the subject. In the case of experience, the less than Cartesian position I described, exploiting the idea that the notion of appearance is essentially disjunctive, establishes that although that category is certainly legitimate, that does nothing to show that worldly circumstances are only externally related to experiences; to think otherwise is to fall into a fully Cartesian conception of the category. (*Ibid.*: 248)

McDowell points out the danger of sliding between saying "Everything seems the same to the subject" and saying "Everything is the same from the subject's point of view". Although he wants to acknowledge that subjects have perspectives on the world and, further, that there is "something that it is like" to enjoy a perspective, he denies that this should be explained by postulating a subjective realm. Indeed, as I described in Section II, one of his arguments against a two-component analysis of thought – which includes a model of internal states – is that it cannot account for a subject's perspective on the world. In Chapter 5, I shall assess an argument against McDowell's picture of experience that takes this element of subjectivity to be sufficient to undermine its grasp of the world.

But the objection that experiences cannot be constituted beyond what seems common between the veridical and the illusory runs sufficiently deep that McDowell's claim that the phenomenology does not vindicate a highest common factor account of experience does not seem enough to lay it to rest. In Chapter 5, I shall look in more detail at the externalism present in McDowell's account of experience and how this affects his epistemological position.

Chapter 5

Experience, knowledge and openness to the world

In this chapter I shall set out the epistemological consequences of Mc-Dowell's approach to the relation of mind and world, which centres on an account of experience. McDowell defends a form of externalism in epistemology but it is one based on the idea that knowledge depends on reasons. This contrasts with most contemporary forms of externalism – such as reliabilism – that dispense with the notion of *reasons* altogether in favour of talk of the reliability of belief-forming mechanisms. On the other hand, by advocating a form of externalism, McDowell's account of knowledge differs from most reason- or justification-based accounts. His account is externalism because being justified – having a "standing in the space of reasons" (McDowell 1998a: 395) – is not something a subject can ensure unaided. It depends, as I shall explain, on the world doing the subject a "favour" (*ibid.*: 405). In the case of perceptual knowledge, the favour is that the world is as appearances suggest it is. But this does not presuppose that appearances *intervene* between subject and world. Thus McDowell's view contrasts both with positions that emphasize the role of the space of reasons but assume that this is a piece of epistemological *internalism*, and with most forms of epistemological externalism.

Four main papers characterize McDowell's position: "Criteria, Defeasibility and Knowledge" (1982), "Knowledge by Hearsay" (1993), "Knowledge and the Internal" (1995a) and "Towards Rehabilitating Objectivity' (2000d). As will become clear, however, these papers develop the account of experience suggested in "Singular Thought and the Extent of Inner Space" (1986), which I discussed in Chapter 4. Rather than outlining the general position first, I shall follow the chronological order of the development of McDowell's thought here and begin with his discussion of knowledge of other minds and Wittgenstein's use of "criteria". This will take up Sections I and II. McDowell's discussion of knowledge of other minds will serve as a model for his account of knowledge more generally.

In Section III, I shall describe McDowell's account of the nature of justification in general. He argues that one should not think of having good reasons as an "internal" matter. By that he means a view in which a subject can ensure that they have good reasons for their beliefs without depending on a worldly contribution. Instead, he argues, a standing in the space of reasons always depends on a "favour" from the world.

In Section IV, I shall assess the extent to which McDowell earns the right to display indifference in the face of scepticism. I shall argue that, while his position cannot block sceptical doubts that are already held, it undermines the motivation for sceptical doubts about the world in the first place. Without that motivation, while sceptical doubts cannot be refuted, it is reasonable merely to be indifferent to them.

I Knowledge of other minds and a conventional view of criteria

Here and in Section II, I shall describe McDowell's contribution in "Criteria, Defeasibility and Knowledge" to the debate among commentators on Wittgenstein on the role of criteria in knowledge of other minds. This will shed light on the way he conceives experience as enabling us to form judgements about the world generally. The general moral is this. McDowell rejects a view in which the criteria for judgements about other minds are forms of behaviour described in a way that does not presuppose mentality. He rejects the view in which judgements about other minds formed on the basis of criteria fall short of the relevant facts (the facts about other minds and mental states). Similarly, he rejects a more general view of experience in which it stops short of the facts (facts about the external world in general).

The standard view of criteria

Wittgenstein deploys the idea of criteria in a number of different contexts, but the context that has been most influential is that of grounding knowledge of other minds. The influential Wittgenstein exegete P. M. S. Hacker, writing in the *Oxford Companion to Philosophy*, defines a criterion thus:

> A standard by which to judge something; a feature of a thing by which it can be judged to be thus and so. In the writings of the later Wittgenstein it is used as a quasi-technical term. Typically, something counts as a criterion for another thing if it is necessarily good evidence for it. Unlike inductive evidence, criterial support is determined by convention and is partly constitutive of the meaning of the expression for whose application it is a criterion. Unlike entailment, criterial support is characteristically defeasible. Wittgenstein argued that behavioural expressions of the "inner", e.g. groaning or crying out in pain, are neither inductive evidence for the mental (Cartesianism), nor do they entail the instantiation of the relevant mental term (behaviourism), but are defeasible criteria for its application. (Honderich 1995)

Key features of this definition are that the criteria of, for example, an inner state like pain are fixed by convention and are partly constitutive of what we mean by pain. Thus groaning and crying out are not mere symptoms but rather part of what we understand by pain. They are connected by definition not induction.

This account of the relation between relevant behaviour and an inner state can be motivated as a response to the problem of other minds prompted by a Cartesian picture. If the relation between mental states and behaviour had to be established through inductive correlations, then the only available correlation would be the one that governed one's own case. This is the basis of the *argument from analogy*. But that inference seems not to license claims about other people. "If I say of myself that it is only from my own case that I know what the word 'pain' means – must I not say the same of other people too? And how can I generalise the *one* case so irresponsibly?" (Wittgenstein 1953: §293). In addition to this challenge, Norman Malcolm presses a further line of thought found in Wittgenstein. If one starts simply from a first person perspective, it is unclear what *sense* one can give to the thought that other people have pain.

> If I do not know how to establish that "someone has a pain" then I do not know how to establish that he has the *same* as I have when I have a pain. You cannot improve my understanding of "He has a pain" by this recourse to the notion of "the same", unless you give me a criterion for saying that someone *has* the same as I

> have. If you do this you will have no use for the argument from analogy; and if you cannot then you do not understand the supposed conclusion of that argument.   (Malcolm 1958: 970)

Thus, unless there were a criterion to give sense to the judgement "he is in pain" the argument from analogy could not be applied. But, if there is a behavioural criterion, that argument is unnecessary.

This is the general shape of the response to a Cartesian form of scepticism about other minds popular among Wittgensteinians in the 1960s and 1970s. Instead of being mere *symptoms* of pain, relevant behaviour (e.g. groaning and crying out) is linked to underlying pain through an a priori conceptual connection that predates empirical enquiry. At the same time, however, the criteria of pain are taken to be *defeasible*.

The reason for this qualification is the following intuition. While, in general, pain behaviour is the expression of underlying pain, on occasion behaviour that resembles pain behaviour in every detail is *not* the expression of pain. It may be the result of acting or pretence. (And equally, genuine underlying pain may sometimes be stoically kept from expression.) As a result, the criterial support that apparent pain behaviour gives for a judgement that someone is in pain is taken to be defeasible. That is, it can, on occasion, be overturned.

The idea that criteria give only defeasible support for a claim is combined with a further assumption, which McDowell describes thus: "if a condition is ever a criterion for a claim, ... then any condition of that type constitutes a criterion for that claim, or one suitably related to it" (1998a: 377). In other words, criteria are *types*. Thus, while on most occasions when instances of some general type of criterion are satisfied the underlying fact for which those instances are criteria also holds, on some occasions the type of criterion is satisfied (by some particular circumstances) but the fact does not hold. In the latter cases, the criterion is satisfied but is nevertheless also defeated.

The connection between criteria and underlying mental states looks at first sight to be closer than that between symptoms and mental states. It seems almost like direct access to the mental states themselves. McDowell's criticism, however, is that it is not close enough to serve the role for which it is intended. As an exegetical device, McDowell suggests contrasting the idea of criterial support with alternative: "the circumstance that someone else is in some 'inner' state can itself be an object of one's experience ... [and that] one can literally perceive, in another person's facial expression or his behaviour, that he is ... in pain" (*ibid.*: 370). In fact, as I shall outline, the position that McDowell advocates is not quite as direct as this.

McDowell's criticism of the standard view of criteria

McDowell deploys two sorts of argument against the standard view of criteria. One is that it is a poor exegesis of Wittgenstein. Rather than describing a technical device in the philosophy of language (as criteria have been taken to be (e.g. Baker 1974)), Wittgenstein uses the word "without ceremony" (McDowell 1998a: 376). Furthermore, this exegesis only seems compelling against a particular background epistemological assumption for which there is no support in Wittgenstein. I shall return to this assumption shortly.

The second kind of argument undermines the effectiveness of this idea of support for judgements about other people's mental states. It is an attack on the idea that perceptual knowledge is supposed to be based "on an experiential intake that falls short of the fact known ... in the sense [of] ... being compatible with there being no such fact" (McDowell 1998a: 373).[1]

To return to McDowell's second line of criticism:

> If experiencing the satisfaction of "criteria" does legitimize ("criterially") a claim to know that things are thus and so, it cannot also be legitimate to admit that the position is one in which, for all one knows, things may be otherwise. But the difficulty is to see how the fact that "criteria" are defeasible can be prevented from compelling that admission; in which case we can conclude, by contraposition, that experiencing the satisfaction of "criteria" cannot legitimize a claim of knowledge. How can appeal to "convention" somehow drive a wedge between accepting that everything that one has is compatible with things not being so, on the one hand, and admitting that one does not know that things are so, on the other? (McDowell 1998a: 372–3)

The worry is this. If one knows something, then it cannot be the

---

1. Knowledge of particular facts *can* be perceptually based on such a limited experiential intake, but only if the subject has a *theory* to augment their reach. But that point cannot be used to defend the idea of criteria, which are supposed to be analytic and contrasted with symptoms. This does, however, mean that McDowell's attack on criteria does not apply to those who defend a "theory theory" approach to knowledge of other minds. The theory theory approach compares knowledge of other minds with knowledge of subatomic particles on the basis of tracks in a cloud chamber (Fodor & Chihara 1965). Such knowledge depends on a theory that explains the tracks by postulating particles as their underlying causes. So knowledge of minds is supposed to depend on a theoretically mediated inference from behaviour. Although McDowell does not consider this view explicitly, it can be criticized on the same grounds as Dummett's advocacy of full-bloodedness in the theory of meaning (see Chapter 3).

case that – "for all one knows" – things may be otherwise. That possibility is ruled out precisely because one *knows* what is the case. But if criteria fall short of the fact that they are supposed to enable one to know, then (in the absence of a further *theory* of, for example, other minds) it seems that they cannot themselves rule out the possibility that the fact does not obtain. So if our everyday concept of knowledge *does* rule this out then one cannot reach such knowledge merely through perception of the satisfaction of criteria. A possible alternative view in which the perceived criteria is supposed merely to be enough to satisfy linguistic *conventions* for the *ascription* of knowledge (explaining "legitimize 'criterially' a claim to know" in the above quote) would also not address this objection.

To reinforce this point, McDowell considers the following hypothetical example. Imagine that there are two subjects who both experience the satisfaction of the criteria, so understood, for an underlying fact – say, someone else being in a particular kind of mental state – but only in one case does that fact *obtain*, that is, the other person really is in that state. (In fact, McDowell suggests that in both cases the criteria are undefeated. It would be better to say that in one case the criteria are defeated, unknown to the subject.) Thus, supposedly, in one case the subject knows that the fact holds while in the other case the subject does not (he or she merely mistakenly thinks it is the case). But, McDowell objects, if experience is the only ground for knowledge in play (there are no theories) and if the experience is the same in both cases (experience of the satisfaction of the criteria) then how can one subject be said to know and the other not, rather than neither be said to know?

> How can a difference in respect of something conceived as cognitively inaccessible to both subjects, so far as the relevant mode of cognition goes, make it the case that one of them knows how things are in that inaccessible region while the other does not – rather than leaving them both, strictly speaking, ignorant on the matter? (*Ibid.*: 374)

What is the alternative to this interpretation of criteria?

II McDowell's account of criteria

I shall now outline McDowell's suggestion and the general epistemological moral he draws. The key idea is this. Rather than assuming that, in the case of pretence, the criteria for mental states are satisfied but are also defeated – by the fact that it is a case of pretence – one can instead understand this as a case of the criteria only *appearing* to be satisfied. This is a rejection of the idea that criteria are *defeasible types* of situation. Instead, McDowell presses the idea that, when criteria are satisfied, one's experience *does not fall short of the facts*. So there cannot be cases where the criteria are satisfied without the fact for which they give criterial support also holding.

McDowell supports this interpretative possibility by considering a passage in which Wittgenstein discusses criteria in a non-mental context.

> The fluctuation in grammar between criteria and symptoms makes it look as if there were nothing at all but symptoms. We say, for example: "Experience teaches that there is rain when the barometer falls, but it also teaches that there is rain when we have certain sensations of wet and cold, or such-and-such visual impressions." In defence of this one says that these sense-impressions can deceive us. But here one fails to reflect that the fact that the false appearance is precisely one of rain is founded on a definition.
>
> (Wittgenstein 1953: §354)

Wittgenstein here rejects the temptation to say that both the fall of a barometer and also sensations of wet and cold (or visual impressions) are mere *symptoms* of rain. Instead, and by contrast with the barometer fall, the connection between the sensations (or the visual impressions) and rain is definitional or criterial. They are used in an explanation of what "rain" means. This thought can, however, be interpreted in two ways. McDowell writes:

> Commentators often take this to imply that when our senses deceive us, criteria for rain are satisfied, although no rain is falling. But what the passage says is surely just this: for things, say, to look a certain way to us is, as a matter of "definition" (or "convention" ...), for it to look to us as though it is raining; it would be a mistake to suppose that the "sense-impressions" yield the judgement that it is raining merely symptomatically – that arriving at the judgement is mediated by an empirical theory. That is quite compatible with this thought ... when our "sense-impressions" deceive us, the fact is not that criteria for rain are satisfied but that they *appear* to be satisfied.   (1998a: 381)

Similarly, in the case of criteria for mental states, pretence can make it *seem* that the criteria for pain, for example, are satisfied when, in fact, they are not. (As will become clearer, pretence serves the same role in the problem of other minds as illusion serves in motivating scepticism about the external world in general.)

Two intuitive objections to McDowell's account

There is a pair of related objections to this approach that McDowell considers at some length. It is worth considering what he says in some detail because the objections also apply more broadly to the generalization of the basic approach to epistemology. It is also related to the "highest common factor" account of experience discussed in Chapter 4.

(i) There must be something in common between cases in which the criteria for a claim are satisfied and cases in which they only appear to be satisfied for there to be the possibility of confusing one with the other.

(ii) If phenomena like criteria are to be of any use in *guiding* judgements, then it must be possible to establish whether they hold without having to establish that the facts, for which they are criteria, hold. Only if this is the case can criteria serve as a *route* to knowledge of the world.

Now, (i) is the objection to a disjunctive account of experience, which I discussed in Chapter 4. Part of McDowell's response to it is to concede that things can *seem* the same to a subject while refusing to *reify* a common element that explains that same-seeming:

> [W]hat is given to experience in the two sorts of case ... [is] the same *in so far as* it is an appearance that things are thus and so; that leaves it open that whereas in one kind of case what is given to experience is a mere appearance, in the other it is the fact itself made manifest.   (McDowell 1998a: 389)

In other words, the phenomenology does not establish evidence for or against the disjunctive, as opposed to the highest common factor, account.

It is worth mentioning here two further arguments deployed by McDowell in "Criteria, Defeasibility and Knowledge" against a highest common factor conception of experience. First, McDowell argues that the passage from Wittgenstein quoted above suggests that the appearance that it is raining allows knowledge that it is raining simply through a shared content. Criteria do not license claims about the world (including mental states) through *inferences*. Instead, the content of appearances *just is* the content of the knowledge acquired. This idea is developed in *Mind and World*, where McDowell argues that experience is always already conceptualized and thus its content can simply be taken over into active judgements (which are much less contentiously thought to be already conceptualized), providing that there is no reason to believe that experience is misleading in a particular case.

If this is a plausible reading of what Wittgenstein has to say, then it raises a further problem for an interpretation based on the highest common factor account. Roughly, that interpretation suffers the same defect as a reified conception of "inner" mental states, described in Chapter 4. The challenge is to explain *how* it is that the content of an appearance can *ever* point beyond itself to a world beyond if it is understood as stopping short of the fact.

This point can be developed to block a second consideration, which makes a highest common factor account, together with a model of inference, attractive. This is the scientifically motivated thought that perception is mediated by what occurs at the retina, and that information received at that surface is common between true and false experiences. Such information has then to be further processed and the processing constitutes a form of implicit hypothesis. This picture motivates the mention of *guidance* by experience (itself conceived on the highest common factor view) mentioned in (ii).

If the idea of information being received at the retina is to shed light on how knowledge is possible, some constraints have to be placed on the account given. Whatever the implicit theory is that licenses inferences from information received at the retina to conclusions about the outer world, it can only use concepts available without begging any questions about the nature of that outer world. This condition cannot be met. That this is so is most obvious in the case of explaining how the concept of *other minds* can be constructed from non-question-begging concepts applicable to what is presented to the retina. McDowell plausibly suggests that this objection also applies generally to knowledge of the external world.

I shall now turn to the more epistemological objection raised above, (ii): that criteria have to serve as *routes to judgement* and thus judgements about them must be more firmly grounded than judgements about the further states for which they are criteria. In the context of knowledge of other minds, there is a clear response to this objection too. (The response in the case of knowledge of the world will become clearer in Section III.)

The objection can be filled out in the context of other minds with a further specification of what is supposed by an objector to McDowell to be the common factor between (as McDowell would put it) cases where criteria are satisfied and cases where they merely seem to be (or cases where they are satisfied and undefeated and cases where they are satisfied but defeated, as his opponents would put it). In both cases the common factor presupposed by the objection is *neutrally described bodily behaviour or movement*. Because access to, and judgements about, such behaviour is taken to be unproblematic while access to other people's *mental* states is taken to be problematic, a route is needed – through a specification of criteria – from one to the other. Thus it seems plausible to insist that judgements about behaviour can be "assured" independently of the further claims about minds that they license.

McDowell's response to this is to press a Wittgensteinian or Strawsonian emphasis on the fundamental role of the concept of a human being (or a "person" in Strawson's vocabulary) in our thinking (Strawson 1959). The main purpose of this is to bring out the expressive nature of human speech and action by contrast with the "alienated" conception of our relation to others that underpins Cartesianism. McDowell denies that experience of other people is limited to their bare behaviour, with mentality hidden behind it. This is the assumption that initiates scepticism about other minds. McDowell's rejection of this assumption picks up a claim from elsewhere in his discussion of Wittgenstein that, to a suitably educated subject, more can be directly perceived in speech behaviour than mere sound (cf. McDowell 1998a: 332). In the context of this more epistemological discussion, he puts the point as follows: "The idea of a fact being disclosed to experience is purely negative; it rejects the thesis that what is accessible to experience falls short of the fact in the sense . . . of being consistent with there being no such fact" (*Ibid*.: 387). This underlying notion can also be applied even in cases where the fact or state concerned is not literally within the experience of a subject. It can be applied:

> in at least some cases of knowledge that someone else is in an "inner" state, on the basis of experience of what he says and does. Here we might think of what is directly available to experience in some such terms as "his giving expression to his being in that 'inner' state"; this is something that, while not itself actually being the "inner" state of affairs in question, nevertheless does not fall short of it in the sense I explained. (*Ibid*.: 387)

Although one person's inner states do not themselves fall within the experience of another person, the fact that they express them does. This idea of expression is *not* one that is consistent with the *absence* of the inner state. So McDowell replaces an account in which all that is visible to an observer is another person's intrinsically brute or meaningless behaviour, standing in need of further interpretation and hypothesis, with one in which that behaviour is charged with expression. This is a repetition of his rejection of psychologism and behaviourism in both the discussion of Wittgenstein on rules and Davidson on truth theories (see Chapters 1 and 3).

By denying that our "access" to the minds of others must proceed through a neutrally described behavioural intermediary (their behaviour), McDowell can offer a much less technically charged account of criteria, which he summarizes thus:

> I think we should understand criteria to be, in the first instance, ways of telling how things are, of the sort specified by "On the basis of what he says and does" or "By how things look"; and we should take it that knowledge that a criterion for a claim is actually satisfied – if we allow ourselves to speak in those terms as well – would be an exercise of the very capacity we speak of when we say that one can tell, on the basis of such-and-such criteria, whether things are as the claim would represent them as being.
>
> (*Ibid*.: 385)

Thus, to summarize, the answer to the epistemological objection raised above, objection (ii), is this. The criteria for other minds do indeed *guide* judgements because what people say and do is visible and audible, and also expressive of minds. So when all goes well, the appearance that the criteria are satisfied means that the criteria really are being satisfied and these criteria (what is said and done) express mental states.

This response may prompt a further objection. How, in general, is one to ensure that the appearance that the criteria are satisfied really means that the criteria are being satisfied? Consider again the two subjects described above. As McDowell describes it, one subject has as an experience a mere appearance, while the other experiences a worldly fact. For this reason, one subject does not have knowledge while the other does. But, since *as far as the subject is aware* having one experience is qualitatively indistinguishable from having the other, how can there be a difference in "what is given to experience"?

This worry is merely exacerbated by a further comment made as a continuation of the last quotation. McDowell goes on to say:

> This flouts an idea we are prone to find natural, that a basis for a judgement must be something on which we have firmer cognitive purchase than we do on the judgement itself; but although the idea can seem natural, it is an illusion to suppose it is compulsory.
>
> (*Ibid.*: 385)

I shall consider this in more detail in Section III in the context of McDowell's general externalist approach to epistemology developed in "Knowledge and the Internal" (1995a). But it is worth noting that the account of experience already given suggests one further response to the worry. In "Criteria, Defeasibility and Knowledge" (1981), McDowell suggests that the worry is based on a powerful intuition that:

> one's epistemic standing on some question cannot intelligibily be constituted, even in part, by matters blankly external to how it is with one subjectively. For how could such matters be other than beyond one's ken? And how could matters beyond one's ken make any difference to one's epistemic standing?
>
> (McDowell 1998a: 390)

McDowell does not contest this assumption but does deny one with which it can be confused:

> epistemic entitlement ought to be something one could display for oneself, as it were from within; the idea being that that would require a non-question-begging demonstration from a neutrally available starting-point, such as would be constituted by the highest common factor. (*Ibid.*: 390)

Given this idea of the nature of epistemic entitlement – that it can be arrived at without the world doing the subject a favour – and its accompanying highest common factor conception of experience, then worldly facts would be *blankly external* to a subject. They would *never* lie within a subject's range of knowledge even when things went well. But that is the picture that McDowell rejects. On his account, the facts are *not* outside experience. Experience can be openness to the world and can thus be experience of the facts.

On a first reading, this response seems simply to go too quickly. It turns on a metaphysical picture in which experience is not of its nature cut off from external facts. It is only cut off in the case of misleading, non-veridical experience that is experience of a mere appearance rather than a fact. But the original objection that it answers appears to presuppose no particular metaphysical view of experience. The objection seems instead to be based merely on the thought that there cannot be a difference between two experiences – one veridical and one not – that does not make a difference to how things seem to the subject. Isn't that simply part of what we mean by experience?

Now, as I have already remarked above, as a phenomenological objection to the disjunctive account, this cuts no ice. McDowell does not deny that mere appearances can *seem* to a subject like experience of the facts. What he does deny is an explanation of such seeming – an explanation of the nature of experience – that postulates a common *ingredient*. But that still leaves a more epistemological objection. What do we want a concept of experience for if not to act as guidance to a subject? Surely if a subject cannot tell the difference between veridical and illusory experience then all they can go on is something common to both?

I think that the best way to understand McDowell's response to this sceptical worry is to place it in the context of a conflict between different perspectives on a knowing subject, which can be labelled "internal" and "external". In Section III, I shall explore this difference. In Section IV, I shall return to assess the extent to which McDowell's position is immune to scepticism.

III Knowledge and the internal

In this section, I shall describe McDowell's more general approach to knowledge about the "external" world. The main idea repeats his criticism of the conventional view of criteria. If perceptual knowledge is possible, then experience must not stop short of the facts. But if *reason* is involved in knowledge in general then it must also be understood as world-involving, even though an implication of that is that having good reasons requires a "favour" from the world. Having good standing in the space of reasons – being justified – is not independent of worldly states of affairs.

A picture of knowledge based on the argument from illusion

In "Knowledge and the Internal" (1995a), McDowell addresses the general significance to epistemology of the argument from illusion and similar arguments. He suggests that it is a widespread mistake to base our ideas of knowledge on an assumption both partly motivated by, but also motivating, that argument. The result is a mistaken conception of the space of reasons as "internal" – thought of in a way I shall explain – which McDowell rejects. He writes:

> Consider the Argument from Illusion. Seeing, or perhaps having seen, that things are thus and so would be an epistemically satisfactory standing in the space of reasons. But when I see that things are thus and so, I take it that things are thus and so on the basis of having it look to me as if things are thus and so. And it can look to me as if things are thus and so when they are not; appearances do not give me the resources to ensure that I take things to be thus and so, on the basis of appearances, only when things are indeed thus and so. If things are indeed thus and so when they seem to be, the world is doing me a favour. So if I want to restrict myself to standings in the space of reasons whose flawlessness I can ensure without external help, I must go no further than taking it *looks* to me as if things are thus and so.
>
> (McDowell 1998a: 396)

The suggestion here is that concentration on the argument from illusion produces a mistaken assumption that we "ought to be able to achieve flawless standings in the space of reasons by our own unaided resources, without needing the world to do us any favours" (*ibid*.: 395–6). This is the sense of independence from an external world and thus of "internalism" that I mentioned above.

In the face of the kind of sceptical doubt that this argument raises, a natural response is to retreat to the idea that one can base judgements on strategies that do not require a favour from the world. Only thus will a sceptical threat be headed off. But there is not, in fact, a promising path back from this internal position to recovering knowledge of the external world. Descartes's recovery of knowledge of the world via grasp of the nature of God is less convincing to a modern eye than his earlier sceptical doubt.

Note that in the passage quoted above McDowell points out that seeing that things are thus and so is a fully satisfactory epistemological position. It is only correct to say of someone that they have seen that things are thus and so if they really are thus and so. From a different person's perspective, things are straightforward. But from one's own perspective, the argument from illusion appears to cast doubt on one's ability to move from the view that things *look* thus and so to the conclusion that they *are*. This parallels the question of how one moves from knowledge of another person's behaviour to knowledge of their mind.

The problem discussed in "Knowledge and the Internal" is more general than the problem of other minds discussed in Section II. In the case of other minds, McDowell rejects the idea that criteria fall short of, rather than embrace, those minds. The criteria are supposed to fall short because they are taken to concern mere bodily behaviour, described in neutral, non-mind-presupposing terms. It is as though behaviour is a kind of veil that prevents one directly seeing other minds and permits at best risky inferences about them. On this mistaken view, a subject can ensure that the criteria for other minds are satisfied but only, according to McDowell, at the risk of making the fact that there really are other minds in play an accidental extra.

In the more general case of responding to the argument from illusion, McDowell offers a similar criticism but this time applying to empirical reasons rather than strictly criteria. Whereas criteria for other minds are taken to concern the veil of behaviour that stands between one subject and other minds, in this more general case empirical reasons are taken to concern a subject's experience, but, like behaviour, are thought of as a kind of veil intervening between the subject and the outside world. On this mistaken approach, possession of good reasons can be ensured by a putatively knowing subject but only at the cost of severing the connection between those reasons and the world.

In total, McDowell outlines five responses to the problem raised by the argument from illusion.

- Scepticism. This is the normal conclusion of the argument from illusion. The resources of reason, thought of as not requiring that the world does one a favour, are insufficient to guarantee knowledge.
- An implausible optimism that there are risk-free methods of basing beliefs about the world on mere appearances.
- A hybrid picture that combines an interiorized conception of justification with an additional external condition: truth.
- Full-blown externalist reliabilism, which rejects McDowell's Sellarsian assumption that knowledge has to do with reasons.
- McDowell's proposal that a standing in the space of reasons is not, after all, independent of worldly favours.

For the moment I shall not consider the first two positions. Mc-Dowell also rejects the fourth – full-blown reliabilism – with the comment that "it is at most a matter of superficial idiom that we do not attribute knowledge to properly functioning thermometers" (McDowell 1998a: 401). He does not aim to dissuade philosophers who take that view, but instead directs his attention to those who share the intuition that knowledge is connected to the possession of reasons but then adopt the third, hybrid, position above.

The hybrid position fits naturally with a traditional analysis of knowledge as justified true belief. Justification is taken to be an "internal" condition and a subject can ensure that it is met. It is a matter of ensuring the pedigree of a belief and thus, hopefully, its reliability or likeliness of truth. But it is merely a necessary, and not a sufficient, condition for knowledge, for which a further, external, condition has also to be met. That further condition is truth.

There are two key difficulties with this position. First, placing truth and reason on different sides of the divide between the internal and external rules out the role that reason is surely supposed to play: ensuring the reliability of methods of arriving at beliefs (McDowell 1998a: 403). The judgement that a method really is reliable, and does not just appear to be so, is one whose correctness depends on a favour from the world. Thus it cannot be established by reason if that is restricted to areas where no such favours are required.[2]

Secondly, the division undermines a central motivation for a concept of knowledge: that knowledge is *not merely accidentally true* belief. On the hybrid conception, the justificatory condition can be met whether or not a belief turns out to be true. Its truth depends on a favour from the world, which in turn seems a mere accidental addition to possession of an internally constituted justification. McDowell makes this point by asking "how can the unconnected obtaining of the fact have any intelligible bearing on an epistemic position that the person's standing in the space of reasons is supposed to help constitute?" (*ibid.*: 403). This picks up the same point made against the conventional view of criteria as defeasible. If so, the obtaining of the fact that is criterially supported seems an accidental extra that cannot contribute to a knower's epistemic standing.

So much, then, for the negative arguments. They suggest that a

2. Note that the hybrid position contrasts with conventional externalist reliabilist epistemology. In the latter case, the reliability of a method of arriving at beliefs is not assessed by a putative knower; it is simply a fact about the method, a worldly fact. Reliability is, as it were, assessed from a perspective external to the knower.

hybrid position – combining an internal conception of reasons with a further external constraint in the form of truth – is unstable. What does that leave? And what can be said in the face of scepticism?

McDowell's positive account

The key positive idea that McDowell defends is that the resources that reason can bring to bear on knowledge claims do not need to be immune to the effects of luck. He rejects the view that "reason must be credited with a province within which it has absolute control over the acceptability of positions achievable by its exercise, without laying itself open to risk from an unkind world" (McDowell 1998a: 442). In other words, on the favoured account, luck enters at a different stage from that in the hybrid picture. Even to enjoy a particular epistemological status – a "standing in the space of reasons" – requires luck. But no further luck is required to transform that degree of justification or warrant into knowledge. This proposal is made more natural, and less revisionary, by three further points of emphasis:

- a comparison with practical reason;
- an anti-intellectual view of knowledge; and
- an anti-reductionist view of the kind of philosophical insight needed in epistemology.

First, McDowell's proposal about reason and knowledge can be compared with a view of practical reasoning, which already seems more natural:

> The concept of what one does, understood as applying to one's interventions in the objective world, cannot mark out a sphere within which one has total control, immune to luck. It is only if we recoil from this into a fantasy of a sphere within which one's control is total that it can seem to follow that what one genuinely achieves is less than one's interventions in the objective world.
>
> (*Ibid.*: 406 n.16)

Although our actions are the result of an interplay between, on the one hand, our beliefs and desires (to adopt, for simplicity, a familiar philosophical slogan) and, on the other, contingent features of the world that shape our abilities for action, this is not taken generally to undermine our responsibility for our actions. (Of course, in particular cases, it can.)

Secondly, McDowell combines his view that having an epistemological standing depends at least in part on a relation to the world
with an anti-intellectualist view of knowledge. This is developed,
largely, in "Knowledge by Hearsay" (1993). We can understand this
anti-intellectualist view by considering McDowell's attitude to a contrast between what he terms "mediated" and "unmediated epistemic
standings".

A mediated epistemic standing is one that depends on rational
relations to other positions. In other words, it is justified by other
positions such as grounded beliefs. An unmediated standing, by contrast, would be one that was foundational, or an "absolute starting
point" (McDowell 1998a: 430). McDowell argues that unmediated
standings are the stuff of epistemological foundationalism and an
instance of the myth of the given (*ibid.*: 431 n.26, 27). Following Sellars, he rejects any such approach to epistemology: a key subject of
Mind and World. In fact, McDowell's discussion of mediated standings
owes much to Sellars's discussion in Section VIII of *Empiricism and
the Philosophy of Mind*, called "Does Empirical Knowledge have a
Foundation?" (Sellars 1997: 68–79).[3] Both Sellars and McDowell take
perception to involve a mediated state. This leads to the question: what
is the relation between one mediated epistemic state and another?

On one approach, which McDowell rejects, a mediated standing in
the space of reasons is one for which an *argument* can be given, by the
knower, from premises that do not beg any epistemic questions about
the status of the position in question. The argument might thus move
from premises about how things look to a conclusion to the effect that
the subject can see that things are thus and so. Such arguments
articulate the kind of rational relations that make up the space of
reasons in general.

McDowell does not deny that there are *some* arguments relevant
to one's epistemological status. If a subject sees (or has seen) that
something is the case, then it must be the case. This follows because
the locution "sees that" is "factive" (McDowell 1998a: 433). What follows the "that" must be a fact. Furthermore, to be a subject capable of
knowledge, the subject must be sensitive to the rational relations
that make up the space of reasons. This is a necessary background
condition. But McDowell does reject the idea that the epistemic
position of seeing that something is the case can be *reduced to* or *con-*

---

3. McDowell's debt to this work and his own criticism of the myth of the given are
   described more fully in Chapter 6.

structed out of something more basic via an argument that the subject of the position could provide:

> What I am proposing is a different conception of what it is for a standing in the space of reasons to be mediated. A standing in the space of reasons can be mediated by the rational force of surrounding considerations, in that the concept of that standing cannot be applied to a subject who is not responsive to that rational force. But that is not to say that the epistemic satisfactoriness of the standing *consists in* that rational force.
>
> (*Ibid.*: 430, original emphasis)

The main argument for this denial picks up a theme from "Knowledge and the Internal" described above: no argument so restricted has a hope of guaranteeing the truth of its conclusion. But truth is indeed required if the subject sees, or has seen, that something is the case. In the context of "Knowledge by Hearsay", an important example is the idea of knowledge by testimony. It is particularly clear in this sort of case that a hearer would not in general be in a position to rule out sources of error in what the speaker says or other factors that would imply that the speaker does not *know* what he or she affirms. Thus, in general, a hearer cannot provide an argument to its truth from what he or she hears said.

Pre-philosophically, however, it seems clear that testimony can indeed provide knowledge: "if a knowledgeable speaker gives intelligible expression to his knowledge, it may become available at second hand to those who understand what he says" (*ibid.*: 417). McDowell's response is to suggest that the attempt to give a reductionist account of epistemic good standing is mistaken. Instead he takes as a primitive the idea – in the case of testimony – that a subject can *hear* at second-hand *how things are*.

> The idea is, then, that one's epistemic standing with respect to what one comes to know by testimony consists in one's, say, having heard from one's informant that that is how things are; not in the compellingness of an argument to the conclusion that that is how things are from the content of a lesser informational state.
>
> (*Ibid.*: 436)

So – and this is the third point flagged above – the tenor of the analysis runs in the opposite direction to what is normal. Rather than attempting to decompose the concept of knowledge into constituent elements that form its epistemological base or foundation,

McDowell suggests that *it* is the most basic concept in play. Justification is thus explicated from the starting-point of knowledge taken as a basic standing in the space of reasons.

The previous quotation continues:

> Not that the subject does not enjoy a lesser informational state. It cannot be true that he heard from so-and-so that things are thus and so unless it is true that he heard so-and-so say that things are that way – a truth that leaves it entirely open whether things are that way. *(Ibid.: 436–7)*

But McDowell suggests that the very idea of having heard that things are thus and so should not be analysed using this lesser state as a starting-point. Similarly, seeing that things are thus and so implies that it seems or appears to the subject that things are thus and so, "a truth that leaves it entirely open whether things are that way". And similarly that should not be the starting-point of an analysis of "seeing that …".

This is reminiscent of the discussion of the relation between behaviour and mental states in the context of the rival accounts of criteria described above. In that context, McDowell suggested that the mistaken view of criteria was driven by a view that access to other people's behaviour was more "assured" than access to their minds. This motivated a felt need for a route *from* a mentally neutral description of behaviour *to* a non-neutral description of other minds. But that approach could be rejected through the realization that the idea of a neutral – mind-free – description of behaviour was a fiction. Once one has been initiated into the relevant concepts one can recognize immediately that the appropriate mentally charged description of expressive behaviour applies. There is no neutral starting-point for an *inference* to a description of other minds.

This difference in philosophical aim lies behind much of the criticism of Blackburn's work in "Knowledge and the Internal". Blackburn draws a contrast between two sorts of epistemic position: those that are *guaranteeing*, defined as making the beliefs formed in the light of them of necessity true; and merely *indicative* states. He goes on to ask whether indicative states, "provided the external circumstances are right", can sustain knowledge (Blackburn 1993: 43). This way of setting up the question looks very like the hybrid framework McDowell has sketched out. Blackburn is working with a conception of epistemic states for which luck plays no part. He goes on to argue that, providing limitations are placed on the range of sceptical alternatives, there are (comparatively) risk-free policies for forming beliefs about the external world on the basis of such informational states.

McDowell rejects this approach on the grounds that it is a matter of mere common sense that the epistemic states Blackburn needs to reconstruct are factive and thus need to guarantee the truth of their contents. This point seems trivial and Blackburn's error inexplicable. But the underlying difference between the two philosophers is *metaphilosophical*. Blackburn is working within the tradition that asks what has to be added to the conditions that

   p is true

and   *x* believes *p*

for *x* to know that *p*. One of the more recent approaches to that question is to specify that the method of acquiring the belief has a particular degree of reliability. This opens up the question: just how reliable? There is then a range of different options with different problems. One might insist that the method *could never* deliver false beliefs. But that seems implausibly strong. Or one might specify a probability of delivering true beliefs of unity but only in the *actual* world; but unless there is also counterfactual reliability, that threatens to convert the justification into a truth-condition and make accidental knowledge possible. Or one might more modestly specify that it preclude only locally relevant alternatives, but then the question is how those are to be specified (for discussion see Gascoigne (2002: 165–97)). Blackburn's discussion of guaranteeing and indicative states is within the broad tradition of offering an analysis of knowledge in simpler terms (whether or not in reliabilist terms). He takes it for granted that knowledge can be analysed.

McDowell, by contrast, rejects the very idea of asking what has to be added to the two conditions for knowledge. He denies that it is a good philosophical question. Instead, he simply takes for granted the idea of epistemic positions that amount to knowledge, and the attempts to dislodge misleading arguments that make everyday cases of knowledge – such as knowledge by hearsay – impossible. This explains the sense in which Blackburn and McDowell do not appear to be talking about the same thing. They are not.[4]

That is not to say that McDowell says nothing further about the underpinnings of epistemic good standing. A major theme of *Mind*

---

4. For a similar starting-point that takes knowledge as a primitive but then develops a systematic account see Williamson (2000).

and World is the connection between our knowledge or beliefs about the world and *experience*. Indeed, according to Rorty:

> McDowell is just the philosopher you want if you fear losing your grip on the notion of "perceptual experience". He does a splendid job of reconciling common turns of speech such as "a glimpse of the world" and "openness to the world" and "answerability to the world" ...   (Rorty 1998: 150)

Rorty goes on to say that "But, of course, I do not *want* such a reconciliation or such a rehabilitation" (*ibid.*: 150). In Chapter 6, I shall discuss how successful McDowell is in this reconciliation of the very idea of openness to the world with his neo-Fregean sympathies. But in the rest of this chapter, I want to examine the anti-sceptical properties of McDowell's position. I shall turn first to the extent to which McDowell's position is externalist and world-involving.

One feature of McDowell's approach is that by construing good epistemic standing as fully external in the sense of requiring that the world does one a favour, justification seems to collapse, more or less, into truth. This is apparent in two sorts of comment that McDowell makes. One is to equate navigating the space of reasons with navigating the world. The second kind of comment occurs when McDowell contrasts his views with those of Rorty. While Rorty stresses the importance of justification over truth because he takes it that access to the latter but not the former is problematic, McDowell thinks that truth is accessible. Rorty shares with Davidson a view, founded in Davidson's case on a transcendental argument, that most of our beliefs must be true. But both assume that we cannot know which beliefs are true. Truth is, in that sense, inaccessible. McDowell describes this view, in which a gulf opens up between us and the world, as describing a form of *mundus absconditus* (McDowell 2000d). As a result of this view of truth, Rorty stresses an emphasis on justification rather than truth, in accordance with pragmatist tradition.

In part, Rorty's view stems from a philosophical view with which McDowell is in sympathy. This is the denial that there is any hope of an account of *how* language and the world are connected that presupposes a sideways-on or extra-linguistic perspective. I have already described McDowell's hostility to this view in his accounts of Wittgenstein, moral judgement and theories of meaning (described in Chapters 1–3). For Rorty, this view takes the form of a rejection of a correspondence theory of truth that pairs sentences and "sentence shaped piece[s] of non-linguistic reality" (Rorty 1991: 4). But Rorty goes on to reject any notion of "normative relatedness" to the world, in McDowell's phrase (McDowell 2000d: 114). McDowell writes:

> Hilary Putnam has argued, to put it in Rorty's words, that "notions like 'reference' – semantical notions which relate language to nonlanguage – are internal to our overall view of the world." ... Rorty's picture is on these lines. If we use an expression like "accurate representation" in the innocent internal way, it can function only as a means of paying "empty compliments" to claims that pass muster within our current practice of claim-making. Now "the representationalist" finds a restriction to this sort of assessment unacceptably parochial. Recoiling from that, "the representationalist" tries to make expressions like "true" or "accurate representation" signify a mode of normative relatedness – conformity – to something more independent of us than the world as it figures in our world view. This aspiration is well captured by Thomas Nagel's image of "trying to climb outside of our own minds". The image fits a conception, or supposed conception, of reality that threatens to put it outside our reach, since the norms according to which we conduct our investigations cannot of course be anything but our current norms. Recoiling from the idea that we are restricted to paying "empty compliments" to bits of our world view, "the representationalist" tries to conceive the relation between what we want to see as our world view and its subject matter from sideways on, rather than from the vantage point of the world view – now only problematically so called – itself.   (*Ibid.*: 114–15)

Rorty rejects the view that the "representationalist" tries to articulate by rejecting the very idea of conformity to a world and stressing instead the role of warranted assertibility.

Recoiling from Rorty's counterintuitive restrictions, McDowell emphasizes the consequence of his own account of experience as openness to the world. This undercuts Rorty's and Davidson's pessimism about the accessibility of truth. But what is more important in the context of this chapter is that McDowell also suggests that *justification* should also be interpreted in terms of conformity to the world. He writes, for example:

> An utterance of "Cold fusion has not been achieved, so far, in the laboratory" has (if I am right about the physics) a warrant, a justifiedness, that consists not in one's being able to get away with it among certain conversational partners, but in – now I disquote,

and implicitly make a claim – cold fusion's not having been achieved, so far, in the laboratory. Here the terms "warranted", "rationally acceptable", etc., have collected an obvious answer, not to the question "to whom?", but to the question "in the light of what?", and the question "to whom?" need not be in the offing at all. (*Ibid*.: 117)

This makes explicit an issue that may have been nagging for some time: McDowell's account of knowledge does not separate, as much as is normal, truth from justification.

A conventional view of the role of the justification condition of a justified true-belief account of knowledge is that it helps to separate those beliefs that are likely to be true from those that are not, on the assumption that one cannot know which of one's beliefs are true. (Of course, of any belief one could not both hold it and not believe it true when questioned.) But given McDowell's argument that an "internal" conception of justification cannot serve that purpose, then justification has to be thought of as fulfilling a different role. In fact, one consequence of the starting-point of McDowell's epistemological account is to downplay the role of justification. In the quotation above, the role of warrant or justification looks more like that of truth. The reason for this is that justification or warrant is not described as an attempt at a reconstructive account of knowledge from non-question-begging elements. Instead, once the temptation of thinking about knowledge from the starting-point of the argument from illusion has been avoided, the need to regain truth by ensuring justification (or more radically to replace truth with justification) falls away.

I can now return to the question raised briefly earlier: to what extent is McDowell's position immune from scepticism?

IV Scepticism

In a recent paper, Simon Glendinning and Max De Gaynesford have criticized McDowell's account on the basis both that it does not really answer the sceptic and that there is a better response available. They make two preliminary points about how McDowell's account potentially opens up a gap between the subject and the world.

First, while McDowell rejects a view of experience as comprising subjective episodes, cut off from the world:

there is nothing in McDowell's argument which suggests he denies a subjective *character* to experience: there is he maintains, "something it is like" to enjoy experiential access to the world (see, eg, 1986: 149). Thus McDowell claims that "nothing could be recognizable as a characterization of this domain of subjectivity if it did not accord a special status to the perspective of the subject" (*ibid*: 160). And he insists that the characterization of inner facts in terms of first person seemings is "the most conspicuous phenomenological fact there is" (*ibid*: 152). It remains to be seen whether the leading thought of the openness view can be sustained against the sceptic while commitment to this conception of the subjective character of experience is maintained.

(Glendinning & De Gaynesford 1998: 23)

Secondly, they point out that, at times, McDowell describes experiences as *effects* using the idiom of a *causal* theory of experience.

His commitment to the idea that a subject's experience of a fact presupposes that it is an effect of or produced by that fact is evident in the following passage: "Suppose someone is presented with an experience that it is raining. It seems unproblematic that if his experience is in a suitable way the upshot of the fact that it is raining, then the fact itself can make it the case that he knows it is raining" [1982: 474] ... We think that there is a deep tension in this position. For on McDowell's terms any putative fact that is supposed to *give rise* to an experience can only be conceived as blankly external to subjectivity.   (*Ibid*.: 26)

They go on to characterize this view of experiences as *upshots* or *effects* of facts as itself resulting from the assumption, described above, that enjoying an experience has a distinctively first person character. With these points in place they advance two further claims, their third and fourth as I summarize them.

Thirdly, McDowell does *not* answer the sceptic. The problem they raise is that on his disjunctive account an experience is *either* an instance of openness to the facts *or* a mere appearance. But a sceptic can happily accept this but press the point that the subject has no decisive reason for telling which is the case *for any particular experience*. Starting from the basis of "any given subject's perceptual standing" no answer can be given (*ibid*.: 29).

For, on the basis of any given subject's perceptual standing (that is, on the basis of "what is given" to its experience) there is no way for it to provide any adequate grounds for "insisting" that either option is true. (*Ibid.*: 29)

McDowell concedes to the tradition that he "can allow what is given to experience in the two sorts of case (deceptive and non-deceptive) to be the same *in so far* as it is an appearance that things are thus and so" (1982: 475). Our view is that the italics do not prevent his account from conceding *too much*. For, from this point of departure, it seems impossible to avoid the threat of scepticism. (*Ibid.*: 30)

The root of their objection is this. In veridical and non-veridical cases, respectively, the questions "What did the subject see?" and "What did the subject fancy they saw?" can receive the same answer. But this fact can be explained in two different ways. One can explain it by saying that in the non-veridical case there was an *illusion* of a certain perceptual content. Or one can say that there is a common element given to experience: identical appearances, although only one of which is a *mere* appearance. Glendinning and De Gaynesford argue that McDowell's emphasis on a subjective character to experience commits him to the latter, and that this leads to scepticism.

Fourthly, they argue that there is an alternative that is (at least more) immune to scepticism:

It might be thought that no theory of perception can avoid extending what is constant to cover what is "given to experience" because there is no way of accounting for the basis of perceptual knowledge except in terms of a subject's first person perceptual standing. In our view, however, there is a genuine alternative; namely, an account which takes its point of departure not from a subject's personal experience but from a living human being's practical activity: the distinctive ways in which it relates itself actively in an environment. (*Ibid.*: 30–31)

This alternative, which owes something to the early Heidegger, stresses the practical over the experiential foundations of openness to the world. The aim is that, by taking a different point of departure, the sceptic's question – Is this veridical experience or mere appearance? – cannot take hold. Furthermore, because it connects an account of how objects in the environment are taken ("seen as") with "practices of verification", cases in which, say, tufts of grass are taken to be (or seen as) rabbits "must be exceptional" (*ibid.*: 31).

Because the favoured account is merely hinted at rather than developed, it is hard to know whether it really can serve as a better alternative to take to avoid scepticism. But it is striking how the phrase the "distinctive ways in which it relates actively in an environment" (*ibid.*: 31), used to characterize it, would also capture part of the role of a theory of sense as described in Chapters 3 and 4. Similarly, the suggestion that perception or "seeing as" should be tied into a broader behavioural pattern is a recapitulation of McDowell's description of the interpretational constraints on a theory of sense.

Thus, in this context, the key challenge to the account sketched out is to be able to capture the "contours of a subjectivity" (*ibid.*: 28, quoting McDowell 1998a: 271) exemplified in patterns of speech and behaviour (which are perhaps combined in practices of verification) without succumbing as easily to scepticism as Glendinning and De Gaynesford suggest McDowell's account does. The suggestion seems to be – although it is not stated – that a transcendental argument based on the practical grounds of content could be deployed for the general truth of beliefs. In the context of the connection forged by McDowell between a neo-Fregean theory of sense and a Davidsonian interpretative truth theory, however, that suggestion is familiar. Davidson argues from premises pertaining to interpretation to the conclusion that in general our beliefs must be true (Davidson 1986a). But even on the assumption that the argument is sound, for any particular belief (or "any given subject's perceptual standing" (*ibid.*: 29)), it still leaves open the question: is it one of the true majority or one of the false minority beliefs? That is the question Glendinning and De Gaynesford say that McDowell's account cannot answer. But why should an account that takes practice rather than experience as the foundation of our openness to the world do any better with this question?

Davidson's argument is relevant here for another reason. In its starkest form it seems to be an argument that beliefs must be largely true even at the risk of distancing an articulation of belief contents from the contours of subjectivity. Put bluntly, if I really were a brain in a, my consolation is that my current beliefs would be true but should be correctly interpreted as being about electrical signals sent by the world-simulating computer rather than being false beliefs about chairs, tables, trees and such like. The problem with this is that it severs the connection between the truth of beliefs and a subject's characteristic perspective on the world. The sceptic can redraw the lines of battle by conceding that a subject's beliefs are largely true but denying that the subject knows what those beliefs are about. A response to scepticism had better, therefore, retain the task of describing the contours of subjectivity.

I think that Glendinning and De Gaynesford's second critical point relies on an unusually uncharitable interpretation of what McDowell says. The main theme of *Mind and World* is an exploration of an account of experience that allows the world to exert a rational control on our thinking. In it, McDowell explicitly rejects causal accounts of experience and adopts what is best characterized as an identity theory of experience and the facts that constitute the world. In Chapter 6, I shall explore this picture and suggest that there are tensions. But the tensions are not the result of adopting an implicit causal theory of perception alongside openness to the world, but result from the need for a Fregean element in describing thought.

One of the arguments for a causal theory of experience is that it can capture the idea that experiences are brought about and partially explained by the world. But this idea can be accommodated by distinguishing between the act or event of experiencing and the content of the experience. In *Mind and World*, McDowell distinguishes between thoughts construed as acts of thinking and thoughts construed as the contents of those acts. Experiences could also be construed in these two different ways. It is the act or events of experiencing that are the effects of interaction with the world. But what is taken in in those experiences is the layout of the world.

This leaves Glendinning and De Gaynesford's first and third points. McDowell certainly does attempt to articulate the contours of subjectivity. Is this starting-point inconsistent with a resistance to scepticism? Note that McDowell himself, in contrast with the interpretation suggested by Glendinning and De Gaynesford, stresses that there is nothing common to both disjuncts in the disjunctive conception of experience. Thus providing that one is not misled, one's experiences take in aspects of the world. This is what is meant by openness to the world. But Glendinning and De Gaynesford are right to state that for any particular experience the sceptic can press the question: is it fact or mere appearance? So if scepticism is already in play, a subject seems to be in no better position than before.

On the other hand, if one of the key motivations for considering a sceptical challenge in the first place is the potential global mismatch between reason and the world, then that has been undercut. By appealing to an external view of epistemic standing, and denying that an internal view makes sense, McDowell's position weaves reasons and the world back together and thus removes a key motivation for scepticism. So if scepticism presupposes a picture of experience or reason that can never reach out to the world, then McDowell's account provides a response before the scepticism can be motivated. This point can be made in the context of "dreaming" scepticism.

In "Singular Thought and the Extent of Inner Space" (1986), McDowell cites Barry Stroud's view that the Cartesian threat of losing the world depends on adherence to a particular principle: "one can acquire worldly knowledge by using one's senses only if one can know, at the time of the supposed acquisition of knowledge, that one is not dreaming" (McDowell 1998a: 238). The problem suggested is that any test that one is not dreaming is subject to the following doubt. Perhaps one is merely dreaming that one has satisfactorily applied the test. But McDowell suggests that this case is not in itself a sufficient explanation of the threat of the loss of the external world because it is not clear what rules out the following natural response. "[O]ne's knowledge that one is not dreaming, in the relevant sort of situation, owes its credentials as knowledge to the fact that one's senses are yielding one knowledge of the environment – something that does not happen when one is dreaming" (*ibid.*: 238).

Only if a sceptical threat of loss of the world is already in play is this response illicit. But scepticism needs an argument if it is to upset our everyday conception of our epistemic predicament. This is why McDowell goes on to suggest the role of a Cartesian account of experience, which is infallibly knowable through and through and thus independent of the world (see Chapter 4). Similarly, the possibility – stressed by Glendinning and De Gaynesford – that when having a particular experience one might be in error rather than directly taking in an aspect of the world is not in itself enough to generate a sceptical doubt. A further argument is needed to make our grip on the world precarious and, in the case of Cartesian doubt, that is just what McDowell undermines.

Michael Williams makes this point about the origins of dreaming scepticism in a conception of experience that runs counter to McDowell's Sellarsian picture. Williams suggests that a key assumption that underpins sceptical doubt is that knowledge of the empirical world can be founded on prior knowledge of experience, independently described:

> In effect, what the argument for [scepticism] ... really shows is
> that there is no way of knowing that we are not dreaming that is

independent of all knowledge of the world: there is no purely experiential test by which to exclude the dream possibility. But this conclusion poses no threat to knowledge of the world unless we have already been given reason to think that such knowledge, by its very nature, always requires grounding in some more primitive stratum of knowledge. The argument for there being no test for determining whether or not we are dreaming turns out to be another way of making the point that knowledge of the world cannot be given a ground in experiential knowledge, which is not a step on the road to scepticism unless it has been established that knowledge of the world stands or falls with the possibility of giving it such a grounding. Once again we have an argument that shows that foundationalist ambitions are likely to be disappointed, but gives no particular reason for entertaining them in the first place.   (Williams 1996: 87)

McDowell's account provides just the context to make rejection of a Cartesian version of foundationalism unattractive and unnatural.

What I have said so far turns on undermining arguments for scepticism that are implicitly based on a Cartesian account of the extent of inner space. But as Williams suggests elsewhere, there is another family of sceptical problems that is worth mentioning briefly here: Agrippan scepticism (Williams 2001: 61). This kind of scepticism is based on the thought that if a justification is offered for a belief then the status of that justification can also always be questioned. Such further justification faces the so-called Agrippan trilemma:

- one can continue to think up fresh justifications for each preceding justification; or
- one can make a dogmatic assumption; or
- one can repeat something already said.

None of these options seem to provide a positive justification for a belief. Again, however, for this to be an independently natural way of generating a sceptical doubt, something has to be added to the trilemma itself: an assumption that a further justification is required.

As is familiar, a standard internal account of knowledge, which requires that one knows that one knows in order to know something, has much greater difficulty with this sort of threat. That requirement ensures that nothing is known until the trilemma is overcome. What might otherwise have been a harmless observation that there is a potentially infinite chain of justifications that can be given for a judgement becomes the impossible requirement that all justifications are given before the judgement is justified.

By contrast, an externalist – whether reliabilist or McDowellian – can argue that the first justification offered may be sufficient for knowledge, even if it is not sufficient to know that one knows. Furthermore, McDowell undermines the contrast between the game of justification on the one hand, and actually getting the world right on the other. Without that contrast, the Agrippan sceptic's further questions seem unnatural and unmotivated. This is why McDowell advocates the right to be indifferent to such doubts.

Chapter 6

Mind and World *and idealism*

In this final chapter, I shall examine McDowell's influential book *Mind and World* (1994), which is based on his John Locke Lectures at Oxford in 1991. I shall first describe some of the main themes of the book and its overall organization before returning to one of the questions that has been implicit in much of the discussion in previous chapters: can McDowell articulate an account of the world or nature that neither is wholly independent of rational subjects nor falls into a form of idealism?

In Section I, I shall set out the central account of experience in *Mind and World*. This starts with a key lesson that McDowell derives from Kant. Experience is always already conceptualized. It lies within the space of reasons. McDowell combines this claim with the idea, discussed in Chapter 5, that experience is a form of openness to the world. The claim that experience has to be thought of as always conceptually structured is defended against an intuitive phenomenological objection. The objection is based on the thought that experience is typically more finely grained than the concepts a subject possesses. But McDowell suggests that experience itself can equip a subject with concepts: demonstrative concepts such as "that colour!" Finally, I outline the transcendental role that experience plays for McDowell's discussion of intentionality in general.

Section II sets out the resistance McDowell predicts there will be to his account of the nature and role of experience. He focuses on the view of nature that arose as a result of the success of natural scientific method. It is this that underpins a narrow view of what is natural and it is this that makes it difficult to realise that experience might be both conceptualized and a *natural* phenomenon, part of the natural world. Drawing on the ideas, discussed in Chapter 2, of a Kantian view of the world and an Aristotelian idea of second nature, McDowell attempts to dismantle the apparent dualism of reason and nature.

In Section III, I shall consider the objection that a combination of a view of experience as openness to the world with a Fregean conception of sense is unstable and leads to idealism. I argue that this objection can be turned aside but only through a careful rethinking of the nature of sense.

I   The role of concepts in experience

The Kantian slogan

The stated overall concern of *Mind and World* is the way that concepts "mediate the relation between minds and world" (McDowell 1994: 3). This is part of McDowell's general concern with the relation between reason and nature. Understanding the role that concepts play in experience and the role that experience plays for intentionality suggests lessons for a proper understanding of nature and second nature.

Mind and World begins by ascribing important insight to a Kantian slogan, but simultaneously warning that it can also prompt a characteristic philosophical dilemma. The slogan is: "Thoughts without content are empty, intuitions without concepts are blind" (Kant 1929: 93, A51, B75). The mention here of content and concepts is in turn related to the dualism between conceptual scheme and content that Davidson describes and rejects in "On the Very Idea of a Conceptual Scheme" (1984: 183–98).

McDowell suggests that the Kantian slogan expresses an important insight into how empirical content is possible by stressing the importance of both concepts and direct experiential intake. But he also warns that accommodating these two aspects has typically led to an "interminable oscillation" between positions that overemphasize each side in turn. It is an oscillation between, on the one hand, coherence theories in which there is no friction between thought and the world and, on the other, the myth of the given, which attempts to ensure such friction but, impossibly, from outside the space of reasons (McDowell 1994: 9). A proper understanding of the Kantian idea should be consistent with Davidson's rejection of the dualism of scheme and content and should unite the role of reason and nature.

Two preliminary points are worth noting. First, as McDowell points out, there is something potentially misleading in the way these familiar ideas are generally transcribed, in that in both the Kantian and Davidsonian context the word "content" has a different sense from recent philosophy of thought. In the latter context, it means representational bearing or meaning.[1] But in both the Kantian phrase and in the dualism of conceptual scheme and content that Davidson rejects, "content" stands for a partial *explanation* of empirical content or meaning and not for that empirical content itself. McDowell suggests that it might be better to talk of the "given" rather than content in both Kant's and Davidson's slogans.

Secondly, McDowell comments elsewhere that *Mind and World* is primarily addressed to a particular philosophical audience: those who are subject to a particular philosophical discomfort as a result of subscribing to particular philosophical intuitions. "Only someone who feels the pull of the thoughts I uncover will be subject to the philosophical discomfort I aim to deal with" (McDowell 1998d: 404). To that extent it does not articulate a freestanding context-independent philosophical theory but rather aims to dissolve a particular felt tension. The difficulties that arise in understanding the relation of thought and the world result only from adopting understandable but misleading assumptions about the rational structure of thought and the way thought needs a worldly input. Elsewhere he says:

> I do not present the Myth of the Given and coherentism as two unsatisfying responses to a problem about thought's bearing on reality – as if philosophers came up with those views in order to deal with a problem that was on the philosophical agenda anyway. Rather, I use the uncomfortable oscillation between these two ways of thinking, in a framework in which they have come to seem the only possibilities, as a way to bring out why there might seem to be a problem about thought's bearing on reality in the first place. (McDowell 2000a: 334)

In broad outline, that tension arises from the following line of thought. Empirical content is portrayed by Kant to be the result of the interplay of the faculties of receptivity and spontaneity, responsible, respectively, for intuitions and concepts. The fact that the faculty that

---

1. Sentences have meaning; thoughts have content; and these can be the same. The further question – touched on in Chapter 4 – of whether thoughts should be identified with their contents, or whether, by contrast, they are the *vehicles* or *bearers* of that content, can be put aside for the moment.

contributes concepts is that of "spontaneity" is suggestive. McDowell suggests that concepts are characterized by rational relations. And, according to Kant, "rational necessitation is not just compatible with freedom but constitutive of it. In a slogan, the space of reasons is the realm of freedom" (McDowell 1994: 5). But emphasis on the freedom associated with conceptual judgements threatens to cut off empirical content from the world so that it degenerates into a "self-contained game". This is the danger of mere coherentism where the only constraint on judgement is coherence with other judgements.

It is in response to this worry that the myth of the given seems, attractively, to provide an external constraint on thought.

> The idea is that when we have exhausted all the available moves within the space of concepts, all the available moves from one conceptually organised item to another, there is still one more step we can take: namely, pointing to something that is simply received in experience. (*Ibid.*: 6)

This final step is a pointing out of the conceptual realm to something given. McDowell suggests that this amounts to construing the space of reasons as more extensive than the space of concepts because the act of pointing still serves as a reason for belief.

But this idea fails. The key objection is simple. The only model we have of a reason for a belief is a relation in which both items related are already conceptualized. So if the final step in giving a reason for an empirical judgement is an extra-conceptual act of pointing, it will not sustain a *rational* friction between belief and the world. We will be exempted from blame for the outermost impacts of the world on us, because we are not responsible for them, the world is. But that idea by itself is not enough to explain the idea that our beliefs are rationally responsive to the world and can thus be right or wrong. "In effect the idea of the Given offers exculpations where we wanted justifications" (*ibid.*: 8).

Thus both coherentism and the myth of the given achieve partial insights. A self-conscious coherentist like Davidson recognizes that "nothing can count as a reason for holding a belief except another belief" and thus rejects any notion of an epistemic intermediary between belief and world (Davidson 1986a: 310). But the cost of this, according to McDowell, is giving up the notion that thought has a bearing on the world. This is what he means by thought's "normative directedness". A subscriber to the myth of the given, on the other hand, can address the idea that there must be worldly input to empirical

beliefs, but fails to respect the argument that only conceptually structured items can play that role.

McDowell's suggestion to resolve this problem is subtly to balance
respect for the Kantian slogan and respect for Davidson's criticism of
the dualism of scheme and content. Thus, although he rejects the
dualism of scheme and content, he does not reject the "duality" (cf.
McDowell 1999: 88). That is, he is happy to talk of the faculties of
receptivity and spontaneity but he denies that they can be understood
in isolation from one another. This picks up a theme from his discussion of theories of meaning (described in Chapter 3). It is impossible to
adopt a stance outside one's conceptual scheme (or the space of reasons,
in McDowell's terminology) to chart the relation between it and the
world with each understood separately (cf. McDowell 1994: 34–6). In
the case at hand, it is possible to understand the role of conceptualized
experience in providing friction between beliefs and the world only "if
we can achieve a firm grip on this thought: receptivity does not make
an even notionally separable contribution to the co-operation" (*ibid.*: 9).

The idea is that for language users – who are thus rational subjects capable of taking a stand in the space of reasons – experience is
to be understood as always already conceptualized. It is not the result
of subsequently clothing in concepts what is initially brutely given in
non-conceptual form. Because it is conceptualized, experience is
partly the product of spontaneity. But the subject is passive in this
bringing of concepts into play. In summary:

> [T]he need for external constraint is met by the fact that experi-
> ences are receptivity in operation. But that does not disqualify
> experiences from playing a role in justification, as the counterpart
> thought in the Myth of the Given does, because the claim is that
> experiences themselves are already equipped with conceptual con-
> tent. This joint involvement of receptivity and spontaneity allows
> us to say that in experience one can take in how things are.
>
> (*Ibid.*: 25)

I shall shortly return to the last sentence.

Experience and the world

The claim that experience is conceptualized, and therefore belongs to
the faculty of *spontaneity*, but at the same time the concepts are
drawn into experience *passively*, without the conscious intent of the

subject, may suggest a tension. How can the same items play both passive and active roles? McDowell stresses, however, that it is only because the same capacities that are implicated in experience are also involved in active judgements that a subject can be counted a subject of experience. Only so can the subject be capable of genuinely judging, for example, that there is a red-coloured surface before them. McDowell argues, following Sellars (see below), that such judgement requires a background of other beliefs about the world. Furthermore "[a]ctive empirical thinking takes place under a standing obligation to reflect about the credentials of the putatively rational linkages that govern it" (*ibid.*: 12). Thus the concepts in play in experience are themselves subject to revision suggesting continuity in their roles in active judgement and passive experience.

To flesh out these claims about the continuity of the roles of concepts, McDowell considers *secondary* qualities because these are the most minimally integrated into our conception of the fabric of the world. (If he can make his point for secondary qualities it should be more obvious for primary qualities.) But even here it is the connection between the concepts when drawn into experience and when used in evolving active judgements that enables a subject to understand experiences as *glimpses* of an enduring world that exists independently of experience. McDowell writes:

> Concepts of colour are only minimally integrated into the active business of accommodating one's thinking to the continuing deliverances of experience, and hence only minimally integrated into possible views of the world. Still, they are so integrated, even if only minimally. No subject could be recognised as having experiences of colour except against a background understanding that makes it possible for judgements endorsing such experiences to fit into her view of the world. She must be equipped with such things as the concept of visible surfaces of objects, and the concept of suitable conditions for telling what something's colour is by looking at it. (McDowell 1994: 30)

Occasions when these concepts are drawn into merely *inner experience*, such as the seeing of colours after a blow to the head, are derived from their involvement in characterizing an *outer* world. Although McDowell thinks that one can only have an understanding of secondary qualities if one has an understanding of how they are experienced by a subject (e.g. a relation between red and looking red) he does not construe the latter as an inner experience:

It is one thing to gloss being red in terms of being such as to look red, and quite another to gloss it in terms of being such as to induce a certain "inner experience" in us. Note that "red" in "looking red" expresses a concept of "outer experience" no less than does "red" in "being red", in fact the very same concept.

(McDowell 1994: 31 n.7)

If, by contrast, an analysis of colour terms started with "inner experiences", it is hard to see how that could generate a conception of properties, albeit with a phenomenal quality, located in objects in the world.

McDowell devotes a separate treatment to inner sense generally. He argues that judgements of sensations are also fully conceptualized and that these concepts are also, of necessity, used in third person judgements. Thus to understand the concept of pain in the first person judgement "I am in pain" requires that one also understands that pain is a general type of state of affairs and one in which another subject can be.[2] But, unlike secondary qualities, sensation concepts are not interconnected with other concepts in such a way as to suggest that such states exist independently of the instantiation of sensation concepts in experiences (e.g. pains).

This difference between judgements of inner and outer sense has to be handled with care, however. It is the basis for the following criticism by Michael Friedman:

> [T]he distinction between passive experience (concerning which we are simply "struck" one way or another, as it were) and active judgment (concerning which we have free choice) is not at all the same as the distinction between that which expresses constraint by an independent objective world and that which does not. The crucial question, in this regard, concerns rather how we distinguish between "inner" and "outer" sense. And McDowell's idea here, if I understand him correctly, is that passively received impressions become experiences of an objective world (and thus impressions of outer sense) only by being *taken as such* by the active faculty of understanding: by being subject, that is, to the perpetually revisable procedure through which the understanding integrates such impressions into an evolving world-conception.

(Friedman 2002: 34–5)

---

2. This picks up comments on Wittgenstein's private language argument discussed in Chapter 1.

McDowell responds to this by clarifying the connection between glimpses of the world and the requirement on a reasonable subject to reflect on his or her worldview:

> But this does not fit the conception of experience I recommend. In my picture, actualizations of conceptual capacities in receptivity are already, in conforming to that specification, at least apparently revelatory of an objective world, and, when all goes well, actually so. They do not need to be turned into experiences with objective purport by being so taken. The point of invoking the perpetual obligation to rethink a world-view is to help make it intelligible that these "passively received impressions" already have objective purport – not to indicate a way in which intellectual activity can somehow make experiences of an objective world out of items that are in themselves less than that.
>
> (McDowell 2002: 273)

Friedman argues that McDowell's account is idealist because the difference between inner states and worldly facts depends merely on what subjects do with their experiences. McDowell's reply is to stress that the phenomenology of outer sense shows it to involve glimpses of the world. The further connection to the reflective role of reason is a transcendental condition on such glimpses. But it does not explain how neutrally described experiences gain their worldly content. In other words, if idealism were separately motivated, Friedman's point would be significant. But, given the starting-point McDowell adopts, there is no reason to go against the everyday assumption that some experiences reveal worldly facts while others are merely inner states.[3]

I shall now return to the claim that the "joint involvement of receptivity and spontaneity allows us to say that in experience one can take in how things are". This suggests two key points. First, the claim that in experience one can take in how things are recapitulates McDowell's disjunctive conception of experience (described in Chapters 4 and 5). Providing one is not misled, experience provides a form of direct openness to the world. Secondly, the notion of experience as openness to the world is a notion of a *conceptualized* uptake. One argument for this is the fact that the content of the experience is the same as the content of a judgement that it can prompt. Of course,

---

3. McDowell also thinks that this understanding of empirical experience is also vital for the very idea of mental states having representational bearing. If one were to deny that experience can reveal worldly facts then it would be mysterious how intentionality was possible at all.

sometimes a subject will not endorse the relevant judgement.[4] But if a subject does endorse an experience in the corresponding judgement then the basis for the judgement – the experience – has the same content as the judgement. The judgement is not based on an *inference* from lesser information. McDowell makes this point in his discussion of criteria (discussed in Chapter 5).

These points are summarized in the following passage:

> In a particular experience in which one is not misled, what one takes in is *that things are thus and so. That things are thus and so* is the content of the experience, and it can also be the content of a judgement: it becomes the content of a judgement if the subject decides to take the experience at face value. So it is conceptual content. But *that things are thus and so* is also, if one is not misled, an aspect of the layout of the world: it is how things are. Thus the idea of conceptually structured operations of receptivity puts us in a position to speak of experience as openness to the layout of reality. Experience enables the layout of reality itself to exert a rational influence on what a subject thinks.
>
> (McDowell 1994: 26)

The idea here is that by construing experience as conceptualized, McDowell can identify the content of experience – when nothing has gone awry – with the same sorts of items that constitute the layout of reality. Experience has the kind of content that is characterized using a "that-clause" and that enables a harmony between it and the facts that collectively constitute the world. On this point, McDowell suggests that he finds it helpful to reflect on Wittgenstein's comment that "When we say, and *mean*, that such-and-such is the case, we – and our meaning – do not stop anywhere short of the fact; but we mean: *this – is – so*" (Wittgenstein 1953 §95). McDowell summarizes:

> in a style Wittgenstein would have been uncomfortable with: there is no ontological gap between the sort of thing one can mean, or generally the sort of thing one can think, and the sort of thing that can be the case. When one thinks truly, what one thinks *is* what is the case. So since the world is everything that is the case (as he himself once wrote), there is no gap between thought, as such, and the world. Of course thought can be distanced from the world by

---

4. McDowell discusses the Müller–Lyer illusion. Once one is familiar with this visual illusion, one will not endorse the judgement that one line is longer than the other. Nevertheless, this is how they continue to seem.

being false, but there is no distance from the world implicit in the
very idea of thought. (1994: 27)

I shall return to this passage later in this chapter. It marks out what
has been called an "identity theory of truth".

These passages occur in the second lecture of *Mind and World*:
"The Unboundedness of the Conceptual". The general thrust of this
lecture is to argue that there is no outer boundary to the conceptual
sphere. While it is possible to point outside the sphere of thinking to
features of the world that are independent of acts of thinking, this is
not to point outside *thinkable* contents or the space of concepts (cf.
ibid.: 39):

> [W]e must not picture an outer boundary around the sphere of
> the conceptual, with a reality outside the boundary impinging
> inward on the system. Any impingements across such an outer
> boundary could only be causal, and not rational ... I am trying to
> describe a way of maintaining that in experience the world
> exerts a rational influence on our thinking. And that requires us
> to delete the outer boundary from the picture ... The facts that
> are made manifest to us ... are not beyond an outer boundary
> that encloses the conceptual sphere ... (*Ibid.*: 34)

This passage captures the general philosophical project that I have
suggested can be read into much of McDowell's previous work: showing how the world can be brought within the space of reasons.

Demonstrative concepts

Before turning to some of the broader metaphysical consequences of
this picture it is worth noting one key idea that helps make McDowell's claim about the conceptual nature of experience more plausible.
In *Mind and World*, Evans plays the role of a subscriber to the myth
of the given (countering Davidson as a coherentist). McDowell suggests that one reason for this is that Evans takes experience to be
more fine grained than the concepts that speakers typically possess.
Evans offers the example of colour experience. He suggests that our
experience can outstrip our conceptual repertoire because even if we
master labels such as "red", "green" or even "burnt sienna", our experience can present us with detail as fine as individual lines on the
spectrum. Thus it seems that experience can contain more detail
than can be linguistically codified.

McDowell's response is to suggest that experience itself can equip a subject with concepts:

> But why should we accept that a person's ability to embrace colour within her conceptual thinking is restricted to concepts expressible by words like "red" or "green" and phrases like "burnt sienna"? It is possible to acquire the concept of a shade of colour, and most of us have done so. Why not say that one is thereby equipped to embrace shades of colour within one's conceptual thinking with the very same determinateness with which they are presented in one's visual experience, so that one's concepts can capture colours no less sharply than one's experiences presents them? (1994: 56)

When presented with a colour experience, a subject with the general concept of "shade of colour" can acquire a particular concept expressed with the demonstrative phrase "that colour" or "that shade". Such a concept is not linguistically codified but, as in the case of singular thoughts (Chapter 4), that need not preclude its being conceptual.

Some further conditions have to be met for it to count as conceptual. The recognitional capacity on which the concept depends needs to last longer than the experience that gives rise to it, even if it is short lived. McDowell writes:

> It is the conceptual content of such a recognitional capacity that can be made explicit with the help of a sample, something that is guaranteed to be available at the time of the experience with which the capacity sets in. Later in the life of the capacity it can be given linguistic expression again, if the course of experience is favourable; that is, if experience again, or still, presents one with a suitable sample. But even in the absence of a sample, the capacity goes on being exploitable as long as it lasts, in thoughts based on memory: thoughts that are not necessarily capable of receiving an overt expression that fully determines their content.
> (*Ibid.*: 57–8)

As long as the capacity has some duration, it can allow a particular experienced shade of colour to play a role in reasoning, via inferences for example, and thus count as genuinely conceptual. While assessing other arguments for non-conceptual content – such as those based on the explanation of conceptual abilities – is outside the scope of this book, the idea of demonstrative concepts can at least counter the most obvious phenomenological objection to the idea that experience is conceptual.

McDowell, Brandom and Sellars and the transcendental role of experience

So far in this chapter I have described how McDowell works to interpret and apply a Kantian slogan: "Thoughts without content are empty, intuitions without concepts are blind". His suggestion is that experience should be understood as already placed in the space of reasons while at the same time revealing aspects of the world. Experience allows the world itself to exercise a rational constraint on thought. This idea is supposed to stop the oscillation between coherentism and the myth of the given. I also began by saying that McDowell thinks of this project as answering, and attempting therapeutically to ease, a particular difficulty. It is not a piece of theory building independent of the history of philosophy. But this description still leaves the question of precisely what role experience is supposed to play in McDowell's account of representational content. One way to get a better understanding of this is to look to the contrast between his work and that of Robert Brandom.

Brandom's philosophy shares some important features with McDowell's. Both philosophers reject reductionist accounts of intentionality: accounts that explain mental content in, for example, causal terms. McDowell describes such approaches as "bald naturalism" (McDowell 1994: 67, 73). Both stress the normative nature of the space of reasons and are indebted to Wittgenstein and Sellars (as well as Hegel). Moreover, both adopt forms of externalism in epistemology while rejecting reliabilism because of its lack of concern with normativity (see Chapter 5).

There are, however, significant differences. Centrally, Brandom's main work, *Making it Explicit* (1994), is a piece of substantial theory building. It aims to give an account of meaning in terms of the social practices of ascribing and undertaking commitments and entitlements. Brandom describes these as forms of "deontic scorekeeping". But no weight is placed on the idea of *experience* shedding light on meaning.

Reviewing *Mind and World*, Brandom suggests that McDowell articulates a key requirement for any account of representational content or objective purport: "the rational constraint constraint". A successful account must "make intelligible how perceptual experience imposes not merely *causal*, but *rational* constraints on thinking" (Brandom 1998: 369). Brandom goes on to argue, however, that traditional epistemological reliabilism, Davidsonian semantic externalism and, implicitly, Brandom's own social scorekeeping approach can all meet this constraint without invoking experience. "We are not told what justifies the move from the need for rational constraint by *the world* to rational constraint by *experience*" (*ibid.*: 373).

McDowell's response emphasizes the subtle role that experience plays in his philosophy:

> I recommend a picture in which experience is actualization of conceptual capacities in sensory consciousness, not as the only theory of perception that meets requirements we can impose on any such theory independently of any particular dialectical context, but as the way to relieve the specific philosophical discomfort that I consider. I mention coherentism and the Myth of the Given, not as competitor theories, but with a view to making the discomfort vivid. I mention bald naturalism, not as a competitor theory, but as opting out of this area of philosophy. My point here is to help bring out what it takes to relieve the discomfort I am concerned with. The discomfort involves wanting to preserve the thought that actualizations of conceptual capacities belong in a *sui generis* logical space of reasons, in the face of a transcendental anxiety it can easily help to generate.
>
> (McDowell 1998d: 403–4)

What is the transcendental anxiety? In the reply to Brandom it is spelled out only implicitly but it clearly concerns the role of experience in what McDowell has come to call "transcendental empiricism". "I do indeed take a transcendentally motivated empiricism to be innocent. Liberated from a certain discardable conception of the natural, it does not present us with a mystery about the very idea of objective purport" (*ibid.*: 405). Thus experience, properly understood, plays a role in disarming a transcendental anxiety. The anxiety concerns the possibility of representational content, objective purport or meaning:

> We can trace some characteristic concerns of modern philosophy to a thought on these lines: if we cannot see conceptual activity as part of a package that includes sensory consciousness of the objective, then the very idea of conceptual activity – which must have objective purport in order to be recognizable as conceptual activity at all – becomes mysterious. And for it to be intelligible that sensory consciousness can be of the objective, we have to be able to see how episodes or states of sensory consciousness can belong

together, in the space of reasons, with the activity of deciding what to think about the world. The thought, innocent in itself, that sensory consciousness is an actualization of natural capacities puts pressure on the possibility of seeing sensory consciousness as belonging with, say, theory-construction in the space of reasons; thereby on the idea of sensory consciousness with objective purport; and thereby against that transcendental background on the very idea of objective purport. It does not relieve this pressure ... to respond ... by giving up the thought that sensory consciousness itself can have objective purport ...   (*Ibid*.: 407)

This is *not* to say that experience combines with neutrally describable mental states to inject them with meaning or content. But if experience of an objective world is precluded by a particular combination of philosophical views, then intentionality as a whole becomes mysterious. In Section II, I shall set out McDowell's further diagnosis of the nature of this conflict: the combination of the recognition of the normative nature of the space of reasons and the idea that experience is a natural event. But it is also worth noting here the connection between transcendental empiricism and Sellars's work.

McDowell spells out his relation to Sellars in both the Woodbridge Lectures and "Transcendental Empiricism" (McDowell 1998e and unpublished). The important connection in this context concerns Sellars's discussion in "Does Empirical Knowledge Have A Foundation?", Section VIII of *Empiricism and the Philosophy of Mind* (Sellars 1997: 68–79). Sellars defends a form of empiricism, on McDowell's plausible interpretation, but one that avoids the myth of the given. Sellars describes (one form of) the myth of the given in the following way:

One of the forms taken by the Myth of the Given is the idea that there is, indeed *must be*, a structure of particular matter of fact such that (a) each fact can not only be noninferentially known to be the case, but presupposes no other knowledge either of particular matter of fact, or of general truths; and (b) such that the noninferential knowledge of facts belonging to this structure constitutes the ultimate court of appeals for all factual claims – particular and general – about the world. It is important to note that I characterized the knowledge of fact belonging to this stratum as not only noninferential, but as presupposing no knowledge of other matter of fact, whether particular or general. It might be thought that this is a redundancy, that knowledge (not belief or conviction, but knowledge) which logically presupposes knowledge of other facts *must* be inferential. This, however, as I hope to show, is itself an episode in the Myth.   (Sellars: 68–9)

He goes on to accept that experience can provide non-inferential knowledge and that such experience can constitute the ultimate court of appeals for factual claims. But he denies the claim that it – the experience that grounds non-inferential knowledge – presupposes no other knowledge of particular matters of fact. The reason for denying this third claim is that Sellars takes there to be a dual dependence between the kind of knowledge expressed in perceptual reports and an overall worldview. (This accords with McDowell's discussion of colour concepts described above.) Sellars suggests that perceptual knowledge has to jump two hurdles. The first concerns the reliability of the perceptual report:

> The second hurdle is, however, the decisive one. For we have seen that to be the expression of knowledge, a report must not only have authority, this authority must *in some sense* be recognized by the person whose report it is. And this is a steep hurdle indeed. For if the authority of the report "This is green" lies in the fact that the existence of green items appropriately related to the perceiver can be inferred from the occurrence of such reports, it follows that only a person who is able to draw this inference, and therefore who has not only the concept *green*, but also the concept of uttering "This is green" – indeed, the concept of certain conditions of perception, those which would correctly be called "standard conditions" – could be in a position to token "This is green" in recognition of its authority. In other words, for a *Konstatierung* "This is green" to "express observational knowledge," not only must it be a *symptom* or *sign* of the presence of a green object in standard conditions, but the perceiver must know that tokens of "This is green" *are* symptoms of the presence of green objects in conditions which are standard for visual perception.
>
> (*Ibid.*: 74–5)

Whether or not Sellars is successful in articulating this requirement (cf. Brandom's study guide in Sellars (1997: 157–9) and McDowell (1998e)) it imposes a dependence of perceptually based knowledge on an overall worldview while Sellars also accepts a dependence in the other direction. McDowell calls dependence of worldview on perceptual knowledge and perceptual knowledge on worldview the first and second dimension of dependence, respectively. Commenting on Sellars approvingly, he describes the transcendental role of experience in his own philosophy:

> For it to be intelligible that experiences have objective content (that, in Sellars's idiom, they contain claims about the objective world), the very capacity for experience must be recognised to depend on antecedent knowledge of the sort that depends on experience in the first dimension. It must be possible to see how what experiences purport to disclose fits into an already pos- sessed world view. This formulation shows how this non-tradi- tional empiricism has a transcendental aspect, in an at least roughly Kantian sense.
>
> And once we see that introducing the second dimension makes this transcendental point, it is easy to find a transcendental as- pect in the first dimension too. The presence of objective content at the upper level of the two-levelled picture is not intelligible independently of the fact that what is at the upper level can be supported by citing elements from the lower level. We cannot make sense of the objective content involved in the idea of a world view – a view of, as we naturally put it, the empirical world – independently of the idea that a world view is supported by facts directly disclosed in experience.   (McDowell unpublished)

The second paragraph outlines the transcendental role of experience for empirical content in general. Only if the empirical content involved in a worldview is supported by experiences can such empirical or objec- tive content be possible.

I shall now turn to McDowell's diagnosis of why his account of experience has not seemed more obvious and explore some of its metaphysical consequences.

II The nature of nature

Animals are perceptually sensitive to their environment. Their sensory interactions are, however, merely natural events. They lie within the natural realm even when this is understood in the narrow sense that dominates contemporary naturalism (described in the Introduction). But given that we share broadly similar sensory systems with animals, how can our sentience be structured by concepts that have no echo in nature? It is thus tempting to suppose instead that sentience is not itself conceptually structured. Its deliverances are only subsequently interpreted so as to place items – not themselves directly given in experience – in the space of reasons.

In a passage quoted in the Introduction (and continued here), Mc-Dowell offers a diagnosis of the source of the perceived difficulty.

> What is at work here is a conception of nature that can seem sheer common sense, though it was not always so; the conception I mean was made available only by a hard-won achievement of human thought at a specific time, the time of the rise of modern science. Modern science understands its subject matter in a way that threatens, at least, to leave it disenchanted, as Weber put the point in an image that has become a commonplace. The image marks a contrast between two kinds of intelligibility: the kind that is sought by (as we call it) natural science, and the kind we find in something when we place it in relation to other occupants of "the logical space of reasons", to repeat a suggestive phrase from Wilfrid Sellars. If we identify nature with what natural science aims to make comprehensible, we threaten, at least, to empty it of meaning. By way of compensation, so to speak, we see it as the home of a perhaps inexhaustible supply of intelligibility of the other kind, the kind we find in a phenomenon when we see it as governed by natural law. It was an achievement of modern thought when this second kind of intelligibility was clearly marked off from the first.   (McDowell 1994: 70–71)

As I set out in the Introduction, McDowell is not attacking scientific method here. Scientific method, and the self-conscious reflection that accompanies it, has been a genuine achievement of the modern era. But at the same time, the assumption that the disenchantment that has successfully underpinned scientific descriptions of the world also exhausts its nature is "not the educated common sense it represents itself as being; it is shallow metaphysics" (McDowell 1998b: 182; cf. McDowell 1994: 82). McDowell uses the phrase "realm of law" to describe the kind of intelligibility found in the natural sciences in which events are explained by subsuming them under laws of nature. He suggests that in the "shallow" and scientistic metaphysical picture, nature is simply equated with realm of law and that this suggests a tension. If the realm of law exhausts nature, the deployment of concepts by the faculty of spontaneity (rooted in the space of reasons) looks unnatural. But this makes our own position in nature, as subjects able to exercise conceptual judgement, mysterious.

McDowell suggests that there are three styles of response to this difficulty:

- bald naturalism, which aims to show how the space of reasons can be constructed from concepts that belong to the realm of law. Reductionist forms of contemporary naturalism fall into this category (McDowell 1994: 73);
- McDowell's favoured position, which affirms the genuine distinctness of the realm of law and the space of reasons and resists "the characteristically modern conception according to which something's way of being natural is its position in the realm of law" (*ibid.*: 74); and
- a position that also affirms the genuine distinctness of the realm of law and space of reasons but claims that the very same things satisfy both kinds of concepts. Davidson's non-reductive anomalous monism is such a position (Davidson 1980). Davidson agrees that the categories picked out in the space of reasons (reasons, mental states, etc.) cannot be systematically mapped onto the categories of the realm of law (states of the brain or nervous system) because the former but not the latter are bound by the "constitutive principle of rationality". But at the same time, he advocates a token-identity theory of items instantiating both sets of concepts. Thus every mental event just is a physical event.

McDowell's rejection of the third position depends on the following argument:

> According to the ontological thesis, the items that instantiate the *sui generis* spontaneity-related concepts have a location in the realm of law. But the concepts are *sui generis* precisely in that it is not by virtue of their location in the realm of law that things instantiate those concepts. So if we go on equating something's place in nature with its location in the realm of law, we are debarred from holding that an experience has its conceptual content precisely as whatever natural phenomenon it is.
>
> (McDowell 1994: 75–6)

The crux of the argument is the last sentence. I think that there are two ideas at work here. One is that Davidson's position precludes the idea that experiences have (conceptual) content as an essential feature, as "whatever natural phenomena they are". This recapitulates McDowell's rejection of the master thesis that mental states are freestanding internal states, independent of the external world (see

Chapters 1 and 4). But a little later in *Mind and World*, McDowell suggests that the problem is ideological not ontological (*ibid.*: 78 n.8). The conceptual content of an experience, understood as an item in the space of reasons, looks supernatural if the natural is taken to be exhausted by the realm of law. That is to say, Davidson can accommodate the physical or neurological properties of experiential states as part of nature (since the states are taken to be physical items in his token-identity theory) but not their content-laden or psychological properties. In fact, these points can be bolstered by considering McDowell's objection to Cartesian and post-Cartesian conceptions of mind that assume that mental states are freestanding states. Given that starting-point, it is hard to see how they can be *about* anything. While Davidson's approach to the philosophy of thought through radical interpretation has much in common with McDowell's approach, his token-identity physicalism appears to suffer this Cartesian weakness.

McDowell thus rejects the third position and assumes that the first position, bald naturalism, should be avoided because it simply opts out of this area of philosophy. It does not take seriously the genuine, according to McDowell, contrast between the space of reasons and realm of law. He suggests that it can seem that the only other available response is a form of rampant Platonism, which is his label for a position that pictures "the space of reasons as an autonomous structure – autonomous in that it is constituted independently of anything specifically human" (*ibid.*: 77). This would involve a "peculiarly bifurcated" (McDowell 1994: 78) account in which humans had both animal natures but also supernatural capacities to resonate to a structure that is wholly independent of anything human (cf. *ibid.*: 78, 88). But, again, this requires taking for granted that the natural is limited to what can be captured within the realm of law.

That assumption can, however, be rejected providing that one can come to construe the role of concepts, both in experience and in active judgement, as "capturing patterns in a way of living" (*ibid.*: 78). McDowell suggests that the best way to accept this alternative to the scientistic view that causes the tension is to think about Aristotle's account of ethics and the notion of second nature. Thinking about ethical judgement is a step towards a proper understanding of how the natural realm is not completely independent of human subjectivity.

I have already described, in Chapter 2, the general shape of McDowell's broadly Aristotelian account of moral or ethical judgement. Aristotle takes for granted the idea that moral judgements answer to external constraints that come into view to those who, through suitable education, have attained an ethical standpoint. The features of that standpoint, and the judgements made from it, do not need to be given an explanation or justification in terms that are understandable without adopting that standpoint. McDowell thus rejects accounts of Aristotle that attempt to explain moral judgement through its contribution to human flourishing with flourishing explained in non-moral terms. In the terminology above, such attempts are forms of bald naturalism.

McDowell suggests instead that a proper education furnishes a subject with a natural ability to recognize the demands that, for example, kindness makes in a particular circumstance. Education moulds the practical wisdom of a subject, and this includes shaping their motivation. But the underlying idea is that education opens the subject's eyes to moral requirements. "The picture is that ethics involves requirements of reason that are there whether we know it or not, and our eyes are opened to them by the acquisition of 'practical wisdom'" (*ibid*.: 79). Thus education enables a subject to be sensitive to a further area of the space of reasons. Such sensitivity is natural but, because it requires education, it is a form of *second nature*.

McDowell concedes that Aristotle's own confidence in the specific ethical outlook he takes for granted might be a form of intellectual smugness (*ibid*.: 81). But, if so, that is not a necessary feature of a broadly Aristotelian form of moral realism. Given that ethical think-ing belongs to the space of reasons, it is under a standing injunction to reflect on its own credentials, on what it takes for granted and what counts as a good reason. It is, in this sense, in the same (Neurathian) boat as empirical thinking. Although there is no possi-bility of stepping outside a moral standpoint to validate or justify it in neutral terms, judgements within it can be scrutinised using other judgements. (In Otto Neurath's simile, a sailor "overhauls his ship whilst it is afloat" (*ibid*.: 81).)

A key element of this account of moral judgement is that, once a subject has attained an appropriate second nature, he or she is capa-ble of responding to demands that are independent of him or her, even if the moral world is not taken to be understandable independently of subjective responses to it. Moral reasons are thus independent of moral subjects, if not "brutely independent". This calls to mind a form of Platonism, but if so it is not rampant Platonism but naturalized Platonism, as I described in Chapter 1. It is only semi-autonomous.

McDowell suggests that this Aristotelian picture of moral judge-ment and second nature can help connect our ability to use concepts and respond to reasons to the natural world. With it in mind, then, it is possible to reject the conflation of the picture of the world that natural science successfully articulates with the totality of what is in nature. It provides a response to Fodor's argument for reductionism (described in the Introduction) that what is natural is either described in a final physics or reducible to it. The overall argument of *Mind and World* is summarized thus:

> In these lectures so far, I have taken perceptual experience as an object lesson, in order to describe a kind of predicament we tend to fall into when we think about aspects of the human condition. I promised to try to uncover a deep-rooted but, as we can come to realize, non-compulsory influence on our thinking that accounts for the predicament. I have now introduced my candidate for that role: the naturalism that leaves nature disenchanted. We tend to be forgetful of the very idea of second nature. I am suggesting that if we can recapture that idea, we can keep nature as it were partially enchanted, but without lapsing into pre-scientific superstition or a rampant platonism. This makes room for a conception of experience that is immune to the philosophical pitfalls I have described.
>
> We need to recapture the Aristotelian idea that a normal mature human being is a rational animal, but without losing the Kantian idea that rationality operates freely in its own sphere. The Kantian idea is reflected in the contrast between the organization of the space of reasons and the structure of the realm of natural law. Modern naturalism is forgetful of second nature; if we try to preserve the Kantian thought that reason is autonomous within the framework of that kind of naturalism, we disconnect our rationality from our animal being, which is what gives us our foothold in nature. (*Ibid.*: 85)

McDowell thus credits Kant with an appreciation of the joint dependence of empirical content on concepts and intuitions and suggests that, by combining this with a broadly Aristotelian notion of second nature, he can prevent that dependence seeming either supernatural or requiring reductionist explanation.

McDowell also draws a second related claim from Kant, summarized in Chapter 2, that I will now briefly recapitulate. This is the claim that the world is constitutively apt for conceptualization. This claim provides a further aspect of the connection of thought and the world, but it also leads to some difficulty, first for Kant, as I will describe here, and then for McDowell, described in Section III.

As I described in Chapter 2, McDowell credits Kant with the realization that the world cannot be, as Hume seems to think, "an ineffable lump, devoid of structure". Instead "an acceptable world-picture consists of articulable, conceptually structured representations. Their acceptability resides in their knowably mirroring the world; that is, representing it as it is" (McDowell 1998b: 178). But if so, McDowell argues, "we cannot suppose [with Hume] that intelligible structure has completely emigrated from the world ... we have to suppose that the world has an intelligible structure matching the structure in the space of *logos*" (*ibid.*). It cannot, after all, be independent of the space of meaningful thought. True judgements can be taken to mirror the world:

> But mirroring cannot be *both* faithful, so that it adds nothing in the way of intelligible order, *and* such that in moving from what is mirrored to what does the mirroring, one moves from what is brutely alien to the space of *logos* to what is internal to it.
>
> (*Ibid.*: 179)

Thus McDowell argues that the world must itself possess the kind of structure picked out by concepts. It must reflect the space of reasons as well as the realm of law. "Kant – to resort to a thumbnail caricature – established that the world ... cannot be constitutively independent of the space of concepts, the space where subjectivity has its being" (*ibid.*: 306). But McDowell goes on to suggest that Kant distorts both these insights. The problem, he suggests, is that Kant does not keep a firm enough grip on the thought that receptivity and spontaneity do not make even notionally separable contributions to their cooperation in experience. Although there is no separation from the standpoint of empirical experience, there is a further "transcendental story" in which there is. (Responding to criticism, McDowell subsequently calls this a "transcendent story" (1998e).) "In the transcendental perspective, receptivity figures as a susceptibility to the impact of a supersensible reality, a reality that is supposed to be independent of our conceptual activity in a stronger sense than any that fits the ordinary empirical world" (McDowell 1994: 41).

This account has to be given from a notional sideways-on perspective, which pictures the supersensible world as lying outside the sphere of the conceptual. "Kant himself preserved a residual role for the idea of something more brutely alien to the realm of thought than that, something that co-operates with mind in the transcendental constitution of the world" (McDowell 1998b: 306). But this is, in effect, a reiteration of the myth of the given. Once the world is outside the conceptual sphere, then it cannot play a rational role in constraining belief. But at the same time, "Once the supersensible is in the picture, its radical independence of our thinking tends to present itself as no more than the independence any genuine reality must have" (McDowell 1994: 42). With the contrast with the supersensible in place, the empirical world is tainted with idealism because it is the product of an interaction with subjectivity, albeit off-stage. McDowell recommends German Idealism precisely because it removes the supersensible while leaving the Kantian account of the intelligibility of the empirical world.

> But Kant's successors saw (in one way or another) that the fundamental thesis, that the world cannot be constitutively independent of the space of concepts, does not require this residual recognition of an "in itself". This tradition is generally known as "German Idealism" ... (but) need not be idealistic in any obvious sense. (McDowell 1998b: 306)

McDowell's reading of the history of philosophy has been called inaccurate. His interpretation of Kant has been criticized for subscribing to Strawson's two-world interpretation. Graham Bird, for example, argues that the arguments against the "monstrous" side of the traditional interpretation should in fact suggest that Kant was more successful than McDowell takes him to have been (Bird 1996: 230 n.15). Equally, Friedman argues that German Idealism was characterized by emphasis on the Kantian faculty of reason rather than understanding (Friedman 2002). But from the point of view of the project of seeing how Kant and Kantianism can be used to shed light on intentionality, this kind of objection is less important. The question that remains is what can be preserved if an account of the noumenal as extra-conceptual is rejected, whether or not Kant took this view.

McDowell characterizes the proper understanding of the world for which he uses the label "German Idealism" as involving the "partial re-enchantment" of nature. But what does this mean? The most explicit account McDowell gives is in the following passage:

> Against Hume, Kant aims to regain for nature the intelligibility of law, but not the intelligibility of meaning. For Kant, nature is the realm of law and therefore devoid of meaning. And given such a conception of nature, genuine spontaneity cannot figure in descriptions of actualizations of natural powers as such. (McDowell 1994: 97)

231

So far this seems to undermine the claim, quoted above, that Kant realized that the world "cannot be constitutively independent of the space of concepts". But that impression is modified as the passage in *Mind and World* continues:

> The point here is one of some delicacy. For Kant, the ordinary empirical world, which includes nature as the realm of law, is not external to the conceptual. In view of the connection between the conceptual and the kind of intelligibility that belongs to meaning, I have suggested that defending that Kantian thought requires a partial re-enchantment of nature ... But it does not require us to rehabilitate the idea that there is meaning in the fall of a sparrow or the movement of the planets, as there is meaning in a text. It is a good teaching of modernity that the realm of law is as such devoid of meaning; its constituent elements are not linked to one another by the relations that constitute the space of reasons. But if our thinking about the natural stops at an appreciation of that point, we cannot properly comprehend the capacity of experience to take in even the meaningless occurrences that constitute the realm of law. We cannot satisfactorily splice spontaneity and receptivity together in our conception of experience, and that means we cannot exploit the Kantian thought that the realm of law, not just the realm of meaningful doings, is not external to the conceptual. The understanding – the very capacity that we bring to bear on texts – must be involved in our taking in of mere meaningless happenings.   (*Ibid.*: 97)

This quotation suggests that the re-enchantment of nature is broader than just the recognition of second nature: our ability as rational subjects to have our eyes opened to normative relations. The suggestion is that extra-human nature is also re-enchanted, even if not to the extent of furnishing meaning in the fall of a sparrow. But the fact that nature is constitutively apt for conceptualization suggests again the worry about idealism, which might be put as follows. If experience is always already conceptualized, and if experience is – at least when appearances are not misleading – a form of openness to the world, then the world itself is always already conceptualized.

In a paper generally hostile to *Mind and World*, Wright puts this point succinctly:

> So – if McDowell is right – not just experience, as a potential justifier of empirical beliefs, but the *real world* in turn, as that

which is to be capable of impinging upon us in a way which induces experiences of determinate content, must be thought of as *conceptual*. We arrive at a conception of experience not merely as something which is intrinsically content-bearing, a passive exercise of concepts, but as also essentially an "openness to the layout of reality", where this openness is a matter of conceptual fit between the experience and the situation experienced. The world, as we must conceive of it, is indeed the Tractarian world: a totality of *facts*, where facts are essentially facts that *P*. Conceptual content, in McDowell's metaphysics, belongs to the very fabric of the world.   (Wright 2002: 147)

Surely this requires an account like Strawson's dark transcendent story of how the world is constructed in accordance with the space of reasons? How can the account avoid idealism?

III The threat of idealism

In this section, I shall return to the issue of idealism, which has been hinted at throughout this book. Does McDowell really escape the charge that reality, on his account, loses a vital element of its independence? I shall examine this question by looking at a particularly pithy expression of it.

A year after the publication of *Mind and World*, Julian Dodd raised the following objection to it in a brief paper (Dodd 1995; see also Dodd 2000). According to Dodd, McDowell's attempt to escape the "intolerable oscillation" between unpalatable alternatives in the philosophy of content in turn falls prey to a vicious dilemma through his identification of the contents of thoughts with facts. This is the result, Dodd argues, of confusing two distinct identity theses that differ in their construal of facts.

- A *robust* identity thesis identifies true thoughts with facts, which are themselves construed along the lines "favoured by correspondence theorists: items with particular objects and properties as constituents, whose totality makes up the world" (Dodd 1995: 161). This "eradicates the gap between content and reality".
- A *modest* identity thesis (by contrast) identifies true thoughts with facts but the further analysis provided is concentrated on the left-hand side of the equation (i.e. on thoughts). Facts are true Fregean

Thoughts "*rather than* occupants of the world" (*ibid*.: 161, original emphasis) and, as Thoughts, have senses, rather than objects, as their constituent components.

Dodd argues that McDowell vacillates between the two, because he (McDowell) argues on the one hand that his thesis is truistic (implying *modesty*) and, on the other, that it provides (*robustly*) an account of the connection between mind and the fabric of the world. Dodd goes on to argue that, because a robust thesis is "beggared for an account of falsehood" (*ibid*.: 163), it is independently unacceptable, and McDowell should settle for a modest thesis. But the cost of that is the loss of an account of mind–world relations (by means of the identity thesis at least) because, if the components of Thoughts are senses, then they are *modes of presentation* of things and not things themselves.

Clearly, if Dodd's dilemma genuinely exhausts the options, then McDowell has not succeeded in his therapeutic metaphilosophical aim of dissolving the key philosophical problems that cluster about the relation of mind and world. The problem here seems to arise from the combination of two McDowellian themes: first, what we may term McDowell's commitment to openness to reality (cf. McDowell 1994: 26, 143), drawn in part from the later Wittgenstein; and, secondly, a neo-Fregean theory of sense (*ibid*.: 106, 179–80). The former asserts that veridical experience involves direct and unmediated access to the world (unmediated, that is, by the epistemic intermediaries; they are still conceptualized).[5]

The latter theme, the neo-Fregean theory of sense described in Chapters 3 and 4, emphasizes the way contact with the world has always to be theorized from a perspective that makes *rational* sense of speech and action. While McDowell speaks throughout *Mind and World* of experience as always already conceptualized, and of the sphere of concepts as having no outer boundary, his understanding of concepts here is given by a neo-Fregean theory of sense: "If we want to identify the conceptual realm with the realm of thought, the right gloss on 'conceptual' is not 'predicative' but 'belonging to the realm of Fregean sense'" (McDowell 1994: 107). So is there really any tension in putting these two themes together?

---

5. McDowell rejects the label "openness to reality conjecture" suggested by a critic, on the grounds that it is not something that stands in need of argument (McDowell 2000a: 338). Nevertheless, the idea of openness does play a characteristically *philosophical* role and is meant to contrast with, for example, a highest common factor conception of experience, as discussed in Chapters 4 and 5.

I think that McDowell faces a difficulty that has parallels in Wittgenstein's treatment of the connection of mental states and worldly events. I shall suggest that McDowell's problems are the "material mode" (i.e. talking about things) analogues of problems that arise, one semantic level higher, in the interpretation of Wittgenstein's comments, expressed in the formal mode (i.e. talking about words and concepts). Among other things, resolving Dodd's challenge to McDowell will involve an interpretation of a neo-Fregean theory of sense that does not turn on a contrast between sense and reference.

As I described earlier in this chapter, McDowell attempts to motivate the idea that experience is a form of direct openness to the world by quoting Wittgenstein's claim that "When we say, and *mean*, that such-and-such is the case, we – and our meaning – do not stop anywhere short of the fact; but we mean: *this – is – so*" (Wittgenstein 1953: §95, quoted in McDowell 1994: 27). He goes on to say that there is no "ontological gap" between the sort of thing one can think, and the sort of thing that can be the case and that, when one thinks truly, what one thinks *is* what is the case. Wittgenstein's discussion in the *Investigations* of what connects content-laden mental states and states of the world occurs in an under-read chapter from which McDowell draws the idea of thought catching reality in its net (Wittgenstein 1953: §§428–65). To shed further light on McDowell's claims, here I shall digress briefly to outline Wittgenstein's discussion.

Wittgenstein focuses his investigation on the question: how can a connection exist between an expectation and an expected event? "I see someone pointing a gun and say 'I expect a report'. The shot is fired. – Well, that was what you expected; so did that report somehow already exist in your expectation?" (*ibid.*: §442). He goes on to reject any explanation of this connection via intermediaries, whether mental items or mysterious "shadows of facts". A key difference from McDowell's account is that Wittgenstein concentrates as much on the possibility of false as true thoughts, since they raise complementary difficulties for the philosophy of content. By focusing on false thoughts, Wittgenstein undermines the idea that, in the example above, the shot is somehow already present in an expectation.

The discussion culminates in two dramatic passages. The first begins:

> One may have the feeling that in the sentence "I expect he is coming" one is using the words "he is coming" in a different sense from the one they have in the assertion "He is coming". But if it were so how could I say that my expectation had been fulfilled? If

> I wanted to explain the words "he" and "is coming", say by means
> of ostensive definitions, the same definitions of these words
> would go for both sentences. (*Ibid.*: §444)

The problem raised here is a symptom of postulating internal
objects to carry or explain content. On any such account, the words
characterizing the content of an expectation would designate one
(internal) object, and those characterizing its fulfilment would designate a different (external) object. Thus the description of the fulfilment condition would have nothing to do with the description of the
content of the expectation. But, as Wittgenstein points out, the words
do have the same meaning. We can, for example, give the same
(ostensive) definitions of them.

Wittgenstein instead proposes to approach the general problem of
the content of intentional states from the perspective suggested by
this response. Instead of seeing linguistic representation as secondary, he proposes that we see it as of primary importance. The *repre-*
sentation of expectations and their fulfilment can provide an answer
to what links the two. The pair of passages continues:

> But it might now be asked: what's it like for him to come? – The
> door opens, someone walks in, and so on. – What's it like for me to
> expect him to come? – I walk up and down the room, look at the
> clock now and then, and so on. – But the one set of events has not
> the smallest similarity to the other! So how can one use the same
> words in describing them? – But perhaps I say as I walk up and
> down: "I expect he'll come in." – Now there is a similarity some-
> where. But of what kind?! (*Ibid.*: §444)

> It is in language that an expectation and its fulfilment make
> contact. (*Ibid.*: §445)

One way of reading these passages is to suppose, with Wright, that
the connection is *forged* through utterances (cf. Wright 1987a, 1989).
This would be to subscribe to a form of semantic anti-realism, which
Wright has proposed in a number of papers to explain the connection,
but which McDowell has convincingly rebutted (see Chapter 1). But a
different approach is to take an interpretation in the style of Wright
as expressing an "empirical" claim about how language mediates
mind–world links, whereas the truth expressed should be construed
as transcendental. It is a transcendental condition that both the
mental state and its fulfilment can be described using related
language. One way of understanding such a transcendental claim is

to say that a condition of possibility of being able to form such content-laden mental states is that one can speak a language of sufficient conceptual richness that their fulfilment conditions can be specified. So understood, however, it is the mental state itself (although thought of as a state of a whole person and not as a free-standing internal configuration of the brain), and not the act of giving it expression, that determines what accords with it (cf. McDowell 1998b: 314–17). Although it is a transcendental condition of possibility for the connection between thought and reality, language does not *directly* mediate that connection.

By contrast with Wittgenstein's discussion, McDowell's comments about the harmony of thought and language escape this ambiguity but nevertheless contain a similarly transcendental claim (to which I shall return). While Wittgenstein's comments are pitched in the formal mode, McDowell, perhaps in order to distance himself from any taint of semantic anti-realism, presents his as ontological claims in the material mode. Experiencing subjects are "open to facts" (McDowell 1994: 72); and "perceptible facts are essentially capable of expressing themselves on perceivers in [experiences]" (*ibid.*: 28). These are the sorts of comments that are summarized in the claim that "one can think, for instance, *that spring has begun*, and that very same thing, that *spring has begun*, can be the case" (*ibid.*: 27, original emphasis).

McDowell goes on to say that this is truistic and cannot slight the independence of reality. In order to reinforce this point, he points out that in equating facts with (true) thoughts, the latter are to be understood, not as acts of thinking – which would amount to idealism – but as thinkable contents. It might be thought that this would be enough to disarm Dodd's objection that if an identity of (true) thoughts and facts is truistic then the facts cannot be the sorts of things that make up the world. But McDowell explicitly combines these claims about our direct openness to reality with claims about the central role of Fregean sense in accounting for a "thinker's competent self-conscious presence in the world" (*ibid.*: 106). "[T]he whole point of the notion of sense is captured by the principle that thoughts differ if a single subject can simultaneously take rationally conflicting stances towards them" (*ibid.*: 180). And the "point of the notion of sense ... is thus tied to our interest in understanding behaviour, and ultimately our interest in understanding – fathoming – people" (McDowell 1998a: 172).

This combination invites Dodd's objection that the identity of thoughts and facts cannot be invoked to connect mind and world if the component parts of thoughts (Thoughts) are senses – as they are in neo-Fregean theory – rather than things. Once this objection is in place, McDowell's quick hint at a solution in the comment that "On a proper understanding of the Fregean apparatus, my exploitation of Wittgenstein's truism ... can indeed be reformulated by saying thought and reality meet in the realm of sense" (McDowell 1994: 180) makes it looks as though the meeting stops thought crucially short of the world. Although talk of Thoughts as facts retains its merely Fregean conception, it seems that there is a kind of mind–world connection that is not accounted for. This is the connection, not between Thoughts and facts, but between thoughts and things.

Responding to a similar objection raised elsewhere by Ian Lyne, McDowell does not seem to see any apparent problem (Lyne 2000: 308). Having re-emphasized the importance of a Fregean distinction between sense and reference, he says rather briskly:

> And there is no conflict with my conception of the world as true thinkables. Lyne evidently cannot comprehend a conception of the world in which, to echo Wittgenstein's *Tractatus*, it breaks up into facts, not objects. It is as if he thinks he knows, without needing to listen to alternatives, that something that does not break up into objects cannot be the world. But Frege shows, precisely, a way to see how something that does not break up into objects can be, to continue the echo of the *Tractatus*, everything that is the case – which seems a fine thing to mean by "the world".
>
> (McDowell 2000a: 339)

And addressing the same point elsewhere, he says:

> Since objects figure in the world by figuring in facts, which are true thinkables, the sense in which objects figure in the world, on the Fregean conception, is the sense in which objects figure in think-ables, in Fregean thoughts. And Frege's terminology of Sinn and Bedeutung is precisely suited for giving expression of this idea. We can introduce the terminology of objects figuring in thoughts, and hence in facts, by saying that for an object to figure in a thought, a thinkable, is for it to be the Bedeutung associated with a Sinn that is a constituent of the thinkable. I see no difficulty in apply-ing such a construal to (for instance) my talk of objects coming into view for us in actualisations of conceptual capacities.
>
> (McDowell 2000c: 94–5)

The problem with these responses is that they do not seem to go far enough towards removing the apparent difficulty here. The problem raised is not so much that the world is not a world of facts but of things; it is rather – to echo McDowell's own comments about the relation between a Kantian world of appearance and the nou- menal – that once a distinction between sense and reference is in play then reference "tends to present itself as no more than the independ- ence any genuine reality must have" (cf. McDowell 1994: 42). Thus the world of facts, understood as neo-Fregean senses, does not seem independent enough. This impression calls for therapeutic dissolu- tion not dismissal.

I think that the best way to approach this point is to return to an element of Dodd's paper. He begins by defining identity theories of truth in contrast with correspondence theories. "Whereas a corre- spondence theorist holds that facts are *extra-linguistic items* which make propositions true, an identity theorist, by contrast, believes true propositions to be facts" (Dodd 1995: 160, emphasis added). But he goes on to define robust *identity* theories as identifying true thoughts with facts conceived in just this way: as extralinguistic items, or "bodily chunks of mind-independent reality". Only so does he think that facts can be conceived as constituting the fabric of the world.

But although, at first sight, this may seem an understandable as- sumption, it cannot survive in a philosophical context that shuns a distinction between scheme and content, and thus it cannot be rea- sonably ascribed to McDowell as an alternative that is implicit in his thinking. It is this distinction between conceptual scheme and worldly content that McDowell rejects when he rejects the sideways- on view of language (see especially McDowell 1994: 146–61):

> What I ... mean to rule out is this idea: that, when we work at making someone else intelligible, we exploit relations we can already discern between the world and something already in view as a system of concepts within which the other person thinks; so that as we come to fathom the content of the initially opaque con- ceptual capacities that are operative within the system, we are filling in detail in a sideways-on picture – here the conceptual system, there the world – that has been available all along ... in outline. (*Ibid.*: 34–5)

> [T]hinking does not stop short of the facts. The world is embrace- able in thought. What I have been urging is that that constitutes a background without which the special way in which experience takes hold of the world would not be intelligible. And the depend- ence is not only in that direction. It is not that we could first

make sense of the fact that the world is thinkable, in abstraction
from experience . . . (*Ibid*.: 33)

McDowell's idea here echoes Davidson's conclusion in "On the
Very Idea of a Conceptual Scheme" (Davidson 1984: 183–98). It is
also implicit in a part of the discussion of why he thinks the identity
of thoughts and facts is not guilty of idealism, which I have not yet
mentioned. As an alternative to the mistaken temptation to take that
identification as a slight to the independence of reality, McDowell
suggests that one might as well take it the other way round. That is,
one might:

take the fact that the sort of thing one can think is the same as
the sort of thing that can be the case . . . as an invitation to understand the notion of the sort of thing one can think in terms of a
supposedly prior understanding of the sort of thing that can be
the case. *And in fact there is no reason to look for priority in either
direction.* (*Ibid*.: 28, emphasis added)

In fact, the last sentence is too weak. Given his endorsement of
Davidson's attack on a dualism of scheme and content, there is a positive reason to abandon the hope of characterizing first facts and thus
then thoughts, or first thoughts and thus then facts. The general
lesson to be learned is that our understanding of the two can only
develop together. We cannot even notionally achieve the perspective
of cosmic exile from which to individuate bodily chunks of reality
independently of the sentences that match up to them.

This provides a partial solution to the problem Dodd raises. One
aspect of the objection is based on a distinction between the conception
of thoughts as extralinguistic bodily chunks of reality and as Fregean
Thoughts "*rather than* occupants of the world" (Dodd 1995: 161). But
this distinction, between robust and modest identity theories, is not
one that fits into the system articulated in *Mind and World*.

So much, then, for one aspect of the problem: accounting for true
thoughts, understood as true thinkables, which are equated with facts
in a way that allows facts to constitute the fabric of the world. Taking
for granted the dismantling of the dualism of scheme and content,
there is no problem in construing true thinkables *both* as possible *contents* of acts of thinking, and as the sort of things that make up the
world. (This will have the consequence of allowing there to be more
facts making up the world than some people would be happy with.
Facts will be individuated as finely as a theory of sense requires.)

This provides the second element of the solution for the problem Dodd raises. By combining the claim of openness to reality with a neo-Fregean theory of sense, McDowell may still seem embarrassed by another aspect of Dodd's objection, summarized in the question: what are the component parts of thoughts? To repeat, the sting in the tail of this question is that McDowell requires that thoughts are senses with nothing but senses as components, and if senses are modes of presentation of things then they are not things themselves, and thought seems to stop short of the world again.

There is, however, a later passage in *Mind and World* in which McDowell appears to consider just this question. He considers the following objection:

> You make it look as if your drift is not idealistic, so long as you consider the world only as something whose elements are *things that are the case*. In that context, you can exploit the claim that it is no more than a truism that when one's thought is true, what one thinks *is* what is the case. But as soon as we try to accommodate the sense in which the world is populated by *things*, by objects (and there had better be such a sense), it will emerge that your image of erasing an outer boundary around the realm of thought must be idealistic in tenor ... [I]t obliterates ... a possibility of direct contact between minds and *objects* which must surely be external to the realm of thought ... (*Ibid.*: 179)

He goes on to comment that objects belong in the realm of reference, not the realm of sense, and thus it may appear that "Wittgenstein's 'truism' yields an alignment of minds with the realm of sense, not with the realm of reference" (*ibid.*: 179). But the response he outlines merely repeats the general moral of post-Evans neo-Fregean thinking. Anticipating that this objection would be raised by a non-Fregean direct-reference theorist, who assumes that Fregean theory can accommodate different senses only by using *descriptive* specifications (based on Russell's theory of descriptions), McDowell reiterates an earlier claim that *de re* senses can also be incorporated into a neo-Fregean theory. That earlier, fuller, passage begins:

> Evans's master thought is that Frege's notion of sense, which Frege introduces in terms of modes of presentation, can accommodate the sorts of connection between thinkers and particular objects [i.e. in singular thoughts] ... The detail of Evans's work spells this out case by case. It explains the various ways in which thoughts focus on

241

particular objects, always placing thinking in its proper context, the
thinker's competent self-conscious presence in the world.
                                                        (*Ibid*.: 106–7)

(It goes on: "That such work can be so little appreciated is a mark of
degeneracy in our philosophical culture" (*ibid*.: 107).) The later
passage ends:

> If the relevant senses are rightly understood, the role of sense, in
> a picture that leaves the relation of thought to the world of facts
> unproblematic, already ensures that there is no mystery about
> how it can be that the relevant thoughts bear on the relevant
> particulars, inhabitants of the realm of reference, in ... non-
> specificatory ways.   (*Ibid*.: 180)

But this response will not by itself turn aside Dodd's objection,
which depends on the distinction between incorporating, in thoughts,
modes of presentation of things (whether descriptive or not) and the
things themselves. The problem is not whether senses are descriptive
but whether, if thoughts contain senses *and not* things, they are really
open to the world. Has McDowell removed the problem about relations
between mind and a world that comprises things as well as facts?

In response to this challenge, one approach would simply be to
abandon McDowell's ontological or material-mode account of the harmony of thought and language. I have tried to argue elsewhere that
one of the advantages of a common thread in both the later Wittgenstein and Davidson's work is that questions such as "What are the
component parts of thoughts?" appear as merely gratuitous scholas-
tic metaphysics (Thornton 1998). By approaching propositional
attitudes strictly from the perspective of their ascription in radical
interpretation, Davidson, for example, manages to do without the
machinery that makes that question appear sensible.

Within McDowell's system, however, the solution to whether
thoughts are open to the world requires rethinking how the notion of
sense should be characterized, taking a cue from his discussion in
"On the Sense and Reference of a Proper Name" (1977) (discussed in
Chapter 3). In undergraduate philosophy teaching, the idea of sense
is usually introduced to solve a number of related problems, most
notably the informativeness of identity statements of the form
"Hesperus is Phosphorus". Having pointed out the inadequacy, in
such cases, of a barely referential theory of meaning, the notion of
sense is introduced to characterize what is *understood* by a speaker

when he or she understands a name. The sense of a name is partially defined by an opposition to the thing that bears the name. *Here* the sense (whether construed as platonic or mental) and *there* the thing. (As McDowell comments above, the sense is also introduced as the "mode of presentation" of the thing, but that remains a merely metaphorical characterization.) But in the context of *Mind and World*, and its removal of an outer boundary to the conceptual sphere, this can look like an illicit distinction between the conceptual and an extraconceptual world of things lying *outside* it. It can look, in other words, as though thoughts, in the realm of sense, can have, in McDowell's phrase above, a *bearing* on things, in the realm of reference, but only by indicating them, either descriptively or non-descriptively, as they lie on the outside of the conceptual realm.

Since Dodd's objection depends on a standard way of understanding the distinction between sense and reference, the route to disarming it requires rethinking the distinction from within the context of *Mind and World*. The key element of this, I suggest, is to recognize the (obvious) fact that even the standard example of Hesperus and Phosphorus is told from a particular perspective within the world, and not from a sideways-on perspective outside it. It provides an object lesson in how an interpretative theory, aimed at fathoming people, should accurately individuate their beliefs so as to reflect the sort of inferences that they will sanction. Thus, for example, what, from our perspective on cosmology, may be unimportant in the explanation of a name, whether verbally or by ostension, may matter to others, and it will be important to reflect this in an interpretation of their utterances. But our account of their beliefs is still an account launched from, and framed in concepts that reflect, our perspective. Even if we resort to acts of pointing to explain what we mean by "Venus", this will not escape the conceptual sphere, as Wittgenstein was at pains to point out.

Given such a minimal conception of the nature of sense, the contrast implicit in Dodd's question between modes of presentation and things is undermined. The abstract distinction between sense and reference serves as a reminder for particular cases that others' networks of beliefs about Venus, say, may differ from ours. Thus a purely referential or extensional theory of meaning would fail to be interpretative. But this does not imply a genuine contrast between knowledge of the sense of a name and knowledge of its reference. (Nor is McDowell's suggestion that this can be glossed as a distinction between knowledge of truths and knowledge of things helpful (McDowell 1998a: 174).) It does not license a genuine contrast between what we understand by names and those things that are named, abstracted from all possible naming practice (think of nameables as akin to thinkables). In particular concrete cases, it makes sense to ask whether a speaker's thoughts concern Venus, some planet or other, "that bright light!", or even, neologizing with McDowell, Hesperus. But it does not make sense to ask whether their thoughts contain that very thing as opposed merely to its conceptualization in the broader realm of sense.

I commented earlier that implicit in McDowell's ontological claims about facts and perceivers there was a transcendental claim that paralleled Wittgenstein's transcendental claim raised at a higher semantic level. It has a bearing on the present issue. One of the slogans of *Mind and World* is that our conception of nature should be re-enchanted. But it is not entirely clear what is meant by nature. On occasions it is used to mean human nature. McDowell argues that our acquired resonance to the space of reasons should be regarded as part of our *second nature*, without the need to reduce it to the realm of law. Similarly, our learnt responses to moral situations requires the moral re-enchantment of the world. McDowell also argues, however, that this idea of re-enchantment should not be confined to these areas, even though the move to re-enchant the world outside meaningful and moral contexts "can look like a regress into a pre-scientific superstition, a crazily nostalgic attempt to re-enchant the natural world" (McDowell 1994: 72) But the move to evade Dodd's question indicates a reason for partially re-enchanting even the natural world. There is a transcendental harmony between thought and the world in that the latter is constitutively apt for conceptualization in accordance with the *sui generis* space of reasons.

At the end of the Introduction, I flagged an issue that I said would be an implicit theme throughout. Is McDowell's use of the philosophical canon consistent with his Wittgenstein-inspired therapeutic conception of philosophy? I have not attempted to answer that question explicitly. What is clear is that by appealing to Kantian, Aristotelian, Davidsonian and Sellarsian ideas and concepts, among others, McDowell provides readers with both a way of rethinking those authors and a set of tools for thinking about particular philosophical problems. At the same time, the particular difficulty of the approach is characteristic of second-hand tools. They have been used by previous owners in ways that are sometimes subtly different from the way McDowell wishes to use them.

Glossary

McDowell deploys a number of characteristic semi-technical terms or phrases that can be broadly defined as follows.

Bald naturalism A conjunction of two views. It claims that the world can be fully described by the natural sciences: the **realm of law**. At the same time, it claims that phenomena that are described or understood in the **space of reasons**, such as beliefs, can also be explained by the **realm of law**. Thus it denies that there is a fundamental distinction between these two logical spaces. The clearest examples are reductionist accounts of the mind.

Blueprint conception of mind The assumption that thoughts relate to objects indirectly via "blueprints" or descriptions in general terms that are satisfied, or not, by particular objects. On this view, thoughts do not depend on objects. The view is undermined, according to McDowell, by a proper understanding of **singular thoughts**.

Cosmic exile A notional perspective or explanatory starting-point, first coined by W. V. Quine. Cosmic exile represents a position outside a practice or lacking the concepts that are under philosophical scrutiny. It is the perspective from which a **sideways-on view** is taken and one that McDowell repeatedly rejects in a number of debates. McDowell uses it to describe, for example, the perspective from which a **full-blooded theory of meaning** is drawn up.

Disjunctive conception of experience The idea that experience is either *of a fact* or *of a mere appearance*. In veridical experience, the fact experienced partly constitutes the experience itself. Thus such experiences are "constitutively open" to the world. The disjunctive conception contrasts with a **highest common factor conception**.

Disenchantment, enchantment, partial re-enchantment McDowell suggests that the rise of modern science was based on the rejection of the medieval view that the world contained a book of moral lessons. Rejection of this view and the methodological adoption of explanation by subsumption under natural laws (the **realm of law**) involves, in Max Weber's phrase, the disenchantment of nature. McDowell's suggestion, however, that concepts and thus the **space of reasons** are involved in the very idea of human experience requires a "partial re-enchantment" of nature.

Full-blooded theory of meaning An interpretation of the aim of a formal theory of meaning based on Davidson's and Tarski's work. A full-blooded theory, by contrast with a **modest theory of meaning**, attempts to explain the meaning of even the primitive terms of the object language in, for example, practical terms. It thus attempts to explain meaning from a starting-point outside meaning: the perspective of **cosmic exile**.

Highest common factor conception of experience The idea that there is a common ingredient in both veridical and illusory experience to explain their similarity to a subject. McDowell suggests that it is motivated by the argument from illusion, which stresses that similarity. But it makes perceptual knowledge impossible because the obtaining of facts is "blankly external" to experience.

Master thesis The thesis that mental states are not essentially relational states and have instead to be connected to aspects of the world by interpretations. McDowell suggests that the master thesis is both a key component of the Cartesian picture of mind and also the key target of Wittgenstein's rule-following considerations. Only with the master thesis in place is Wittgenstein's **regress of interpretations** threatened. Thus it is the master thesis that leads to the apparently forced choice between a **regress of interpretations** – and thus scepticism about meaning and mental content – and **rampant Platonism**.

Modest theory of meaning An interpretation of the aim of a formal theory of meaning based on Davidson's and Tarski's work. A modest theory, by contrast with a **full-blooded theory of meaning**, does not attempt to account for the primitive terms of a language in a more basic way. It thus cannot explain meaning in meaning-free terms.

Myth of the given Wilfrid Sellars's term for a version of epistemological foundationalism based on the idea that there are foundational beliefs that are non-inferentially arrived at, presuppose no other beliefs and constitute the ultimate court of appeal for factual claims. McDowell suggests that the myth of the given and coherentism can appear to present a dilemma for an account of intentionality. Avoiding both options is a key aim of *Mind and World*.

Naturalized Platonism In response to some commentators who take the later Wittgenstein to have argued against the normativity and ratification independence of rules (and intentional mental states), McDowell advocates naturalized Platonism. Rules normatively prescribe their correct application. By contrast with the view that rules are ratification dependent, McDowell's naturalized Platonism takes rules to determine their correct application without the need for intervening ongoing judgements. But by contrast with **rampant Platonism**, the *institution* of rules does, however, depend on subjects who can make judgements.

Openness to the world The idea that experiences are, of their very nature, potentially (that is, when true) a way in which the world makes itself available to subjects. McDowell suggests that only a **disjunctive conception of experience**, by contrast with a **highest common factor conception of experience**, allows this.

Rampant Platonism The idea that the normative prescriptions that rules impose on their correct application is fully independent of human subjectivity. McDowell argues that this is a target of Wittgenstein's rule-following considerations. It is also invoked in the idea of an interpretation that needs no further interpretations, used, vainly, to head off the threat of scepticism in the face of the **regress of interpretations**.

Ratification dependence The idea that rules – such as the rules that govern the correct application of words – do not determine their correct application until applied in actual judgements. Meaning is thus moulded by ongoing human use. It is a view held by some interpreters of Wittgenstein, but it is rejected by McDowell.

Realm of law The name McDowell uses to characterize the kind of explanation deployed by the natural sciences. The realm of law provides explanation of phenomena by subsuming them under natural laws. This contrasts with the intelligibility of the **space of reasons**.

Receptivity The label McDowell takes from Kant for the ability (or Kantian faculty) to take in aspects of the world in experiences: it governs pre-conceptual "intuitions", in Kant's vocabulary, or Humean impressions. McDowell argues, however, that experiences always combine such an intake with a conceptual structure. In other words, receptivity always operates in conjunction with **spontaneity**. Properly speaking, there are no such things as intuitions or impressions.

Regress of interpretations The fate, according to the later Wittgenstein's rule-following considerations, of theories of understanding or mental content that deploy an inner representation. Such representations would only have determinate content under an interpretation, however, and that interpretation, on the theory in question, has itself to be encoded in a further representation. This leads to a regress and thus either to scepticism about the possibility of meaning or mental content or to **rampant Platonism**. McDowell suggests that Wittgenstein uses the regress of interpretations to undermine the **master thesis**.

Scheme–content dualism A dualistic explanation of the relation of the structure of language or mental concepts and either experience or the world. A worldview comprising a set of empirical beliefs is supposed to result from the ordering of a structureless world or structureless experiences by a scheme of concepts. McDowell adds to Davidson's criticisms of this dualism in *Mind and World*.

Second nature The capacities of a subject that are natural but that have to be instilled through education. McDowell suggests that the ability to respond to reasons – including moral reasons – is an aspect of human second nature. This enables him to locate such reasons in nature without invoking **bald naturalism**.

Secondary qualities Qualities such as colours, tastes and smells that, according to McDowell, have to be understood through an understanding of the experience to which they give rise in suitable subjects. They are thus "sensory" qualities.

Sideways-on view A notional philosophical explanatory perspective on a set of concepts or practices that does not presuppose the resources of those concepts and practices and aims to articulate their relation to relevant worldly features. The sideways-on view requires the cogency of the perspective of **cosmic exile**, and is repeatedly rejected by McDowell. In *Mind and World*, it is linked to the idea that the world itself lies outside conceptual understanding and impacts on judgement only causally rather than rationally.

Singular thoughts Thoughts that are (partly) constituted by relations to objects. These contrast with descriptive thoughts, which latch on to objects that satisfy a description. Russell's theory of descriptions provides a codification of descriptive thoughts according to which something can still be successfully thought, even if nothing satisfies the description. The thought is false rather than meaningless. Russell's analysis suggests that descriptive thoughts make general claims about the world. Singular thoughts, by contrast, require the existence of the relevant object. Demonstrative thoughts such as *"That* is the best cat in the world" are examples.

Space of reasons A metaphorical name taken from Sellars for the rational structure of beliefs and concepts. McDowell explicitly mentions relations of implication and probabilification as examples of the relations that structure the space. The space of reasons is contrasted with the **realm of law**.

Spontaneity The label McDowell takes from Kant for the ability (or Kantian faculty) to deploy concepts. Paradigmatically, they are deployed in active judgement. But according to McDowell concepts, and thus spontaneity, are also involved in experiences.

Thinkables In *Mind and World*, McDowell argues that the sort of thing that one can think is the sort of thing that can be the case: a fact. But identifying facts and thoughts risks the charge of idealism. Thus McDowell distinguishes thoughts understood as acts of thinking from thoughts as the contents of those acts: the thinkables. Facts are true thinkables.

Vehicles of content McDowell distinguishes two views of concepts. On one view, concepts are aspects of the content of thoughts. On the other they are vehicles of those contents. The latter view requires that thoughts can be codified in inner mental representations. This, he argues, is both falsified by the existence of **singular thoughts**, which cannot be so codified, and is also an instance of the **master thesis**, which is a target of Wittgenstein's later philosophy.

Guide to further reading

Chapter 1

Marie McGinn's *Wittgenstein and the Philosophical Investigations* (1997) is a slim introduction to the *Investigations*. The most thorough interpretative work is the four-volume commentary by Gordon Baker and Peter Hacker (Baker & Hacker 1980, 1985; Hacker 1990, 1996). My *Wittgenstein on Language and Thought* (Thornton 1998) relates Wittgenstein's views on philosophy of content to the contemporary debate.

There is a vast literature on Wittgenstein's account of rule-following, but the collection *Rule-Following and Meaning* (Miller & Wright 2002) gathers some key papers together, including Paul Boghossian's "The Rule-Following Considerations" (1989), which is a thorough survey of the debate.

Chapter 2

Alex Miller's *An Introduction to Contemporary Metaethics* (2003) is an excellent overview. David McNaughton's *Moral Vision* (1998) is an introduction to moral particularism, especially the work of Jonathan Dancy and McDowell. The collection *Moral Particularism* (Hooker & Little 2000) gathers recent work, although it concentrates more on Dancy than McDowell. Dancy's particularism about reasons is generalized in *Practical Reality* (2000). A good statement of Simon Blackburn's moral philosophy is his *Ruling Passions* (2000).

Chapter 3

Donald Davidson's major papers on theories of meaning are gathered in *Inquiries into Truth and Interpretation* (1984). A good overview of Davidson's philosophy of language – although it also includes his philosophy of mind – is Simon Evnine's *Donald Davidson* (1991). Michael Dummett's major papers are gathered in *The Seas of Language* (1993). Crispin Wright's early papers on philosophy of language are collected in *Realism, Meaning and Truth*, (1987b).

Good introductions to philosophy of language are Miller's *The Philosophy of Language* (1998) and Michael Luntley's *Contemporary Philosophy of Thought and Language* (1999). A robust criticism of theories of meaning can be found in *Language, Sense and Nonsense* (Baker & Hacker 1984a).

Chapter 4

The locus classicus of neo-Fregean work on singular thought is Gareth Evans's *The Varieties of Reference* (1982). François Recanati's *Direct Reference* (1993) presents a summary of recent Anglo-American thinking, as well as Recanati's own views. The final chapters of Luntley's *Contemporary Philosophy of Thought and Language* (1999) focus on singular thought.

Chapter 5

In its original publication, McDowell's "Knowledge and the Internal" (1995a) was paired with one by Robert Brandom: "Knowledge and the Social Articulation of the Space of Reasons" (1995). This is a good place to start in comparing and contrasting their different philosophical projects. Brandom's definitive statement (so far) is his *Making it Explicit* (1994), but the collection *Articulating Reasons* (2000) gives a shorter overview. Debate about whether McDowell does provide reason to shrug off scepticism has continued, and recent papers include Wright (2002) and Pritchard (2003).

Timothy Williamson develops a systematic theory that nevertheless starts with the premise that knowledge is a primitive in his *Knowledge and Its Limits* (2000). Michael Williams's discussion of scepticism in *Unnatural Doubts* (1996) makes for an interesting comparison with McDowell's brief discussion. A good short introduction to epistemology is Williams's *Problems of Knowledge* (2001) and one to philosophical scepticism is Neil Gascoigne's *Scepticism* (2002).

Chapter 6

There has been much critical work on McDowell's *Mind and World*. This includes volume 58 of *Philosophy and Phenomenological Research* (1998), which contains McDowell's précis of *Mind and World*, a number of papers by commentators and McDowell's response. The recent collection *Reading McDowell* (Smith 2002) contains criticism and a response. Also of interest, if mainly for McDowell's reponse, is volume 31 of *Journal of the British Society for Phenomenology* (1998) and the edited collection *John McDowell: Reasons and Nature* (Willaschek 2000), which contains McDowell's recent paper "Experiencing the World" (2000b).

Wilfrid Sellars's influential essay "Empiricism and the Philosophy of Mind" (1997) has been reprinted twice recently with commentaries; the edition cited has a study guide by Brandom. *Knowledge, Mind and the Given* (DeVries & Triplett 2000) contains a longer commentary.

Bibliography

Works by John McDowell

1976   "Truth-Conditions, Bivalence, and Verificationism". In *Truth and Meaning: Essays in Semantic*, J. McDowell & G. Evans (eds), 44–66. Oxford: Clarendon Press. Reprinted in *Meaning, Knowledge and Reality*, 3–28.

1977   "On the Sense and Reference of a Proper Name", *Mind* **86**, 159–85. Reprinted in *Meaning, Knowledge and Reality*, 171–98.

1978   "Physicalism and Primitive Denotation: Field on Tarski", *Erkenntnis* **13**, 131–52. Reprinted in *Meaning, Knowledge and Reality*, 132–54.

1979   "Virtue and Reason", *Monist* **62**, 331–50. Reprinted in *Mind, Value and Reality*, 50–73.

1980   "Meaning, Communication and Knowledge. In *Philosophical Subjects: Essays presented to P. F. Strawson*, Z. van Straaten (ed.), 117–39. Oxford: Clarendon Press. Reprinted in *Meaning, Knowledge and Reality*, 29–50.

1981   "Anti-realism and the Epistemology of Understanding". In *Meaning and Understanding*, H. Parrot & J. Bourveresse (eds), 225–48. Berlin: de Gruyter. Reprinted in *Meaning, Knowledge and Reality*, 314–43.

1982   "Criteria, Defeasibility and Knowledge", *Proceedings of the British Academy* **68**, 455–79. Reprinted in *Meaning, Knowledge and Reality*, 369–94.

1983   "Aesthetic Value, Objectivity and the Fabric of the World". In *Pleasure, Preference and Value: Studies in Philosophical Aesthetics*, E. Schaper (ed.), 1–16. Cambridge: Cambridge University Press. Reprinted in *Mind, Value and Reality*, 112–130.

1984a   "De Re Senses", *Philosophical Quarterly* **34**, 283–94. Reprinted in *Meaning, Knowledge and Reality*, 214–27.

1984b   "Wittgenstein on Following a Rule", *Synthese* **58**, 325–63. Reprinted in *Mind, Value and Reality*, 221–62.

1985a   "Functionalism and Anomalous Monism". In *Actions and Events: Perspectives on the Philosophy of Donald Davidson*, E. LePore & B. P. McLaughlin (eds), 387–98. Oxford: Blackwell. Reprinted in *Mind, Value and Reality*, 325–40.

1985b   "Values and Secondary Qualities". In *Morality and Objectivity: A Tribute to J. L. Mackie*, T. Honderich (ed.), 110–25. London: Routledge & Kegan Paul. Reprinted in *Mind, Value and Reality*, 131–50.

1986   "Singular Thought and the Extent of Inner Space". In *Subject Thought and Context*, P. Pettit & J. McDowell (eds), 137–68. Oxford: Clarendon Press. Reprinted in *Meaning, Knowledge and Reality*, 228–59.

1987a   "In Defence of Modesty". In *Michael Dummett: Contributions to Philosophy*, B.

Taylor (ed.), 59–80. Dordrecht: Nijhoff. Reprinted in *Meaning, Knowledge and Reality*, 87–107.

1987b   "Projection and Truth in Ethics". Lindley Lecture, University of Kansas. Pamphlet, Department of Philosophy, University of Kansas. Reprinted in *Mind, Value and Reality*, 151–66.

1989   "One Strand in the Private Language Argument", *Grazer Philosophische Studien* **33/34**, 285–303. Reprinted in *Mind, Value and Reality*, 279–96.

1991   "Intentionality and Interiority in Wittgenstein". In *Meaning Scepticism*, K. Puhl (ed.), 148–69. Berlin: de Gruyter. Reprinted in *Mind, Value and Reality*, 297–321.

1992a   "Putnam on Mind and Meaning", *Philosophical Topics* **20**(1) (Spring), 35–48. Reprinted in *Meaning, Knowledge and Reality*, 275–91.

1992b   "Meaning and Intentionality in Wittgenstein's Later Philosophy", In *Midwest Studies in Philosophy 17: The Wittgenstein Legacy*, P. A. French, T. E. Uehling, Jr., & H. K. Wettstein (eds), 40–52. Notre Dame, IN: Notre Dame University Press. Reprinted in *Mind, Value and Reality*, 263–78.

1993   "Knowledge by Hearsay". In *Knowing from Words: Western and Indian Philosophical Analysis of Understanding and Testimony*, B. K. Matilal & A. Chakrabarti (eds), 195–224. Synthese Library, 230. Dordrecht: Kluwer. Reprinted in *Meaning, Knowledge and Reality*, 414–43.

1994   *Mind and World*. Cambridge, MA: Harvard University Press.

1995a   "Knowledge and the Internal", *Philosophy and Phenomenological Research* **55**, 877–93. Reprinted in *Meaning, Knowledge and Reality*, 395–413.

1995b   "Two Sorts of Naturalism". In *Virtues and Reasons: Philippa Foot and Moral Theory, Essays in Honour of Philippa Foot*, R. Hursthouse, G. Lawrence & W. Quinn (eds), 149–79. Oxford: Clarendon Press. Reprinted in *Mind, Valueand Reality*, 167–97.

1997   "Another Plea for Modesty". In *Language, Thought and Logic: Essays on the Work of Michael Dummett, R.* Heck (ed.), 105–29. *Oxford: Oxford University Press*. Reprinted in *Meaning, Knowledge and Reality*, 108–31.

1998a   *Meaning, Knowledge and Reality*. Cambridge, MA: Harvard University Press.

1998b   *Mind, Value and Reality*. Cambridge, MA: Harvard University Press.

1998c   "Precis of *Mind and World*", *Philosophy and Phenomenological Research* **58**, 365–8.

1998d   "Reply to Commentators", *Philosophy and Phenomenological Research* **58**, 403–31.

1998e   The Woodbridge Lectures: "Having the World in View: Sellars, Kant, and Intentionality", *Journal of Philosophy* **95**, 431–91

1999   "Scheme–Content Dualism". In *The Philosophy of Donald Davidson*, L. E. Hahn (ed.), 87–104. Chicago, IL: Open Court.

2000a   "Comments", *Journal of the British Society for Phenomenology* **31**, 330–43.

2000b   "Experiencing the World". In *John McDowell: Reasons and Nature*, M. Willaschek (ed.), 3–18. Munster: Lit Verlag.

2000c   "Responses". In *John McDowell: Reasons and Nature*, M. Willaschek (ed.), 91–114. Munster: Lit Verlag.

2000d   "Towards Rehabilitating Objectivity". In *Rorty and his Critics*, R. B. Brandom (ed.), 109–23. Oxford: Blackwell.

2002   "Responses". In *Reading McDowell*, N. Smith (ed.), 269–305. London: Routledge.

unpublished   "Transcendental Empiricism".

Works by other authors

Ayer, A. J. 1946. *Language, Truth and Logic*. New York: Dover Publications.
Baker, G. P. 1974. "Criteria: A New Foundation for Semantics", *Ratio* **16**, 156–89.

Baker, G. P. & P. M. S. Hacker 1980. *Wittgenstein: Understanding and Meaning*. Oxford: Blackwell.

Baker, G. P. & P. M. S. Hacker 1983. *Wittgenstein's Philosophical Investigations*. Oxford: Blackwell.

Baker, G. P. & P. M. S. Hacker 1984a. *Language, Sense and Nonsense*. Oxford: Blackwell.

Baker, G. P. & P. M. S. Hacker 1984b. *Scepticism, Rules and Language*. Oxford: Blackwell.

Baker, G. P. & P. M. S. Hacker 1985. *Wittgenstein: Rules, Grammar and Necessity*. Oxford: Blackwell.

Bermúdez, J. L. 2001. "Review of Jerry Fodor, *The Mind Doesn't Work That Way: The Scope and Limits of Computational Psychology*", *Philosophical Quarterly* **51**, 549–52.

Bilgrami, A. 1992. *Belief and Meaning*. Oxford: Blackwell.

Bird, G. 1996. "McDowell's *Kant: Mind and World*", *Philosophy* **71**, 219–43.

Blackburn, S. 1984a. "The Individual Strikes Back", in *Synthese* **58**, 281–301.

Blackburn, S. 1984b. *Spreading the Word*. Oxford: Oxford University Press.

Blackburn, S. 1993. *Essays in Quasi-Realism*. Oxford: Oxford University Press.

Blackburn, S. 2000. *Ruling Passions*. Oxford: Oxford University Press.

Boghossian, P. A. 1989. "The Rule-Following Considerations", *Mind* **98**, 507–49.

Brandom, R. 1994. *Making It Explicit*. Cambridge, MA: Harvard University Press.

Brandom, R. 1995. "Knowledge and the Social Articulation of the Space of Reasons", *Philosophy and Phenomenological Research* **55**, 895–908.

Brandom, R. 1998. "Perception and Rational Constraint", *Philosophy and Phenomenological Research* **58**, 369–74.

Brandom, R. 2000. *Articulating Reasons* Cambridge, MA: Harvard University Press.

Brentano, F. 1995. *Psychology from an Empirical Standpoint*. London: Routledge.

Burge, T. 1977. "Belief *de re*", *Journal of Philosophy* **74**, 338–62.

Cavell, S. 1969. *Must We Mean What We Say?: A Book of Essays*. New York: Scribner.

Child, W. 1992. "Vision and Experience: The Causal Theory and the Disjunctive Conception", *Philosophical Quarterly* **42**, 297–316.

Child, W. 1994. *Causality, Interpretation and the Mind*. Oxford: Oxford University Press.

Dancy, J. 1993. *Moral Reasons*. Oxford: Blackwell.

Dancy, J. 2000. *Practical Reality*. Oxford: Oxford University Press.

Davidson, D. 1980. *Essays on Actions and Events*. Oxford: Oxford University Press.

Davidson, D. 1984a. *Inquiries into Truth and Interpretation*. Oxford: Oxford University Press.

Davidson, D. 1984b. "On the Very Idea of a Conceptual Scheme". In *Inquiries into Truth and Interpretation*, 183–98. Oxford: Oxford University Press.

Davidson, D. 1986a. "A Coherence Theory of Truth and Knowledge". In *Truth and Interpretation*, E. LePore (ed.), 307–19. Oxford: Blackwell.

Davidson, D. 1986b. "A Nice Derangement of Epitaphs". In *Truth and Interpretation*, E. LePore, (ed.), 433–46. Oxford: Blackwell.

Davidson, D. 1990. "The Structure and Content of Truth" (The Dewey Lectures 1989), *Journal of Philosophy* **87**, 279–328.

Davidson, D. 1993. "Reply to Jerry Fodor and Earnest Lepore". In *Reflecting Davidson*, R. Stoecker (ed.), 77–84. Berlin: de Gruyter.

DeVries W. A. & T. Triplett (eds) 2000. *Knowledge, Mind and the Given*. Indianapolis, IN: Hackett.

Dodd, J. 1995. "McDowell and Identity Theories of Truth", *Analysis* **55**, 160–65.

Dodd, J. 2000. *An Identity Theory of Truth*. Basingstoke: Macmillan.

Dummett, M. 1987. "Reply to John McDowell". In *Michael Dummett: Contributions to Philosophy*, B. Taylor (ed.), 253–68. Dordrecht: Nijhoff.

Dummett, M. 1993. *The Seas of Language*. Oxford: Oxford University Press.

Evans, G. 1982. *The Varieties of Reference*. Oxford: Oxford University Press.

Evnine, S. 1991. *Donald Davidson*. Oxford: Polity.

Fodor, J. 1987. *Psychosemantics: The Problem of Meaning in the Philosophy of Mind.* Cambridge, MA: MIT Press.
Fodor, J. & C. Chihara 1965. "Operationalism and Ordinary Language: A Critique of Wittgenstein", *American Philosophical Quarterly* **2**, 281–95.
Frege, G. 1950. *The Foundations of Arithmetic: A Logico-Mathematical Enquiry into the Concept of Number*, J. L. Austin (trans.). Oxford: Blackwell. [*Grundlagen*]
Frege, G. 1964. *The Basic Laws of Arithmetic.* Berkeley, CA: University of California Press.
Friedman, M. 2002. "Exorcising the Philosophical Tradition". In *Reading McDowell*, N. Smith, (ed.), 25–57. London: Routledge.
Gascoigne, N. 2002. *Scepticism.* Chesham: Acumen.
Glendinning, S. & M. De Gaynesford 1998. "John McDowell on Experience: Open to the Sceptic?", *Metaphilosophy* **29**, 20–34.
Goodman, N. 1983. *Fact, Fiction, and Forecast.* Cambridge, MA: Harvard University Press.
Godfrey-Smith, P. 1989. "Misinformation", *Canadian Journal of Philosophy* **19**, 533–50.
Grice, H. P. 1957. "Meaning", *Philosophical Review* **66**, 377–88.
Grice, H. P. 1961. "The Causal Theory of Perception", *Proceedings of the Aristotelian Society* supplementary volume **35**, 121–52.
Hacker, P. M. S. 1987. *Appearance and Reality.* Oxford: Blackwell.
Hacker, P. M. S. 1990. *Wittgenstein: Meaning and Mind.* Oxford: Blackwell.
Hacker, P. M. S. 1996. *Wittgenstein: Mind and Will.* Oxford: Blackwell.
Haugeland, J. 1982. "Weak Supervenience", *American Philosophical Quarterly* **19**, 93–103.
Hooker, B. & M. Little 2000. *Moral Particularism.* Oxford: Oxford University Press.
Horwich, P. 1990. *Truth.* Oxford: Oxford University Press.
Kant, I. 1929. *Critique of Pure Reason*, N. Kemp Smith (trans.). London: Macmillan.
Kaplan, D. 1979. "Dthat. In *Contemporary Perspectives in the Philosophy of Language*, P. French (ed.), 383–400. Minneapolis, MN: University of Minnesota
Kirkham, R. L. 1992. *Theories of Truth.* Cambridge, MA: MIT Press.
Kripke, S. 1982. *Wittgenstein on Rules and Private Language.* Oxford: Blackwell.
Lear, J. 1982. "Leaving the World Alone", *Journal of Philosophy* **79**, 382–403.
LePore, E. 1986. *Truth and Interpretation: Perspectives on the Philosophy of Donald Davidson.* Oxford: Blackwell.
Loewer, B. & G. Rey 1991. *Meaning in Mind: Fodor and his Critics.* Oxford: Blackwell.
Luntley, M. 1991. "The Transcendental Grounds of Meaning and the Place of Silence". In *Meaning Scepticism*, K. Puhl (ed.), 170–88. Berlin: de Gruyter.
Luntley, M. 1999. *Contemporary Philosophy of Thought and Language.* Oxford: Blackwell.
Lyne, I. 2000. "Openness to Reality in McDowell and Heidegger: Normativity and Ontology", *Journal of the British Society for Phenomenology* **31**, 300–13.
McGinn, M. 1997. *Wittgenstein and the Philosophical Investigations.* London: Routledge.
Mackie, J. L. 1977. *Ethics: Inventing Right and Wrong.* Harmondsworth: Penguin.
McNaughton, D. 1998. *Moral Vision.* Oxford: Blackwell.
Malcolm, N. 1958. "Knowledge of Other Minds", *The Journal of Philosophy* **55**, 969–78.
Millikan, R. G. 1984. *Language, Thought and Other Biological Categories.* Cambridge, MA: MIT Press.
Miller, A. 1998. *The Philosophy of Language.* London: UCL Press.
Miller, A. & C. Wright (eds) 2002. *Rule-Following and Meaning.* Chesham: Acumen.
Miller, A. 2003. *An Introduction to Contemporary Metaethics.* Cambridge: Polity.
Miller, A. 2004. "Rule-Following and Externalism', *Philosophy and Phenomenological Research* **68**, 127–140.
Nagel, T. 1986. *The View from Nowhere.* Oxford: Oxford University Press.
Papineau, D. 1987. *Reality and Representation.* Oxford: Blackwell.
Papineau, D. 1993. *Philosophical Naturalism.* Oxford: Blackwell.

Bibliography

Peacocke, C. 1992. *A Study of Concepts*. Cambridge, MA: MIT Press.
Peacocke, C. 1993. "Externalist Explanation", *Proceedings of the Aristotelian Society* **93**, 203–30.
Perry, J. 1977. "Frege on Demonstratives", *Philosophical Review* **86**, 474–97.
Perry, J. 1979. "The Problem of the Essential Indexical", *Noûs* **22**, 1–18.
Pritchard, D. 2003. "McDowell on Reasons, Externalism and Scepticism", *European Journal of Philosophy* **11**, 273–94.
Putnam, H. 1975. "The Meaning of Meaning". In *Mind, Language and Reality*, 215–71. Cambridge: Cambridge University Press.
Ramsey, F. P. 1927. "Facts and Propositions", *Proceedings of the Aristotelian Society*, **7**, 153–70.
Recanati, F. 1993. *Direct Reference*. Oxford: Blackwell.
Rorty, R. 1991. *Objectivity, Relativism and Truth*. Cambridge: Cambridge University Press.
Rorty, R. 1998. *Truth and Progress*. Cambridge: Cambridge University Press.
Russell, B. 1917. "Knowledge by Acquaintance and Knowledge by Description". In *Mysticism and Logic*, 152–67. London: George Allen and Unwin.
Searle, J. 1958. "Proper Names", *Mind* **67**, 166–73.
Sellars, W. 1997. *Empricism and the Philosophy of Mind*. Cambridge, MA: Harvard University Press.
Smith, N. (ed.) 2002. *Reading McDowell*. London: Routledge.
Snowdon, P. 1981. "Perception, Vision and Causation", *Proceedings of the Aristotelian Society* supplementary volume, **81**, 176–92.
Sterelny, K. 1990. *The Representational Theory of Mind*. Oxford: Blackwell.
Stoecker, R. (ed.) 1993. *Reflecting Davidson*. Berlin: de Gruyter.
Strawson, P. F. 1959. *Individuals*. London: Methuen.
Strawson, P. F. 1975. "Perception and its Objects". In *Perception and Identity*, G. F. Macdonald (ed.). Ithaca, NY: Cornell University Press.
Strawson, P. F. 1979. "Perception and its Objects". In *Perception and Identity: Essays Presented to A. J. Ayer with his Replies to Them*, G. F. Macdonald (ed.), 41–60. London: Macmillan.
Strawson, P. F. 1992. *Analysis and Metaphysics*. Oxford: Oxford University Press.
Thornton, T. 1998. *Wittgenstein on Language and Thought*. Edinburgh: Edinburgh University Press.
Weiss, B. 2002. *Michael Dummett*. Chesham: Acumen.
Williams, B. 1978. *Descartes: The Project of Pure Enquiry*. Harmondsworth: Penguin.
Williams, M. 1996. *Unnatural Doubts*. Princeton, NJ: Princeton University Press.
Williams, M. 2001. *Problems of Knowledge*. Oxford: Oxford University Press.
Williamson, T. 2000. *Knowledge and its Limits*. Oxford: Oxford University Press.
Wittgenstein, L. 1953. *Philosophical Investigations*. Oxford: Blackwell.
Wittgenstein, L. 1958. *The Blue and Brown Books*. Oxford: Blackwell.
Wright, C. 1980. *Wittgenstein on the Foundations of Mathematics*. London: Duckworth.
Wright, C. 1984. "Kripke's Account of the Argument Against Private Language", *Journal of Philosophy* **81**, 759–78.
Wright, C. 1986. "Rule Following, Meaning and Constructivism". In *Meaning and Interpretation*, C. Travis (ed.), 271–97 Oxford: Blackwell.
Wright, C. 1987a. "On Making Up One's Mind: Wittgenstein on Intention". In *Logic, Philosophy of Science and Epistemology: Proceedings of the 11th International Wittgenstein Symposium*, P. Weingartner & G. Schurz (eds), 391–404. Vienna: Holder-Pichler-Tempsky.
Wright, C. 1987b. *Realism, Meaning and Truth*. Oxford: Blackwell.
Wright, C. 1988. "Moral Values, Projection and Secondary Qualities", *Proceedings of the Aristotelian Society* supplementary volume **62**, 1–26.
Wright, C. 1989. "Wittgenstein's Rule Following Considerations and the Central Project of Theoretical Linguistics". In *Reflections on Chomsky*, A. George (ed.), 233–64. Oxford: Blackwell.

John McDowell

Wright, C. 1991. "Wittgenstein's Later Philosophy of Mind: Sensation, Privacy and Intention". In *Meaning Scepticism*, K. Puhl (ed.), 126–47. Berlin: de Gruyter.
Wright, C. 1992. *Truth and Objectivity*. Cambridge, MA: Harvard University Press.
Wright, C. 2002. "(Anti-)Sceptics Simple and Subtle: G. E. Moore and John McDowell", *Philosophy and Phenomenological Research* **65**, 330–48.

Index